North Korea

ASIA/PACIFIC/PERSPECTIVES

Series Editor: Mark Selden

Crime, Punishment, and Policing in China edited by Børge Bakken

Woman, Man, Bangkok: Love, Sex, and Popular Culture in Thailand by Scot Barmé

Making the Foreign Serve China: Managing Foreigners in the People's Republic by Anne-Marie Brady

Marketing Dictatorship: Propaganda and Thought Work in China by Anne-Marie Brady

Collaborative Nationalism: The Politics of Friendship on China's Mongolian Frontier by Uradyn E. Bulag

The Mongols at China's Edge: History and the Politics of National Unity by Uradyn E. Bulag

Transforming Asian Socialism: China and Vietnam Compared edited by Anita Chan, Benedict J. Tria Kerkvliet, and Jonathan Unger

China's Great Proletarian Cultural Revolution: Master Narratives and Post-Mao Counternarratives edited by Woei Lien Chong

North China at War: The Social Ecology of Revolution, 1937–1945 edited by Feng Chongyi and David S. G. Goodman

Little Friends: Children's Film and Media Culture in China by Stephanie Hemelryk Donald

Beachheads: War, Peace, and Tourism in Postwar Okinawa by Gerald Figal

Gender in Motion: Divisions of Labor and Cultural Change in Late Imperial and Modern China edited by Bryna Goodman and Wendy Larson

Social and Political Change in Revolutionary China: The Taihang Base Area in the War of Resistance to Japan, 1937–1945 by David S. G. Goodman

Islands of Discontent: Okinawan Responses to Japanese and American Power edited by Laura Hein and Mark Selden

Women in Early Imperial China, Second Edition by Bret Hinsch

Civil Justice in China: Past and Present by Philip C. C. Huang

Local Democracy and Development: The Kerala People's Campaign for Decentralized Planning by T. M. Thomas Isaac with Richard W. Franke

Hidden Treasures: Lives of First-Generation Korean Women in Japan by Jackie J. Kim with Sonia Ryang

North Korea: Beyond Charismatic Politics by Heonik Kwon and Byung-Ho Chung

Postwar Vietnam: Dynamics of a Transforming Society edited by Hy V. Luong

The Indonesian Presidency: The Shift from Personal towards Constitutional Rule by Angus McIntyre

Nationalisms of Japan: Managing and Mystifying Identity by Brian J. McVeigh

To the Diamond Mountains: A Hundred-Year Journey through China and Korea by Tessa Morris-Suzuki

North Korea

Beyond Charismatic Politics

Heonik Kwon

and

Byung-Ho Chung

ROWMAN & LITTLEFIELD PUBLISHERS, INC.
Lanham • Boulder • New York • Toronto • Plymouth, UK

Published by Rowman & Littlefield Publishers, Inc.
A wholly owned subsidiary of The Rowman & Littlefield Publishing Group, Inc.
4501 Forbes Boulevard, Suite 200, Lanham, Maryland 20706
www.rowmanlittlefield.com

Estover Road, Plymouth PL6 7PY, United Kingdom

British Library Cataloguing in Publication Information Available

Library of Congress Cataloging-in-Publication Data
Heonik Kwon, 1962–
    North Korea : beyond charismatic politics / Heonik Kwon and Byung-Ho Chung.
        p.   cm.
    Includes bibliographical references and index.
    ISBN 978-0-7425-5679-9 (cloth : alk. paper) — ISBN 978-1-4422-1577-1 (electronic)
    1. Korea (North)—Politics and government. I. Chung, Byung-Ho, 1955– II. Title.
    JQ1729.5.A58C58 2012
    320.95193—dc23

                                            2011045117

∞™ The paper used in this publication meets the minimum requirements of American
National Standard for Information Sciences—Permanence of Paper for Printed Library
Materials, ANSI/NISO Z39.48-1992.

Printed in the United States of America

Contents

Illustrations

Acknowledgments

Several institutions and many friends and colleagues have helped us to see this project through. We thank the Korea Research Foundation and the British Academy for supporting our work in the early stage. The completion of this work was supported by an Academy of Korean Studies grant funded by the Korean government (MEST) (AKS-2010-DZZ-3104). The Information Center on North Korea at South Korea's Ministry of Unification has provided most generous assistance in searching for and locating primary sources. Good Friends, Yonhap News, and Liu Jae Soo provided material for illustrations. Three postgraduate students at Hanyang University helped with compiling the illustrations and bibliography. We thank Jung Woo-Chang, Christina Hyunim Kim, and An Jong-Soo. Many ideas presented in this book grew out of a postgraduate seminar on North Korean culture at Hanyang University that we taught jointly in the autumn of 2008. We are grateful to Cho Hung-Youn, Bae Kidong, Lee Hee-Soo, Ahn Shin-Won, and Song Do-Young for the invitation.

Parts of this book were presented in lectures and seminars held at the University of North Korean Studies in Seoul, the School of Oriental and African Studies of the University of London, the London School of Economics and Political Science, the University of Cambridge, and the Max Planck Institute in Göttingen, as well as in Ann Arbor, Toronto, Hong Kong, Copenhagen, and Washington, DC. The meetings in Hong Kong and Toronto, in particular, provided important momentum in our consideration of North Korea's recent history through Max Weber's insights into the historical life of revolutionary charismatic authority. We are grateful to Andre Schmid, Michael Shin, Youngju Ryu, Charles Armstrong, Chun Kyung-Soo, Hamm Taik-Young, Tam Ngo, Peter van der Veer, Camilla Sørensen, Ed Simpson, Mark Morris, and Barak Kushner. Heonik Kwon extends special thanks to his colleagues at the London School of Economics, Deborah James and Charles Stafford, and to Lee Moon-Woong, emeritus professor of anthropology at Seoul National University, whose pioneering article published in 1976 has been an inspiring guide throughout the long preparation for this volume.

Byung-Ho Chung delivered presentations at the University of Illinois, Urbana-Champaign, the University of Hawaii, Waseda University, and the City University of Hong Kong. We thank David W. Plath, Nancy Abelmann, Geoffrey White, Ito Abito, and Jonathan London for their kind invitations. His ten visits to

North Korea were made possible by kind assistance from several nongovernmental organizations as well as from the North Korean and South Korean administrations. Many other friends also provided support. Among them are Han S. Park, Hagen Koo, Hyong Kyu Rhew, John Feffer, Courtland W. Robinson, Suh Sung, Takizawa Hideki, Yoshida Yasuhiko, Cho Hyung, Cho-Han Hejoang, Kwon Hyuk-Beom, Jun Woo-Taek, Kim Young-Soo, Lee Gi-Beom, Lee Woo-Young, Lee Tae-Joo, Lee Soo-Jung, Lee Hyang-Kyu, Whang Sang-Ik, Jang Soo-Hyun, Pak Sun-Young, Chung Gene-Woong, and Chung Jean-Kyung. Byung-Ho Chung extends special thanks to the late South Korean journalist and eminent public intellectual Lee Young-Hee, who showed keen interest in and supported the project despite his failing health during his last years.

Susan McEachern and Mark Selden have provided an abiding support throughout, and we are grateful for their enthusiasm and critical intervention. The comments from the anonymous reviewer were immensely helpful not only in tightening the argument but also in clarifying the broad conceptual framework within which we discuss the evolution of North Korea's stateliness. The editors of three journals kindly allowed us to reuse materials first published with them: "North Korea's Politics of Longing," *Critical Asian Studies* 42 (2010): 3–24; "North Korea's Theatre State," *Korean Studies Forum* 4 (2010): 27–54; and "Kŭkchangkukka bukhanŭi sangjingkwa ŭirye [Symbol and ritual in the theater state of North Korea]," *T'ongilmunjaeyŏn'gu* [Korean journal of unification affairs] 22 (2010): 1–42.

Finally, we are deeply obliged to our friends and interlocutors of North Korean origin. They taught us how to read and think through North Korean literature and art; the analysis put forward in this book stems, to a great extent, from their knowledge and wisdom. Kim Suk Jong has been particularly forthcoming, at times even going against her need to protect herself from recalling some of her past experiences in North Korea. This book is dedicated to the children in North Korea who, like Suk Jong's children, have been struggling through the Arduous March so courageously.

Introduction

North Korea is commonly referred to as one of the world's most secluded and enigmatic places. There is no doubt that the country's state hierarchy is bent on keeping its society away from the gaze of the outside world and its population from discovering a way of life other than that offered within. There is also no doubt that the country's leadership has a strong interest in maintaining an enigmatic appearance to its 24 million citizens. The prevailing interest involves the state's willingness to go a long way to apply coercive measures against individuals and their families who happen to fall from the webs of extraordinary and enchanting political and moral symbols that are spun around the historical integrity of the North Korean way of life.

However, there is actually no mystery about the North Korean political system. The North Korean state is not an enigmatic entity and never has been. North Korea had a highly skilful political leader who knew how to build an aura of captivating charismatic power. This leader understood the efficacy of this power for mobilizing the masses toward ambitious political goals, and he was committed to keeping that power not only during his lifetime but also beyond the time of his rule. Modern world history abounds with similar charismatic, visionary leaders and the stories of their rises and falls. The same is true in the political history of the communist world that constituted the moiety of the Cold War international order. This world was distinct from the other half of the global order of the era not only in terms of modes of regulating economic lives but also in its ways of pursuing the modern ideal of a secular, disenchanted society free of traditional beliefs and backward ideas. We know that the disenchantment of society pursued in revolutionary socialist polities involves much more explicit and conscious intervention by state power than in liberal capitalist societies. However, we also know that the performance of secular revolutionary politics, while aiming at demystifying traditional religious norms and mystical ideas, nevertheless often involves the mystification of the authority and power of the revolutionary leadership.

The evolution of North Korea's postcolonial political system has been no exception to this well-trod general trend of modern revolutionary politics. North Korean leaders imported foreign political ideas from other, more powerful states, particularly the Soviet Union, and transformed them according to their own aims, adding some creative indigenous elements and facades. North Korea's political genesis is fundamentally no different from the experience of many other newly independent postcolonial states of the twentieth century, which, while consolidating a political community by applying the established techniques of state and nation building borrowed from the earlier European exemplars, typically claimed that the process was an exclusively indigenous, national art of politics. From this perspective, the North Korean political system is just as modern and as much a product of interaction with global modernity as any other political system existing in the world. In this respect, Bruce Cumings is right to claim that North Korea is nothing more and nothing less than "another country" in the modern world.[1]

Whereas the character of the North Korean postcolonial political system is not unique in history, North Korea is unique in maintaining this particular character for longer than any other state entity born in the Cold War era and, indeed, way beyond the end of the Cold War as the prevailing geopolitical order of the twentieth century. The early North Korean political order centered on an able and preeminent personality, as were the orders of other revolutionary states known in the history of the Cold War. This personality, Kim Il Sung, was in substance and form no more extraordinary than other leading twentieth-century revolutionaries—notably, Joseph Stalin and Mao Zedong. These leaders all had prestigious careers in emancipatory political movements and led a mass-based yet elite political organization that, harboring the principle of democratic centralism, focused on mass mobilization for radical social transformation. They all grasped the central importance of modern technology in politics, including the effectiveness of print technology, art, theater, and drama in mobilizing the masses. They also knew very well that the elite revolutionary vanguard organization was not always an easy family to run and that, at times, the efficient functioning of this organization required an exceptional, charismatic leader whose authority went beyond the realm of institutional politics.

The historical lives of these charismatic revolutionary leaders of the twentieth century can be discussed not only in terms of comparative history but also according to the conceptual premises of historical sociology—most notably, those of eminent theoretician of modern politics Max Weber. Weber was interested in the typology of modern political power and authority, including charismatic authority.[2] No matter how strange the phenomenon appears to rational eyes, for Weber, the enchanting power of charismatic authority is a thoroughly intelligible historical and social phenomenon whose nature is no more mysterious than that of traditional authority (i.e., the authority of a patriarch or emperor) or that of modern bureaucracy and legal systems. Weber understood that all these forms of human authority are imperfect, although all of them, despite their imperfect nature, aspire to perfection and frequently claim to have attained it. When an extraordinary-appearing charismatic authority appears on the horizon, according to Weber, the circumstances of its rise may be other than ordinary; nevertheless, its nature is nothing but extraordinary. In Weber's view, there is nothing miraculous about the miracle-claiming personality. Weber makes it clear that charismatic authority exists only because of the imperfection of other authorities. Charismatic person-alities erupt in history in situations of radical social upheaval, when the society's aspiration for change can no longer be contained within the routine traditional or-der or satisfied by the existing legal-bureaucratic order. Weber also makes it clear, however, that the historicity of charismatic authority, because it originates in ex-traordinary times of social crisis, is limited in time and eventually dwindles away as the society recovers from the upheaval and returns to a routine, everyday order. Most of the charismatic, cultic state personalities of the Cold War era underwent a dramatic rise and fall, following the historical destiny of charismatic authority envisioned by Weber at the turn of the twentieth century—except in North Korea.

The exceptional character of the North Korean political system lies, therefore, not in the specific relationship between the state and the society anchored in what we commonly call the cult of personality but rather in the fact that this particular mode of rule has shown a remarkable resilience, defying the contrary historical trend found in most other revolutionary societies. The durability of this form of politics is an exception also in a theoretical sense, going against the historically impermanent nature of charismatic politics rendered in the Weberian exposition of modern political power and authority. The puzzle of the North Korean political system is therefore not the practice of an extraordinary cult of personality but the extraordinary continuity of this practice. In today's North Korean political termi-nology, the country's unique, protracted, and cross-generational charismatic poli-tics is called, to name just two among many other expressions, "legacy politics" (*yuhun jŏngch'i*) or "politics of longing" (*gǔriumǔi jŏngch'i*) (see chapter 1).[3]

This book explores the historical origins and contemporary realities of North Korea's enduring charismatic politics. It questions how the North Korean politi-cal system overcame the impermanent nature of charismatic authority and how it achieved what Weber calls the "routinization of revolutionary charisma" for such an astonishingly long period and in an apparently hereditary form of succession of rule.[4] As shown by recent events in North Korea (see the conclusion to this volume), North Korea's hereditary legacy politics continues many years after the founder of the North Korean polity passed away in 1994. These events publicized who the country's new inheritor of Kim Il Sung's preeminent legacy should be after the time of Kim Jong Il, the recently deceased leader of North Korea and Kim Il Sung's eldest son, who had ruled North Korea for the past seventeen years. The succession from Kim Il Sung to Kim Jong Il was "the communist world's first hereditary transfer of power" and began as early as the start of the 1970s.[5] Contemporary North Korean accounts extend the origin of this process further to the outset of the 1960s and even as far back as the time of the Korean War (1950–1953). These claims represent the powerful efforts in North Korea, as in other socialist polities, to appropriate and rewrite history in the service of a specific political goal. These historical revisions are intended not merely to bring greater honor and dignity to the country's iconic leader but also to appropriate the author-ity and majesty of the leader's persona to facilitate a desired future—particularly, the continuity of the political order free from the risk of a rupture in the political life of the charismatic authority. In this respect, the evolution of North Korea's statehood has been an epic struggle against the impermanent nature of charismatic authority and against the mortality of this authority, to which all other charismatic personas of the twentieth century eventually succumbed.

It may require no less than the brilliance of a genius or a major technological innovation to change the course of nature. When the change is about altering the life cycle of a charismatic political authority, the power required to make this change must involve a major invention in the art of state politics. In North Korea, this invention, above all, has taken the form of the technology of mass social mobilization and mass political literacy. The importance of this technology is familiar within the existing literature regarding modern politics. For instance, scholars of modern nationalist ideologies have long highlighted the centrality of print technology in the construction of national unity and common national consciousness.[6] In the study of revolutionary socialist state politics, investigation often extends to other technologies of mass politics: songs, drama and cinema, mass rallies and spectacles, and other similar instruments of display and the dissemination of ideas.[7] North Korea describes these diverse modes of display broadly as "revolutionary art" (*hyŏkmyŏng yesul*) and has brought their dissemination to a high level.[8]

Contemporary North Korean art historians claim that the country's revolutionary art underwent a major revolution in the early 1970s and that this revolution was achieved thanks to the genius and guidance of the then future leader of North Korea, Kim Jong Il. It is a widely acknowledged fact among observers that the Kim Jong Il–led artistic revolution in the 1970s was integral to the succession of power from the country's founding hero to his eldest son. With respect to this, Wada Haruki, one of the most astute observers of North Korea, has coined the idea of the "theater state," following anthropologist Clifford Geertz's classical study of ritual politics and spectacles of power in Indonesia. Wada presents the idea as a paradigm for the North Korean political process and development in the era of Kim Jong Il (see chapter 2).[9]

Although the empirical material introduced in this book closely relates to exploring the nature of North Korea's theater state and therefore centers on the examination of works of public art and mass spectacle, we frame this volume as a study of the North Korean state rather than North Korea's state art. Several excellent monographs have recently come out in both fields. Most notable is Charles Armstrong's meticulous study of North Korea's early state-building process, in which he investigates, among other things, the preeminence of arts and mass rituals in North Korea's revolutionary politics.[10] Tatiana Gabroussenko's *Soldiers on the Cultural Front* offers a fascinating history of early North Korean literary production, focusing on the diversion of North Korean literary art from classical socialist realist art.[11] Suk-Young Kim's *Illusive Utopia* examines other genres of North Korean public art, such as musicals and monuments, in ways similar to those explored in this book—with an eye to the role of art as an instrument of propaganda and political indoctrination.[12] Scholars in South Korea have recently made available a large body of other highly informative works on North Korea's art and politics.[13] In writing this book, we benefited greatly from these emerging works of scholarship in the rapidly growing field of social and cultural historical studies of North Korea. The importance of public art in socialist political processes is much studied, and the field of North Korean studies undoubtedly has much to learn from, as well as to contribute to, the existing body of work in comparative socialism. The revolutionary politics of North Korea is not a thing of the past, unlike most other former or existing socialist polities, but very much part of contemporary history. Hence, the study of North Korea's politics of art can also contribute to the current scholarly and policy debates on the future of North Korea and the country's place in the global order.

The present book is neither strictly a cultural historical study of North Korea's socialist realist art nor entirely an analysis of North Korea's domestic and international politics. Rather, it hopes to bridge these two spheres of investigation by dealing with a powerful political aspiration that has shaped North Korea's art and politics for the past decades, without an understanding of which both its politics and art would remain mysterious. Contemporary North Korean literature expresses this aspiration through the idiom of "legacy politics" or "moral loyalty politics (*dodŏk ŭriŭi jŏngch'i*)" and with slogans such as "Let us be faithful [to the legacy] across generations."[14] In this book, we consider the aspiration to be the pursuit of a historically durable, transcendental charismatic authority, and we approach it as the principal leitmotif in the evolution of the state of North Korea. The single-minded pursuit of this aspiration, as we will see, has destroyed the distinction between public art and state politics. The result was the birth of a powerful modern theater state whose mission is to resist, via the man-made politics of art, the natural mortality of charismatic authority.[15] North Korea asserts, "The power of thought knows no limits."[16] We need to know about North Korea's epic struggle to actualize this limitless power of thought and the insurmountable obstacles that its long struggle for unlimited power faces today.

Notes

1. Bruce Cumings, *North Korea: Another Country* (New York: The New Press, 2004).

2. Max Weber, *The Theory of Social and Economic Organization*, edited by Talcott Parsons (New York: The Free Press, 1947).

3. Heonik Kwon, "North Korea's Politics of Longing," *Critical Asian Studies* 42 (2010): 3–24.

4. Weber, *The Theory of Social and Economic Organization*, 389. This concept is discussed in chapter 2 of the present volume.

5. The quote is from "North Korea Confirms Kim Jong-Il's Son Will Take Over as Leader," *Guardian*, October 8, 2010.

6. Benedict Anderson, *Imagined Communities: Reflections on the Origin and Spread of Nationalism* (New York: Verso, 1991). See also Hong Kal, *Aesthetic Constructions of Korean Nationalism: Spectacle, Politics, and History* (New York: Routledge, 2011); Alexander Woodside, *Community and Revolution in Modern Vietnam* (Boston: Houghton Mifflin, 1976); Shawn Frederick McHale, *Print and Power: Confucianism, Communism, and Buddhism in the Making of the Modern Vietnam* (Honolulu: University of Hawaii Press, 2008), 102–42; Glen Peterson, *The Power of Words: Literacy and Revolution in South China, 1949–95* (Vancouver: University of British Columbia Press, 1998).

7. Among the most notable examples is Christel Lane, *Rites of Rulers: Ritual in Industrial Society—the Soviet Case* (Cambridge: Cambridge University Press, 1981). See also Jeffrey Brooks, *Thank You, Comrade Stalin!: Soviet Public Culture from Revolution to Cold War* (Princeton, NJ: Princeton University Press, 2000).

8. Kim Il Sung, *Hyŏkmyŏngjŏk munhakyesulŭl ch'angjakhalde daehayŏ* [On creating revolutionary literature and art] (Pyongyang: Workers' Party Press, 1978); Sahoigwahakch'ulp'ansa [Social science press], *Hangil hyŏkmyŏng munhakyesul: Kyŏngaehanŭn suryŏng Kim Il Sung dongjiŭi t'ansaeng yesundolkinyŏm* [Anti-Japanese revolutionary literature and art: In celebration of the sixtieth birth anniversary of the esteemed supreme leader Kim Il Sung] (Pyongyang: Social Science Press, 1971).

9. Haruki Wada, *Kitachōsen: Yūgekitai kokka no genzai* [North Korea's partisan state today] (Tokyo: Iwanami shoten, 1998); Clifford Geertz, *Negara: The Theatre State in Nineteenth-Century Bali* (Princeton, NJ: Princeton University Press, 1980).

10. Charles K. Armstrong, *The North Korean Revolution, 1945–1950* (Ithaca, NY: Cornell University Press, 2003).

11. Tatiana Gabroussenko, *Soldiers on the Cultural Front: Developments in the Early History of North Korean Literature and Literary Policy* (Honolulu: University of Hawaii Press, 2010).

12. Suk-Young Kim, *Illusive Utopia: Theater, Film, and Everyday Performance in North Korea* (Ann Arbor: University of Michigan Press, 2010).

13. Among the many recent publications are Woo-Young Lee, "Munhakyesulŭl tonghaesŏ bon Kim Jong Il sidaeŭi bukhan [North Korea in the era of Kim Jong Il seen through its literature and art]," *Kyŏngjewa sahoi* [Economy and society], no. 49 (2001): 102–23; Young-Sun Chun, "Bukhanŭi daejipdanch'ejoyaesulgongyŏn 'Arirang' ŭi jŏngch'ijŏk munhakyesuljŏk ŭimi [The socio-political and literary-artistic meanings of North Korea's Arirang Festival]," *Jungsoyŏngu* [Sino-Soviet affairs] 26, no. 2 (August 2002): 131–58; Young-Sun Chun, "Bukhan 'Arirang' ŭi hyŏndaejŏk pyŏnyonggwa ŭimi [Contemporary transformation and meaning of North Korea's Arirang Festival]," *Hyŏndaebukhanyŏn'gu* [North Korean studies review] 14, no. 1 (2011): 40–75; Young-Jung Park, *21segi bukhan kongyŏnyesul daejipdanch'ejowa yesulgongyŏn*

Arirang [North Korean collective gymnastics mass performance, Arirang, in the 21st century] (Seoul: Wŏlin, 2007).

14. U-Chol Yun, *Josŏnrodongdangŭi dodŏk ŭriŭi jŏngch'i* [The moral-loyalty politics of the Workers' Party] (Pyongyang: Social Science Press, 2005); Ha-Chol Chun, *Suryŏngnimŭn yŏngwŏnhi uriwa hamkke kyesinda* [The supreme leader is forever with us] (Pyongyang: Workers' Party Press, 1994). The slogan "Let us be faithful [to the leadership] across generations [*Daerŭl iŏ chungsŏnghaja*]" first appeared as part of North Korea's public language in 1974. See "Hyŏkmyŏngjŏnt'ongŭl daerŭl iŏ pitnage kyesŭngbalchŏnsikija [Let us be faithful (to the leadership) across generations]," *Rodong Sinmun*, April 25, 1974.

15. The term "theater state" is from Geertz, *Negara*. See chapter 2 of the present volume.

16. Quoted from "Kangkye jŏngsinŭro ŏksege ssawŏnagaja [Let's struggle along forcefully in the spirit of Kangkye]," *Rodong Sinmun*, April 22, 2000. Kangkye is in northernmost part of the Korean peninsula, a place that Kim Jong Il praised as having shown, during the time of famine, a heroic endurance of hardship and unwavering commitment to the party.

1

The Great National Bereavement, 1994

For anthropologists, doing research normally entails a long immersion in the rhythms of everyday life in the society or community that they are attempting to understand. This includes a careful survey of the existing literature about the society, learning its language, and, when the time comes to do the fieldwork, making patient efforts to be accepted by the community so as to enter the dynamic, exciting milieu of communal cultural life. This established and cherished way of practicing anthropology cannot be applied to North Korea, however. North Korean society is one of the most sheltered and jealously guarded in the contemporary world; it is also an intensely proud political society and invests heavily in preventing outsiders from seeing anything that might make a negative impression. This is familiar to all foreign visitors to Pyongyang and elsewhere in North Korea, and it appears frequently in their reports and reminiscences. The situation is quite discouraging for anthropologists. The author of this book did fieldwork in the former Soviet Union and later in rural Vietnam. Although he became familiar, while conducting fieldwork in these places, with the state hierarchy's regulation of movement and investigative activity, this never approached the intensity of control over foreign visitors in North Korea. Coauthor Byung-Ho Chung has on a number of occasions visited North Korea as well as China's borders with North Korea since the mid-1990s. He also has had extensive humanitarian and research experience with North Korean youth migrants now settled in China and South Korea. However, like all other foreign visitors to this land, which is proud of its revolutionary heritage and its self-reliant economy and politics, he was always carefully taken care of by the minders assigned to him by the authorities and had few chances to get to know ordinary North Koreans. Yet, even in a highly controlled society that allows outsiders very limited contact with the actual lived reality of its citizens, one experiences fleeting moments of revelation and catches glimpses of truth.

In Pyongyang, in the beginning of 2000, Byung-Ho Chung joined a South Korean humanitarian mission to North Korea and had an experience that left a lasting impression. After a series of meetings with the mission's North Korean counterparts about the impact of the country's food and health crisis on schoolchildren,

members of the mission were invited on a tour of the city's important monuments, museums, and memorials (most foreign visitors to the reclusive country
are expected to join in such a tour and pay respect to the sites). The group saw
the imposing Tower of Self-Reliance, erected in 1982, and the new, sumptuous
Mankyŏngdae Children's Palace, completed in 1989, before heading to a more
recent memorial complex. Their North Korean guide was eager to make clear that
all these monuments were built under the direction of Kim Jong Il and dedicated
to the honor and authority of the nation's supreme leader, Kim Il Sung. The guide
also explained that the more recent monuments built after the death of Kim Il
Sung in 1994 arose out of the Dear Leader Kim Jong Il's profound respect for
the eternal memory of the Great Leader Kim Il Sung and that the sites can only
be fully appreciated with the knowledge that they demonstrate the Dear Leader's
sublime filial piety toward the nation's founding father.

After the visit, Byung-Ho Chung had a chance to walk alongside the guide
away from other members of the group and accompanying North Korean officials. He asked the guide how people in North Korea managed to complete such
large memorial projects during such a difficult time. He did not have to explain
what he meant by a difficult time, knowing that the guide would understand he
was referring to the time of the Arduous March—the North Korean name for the
period of extreme energy and food shortages that devastated the country during
the second half of the 1990s.[1] The famine and accompanying epidemic crisis reportedly killed more than half a million people (some reports claim up to 2 million victims).[2] Upon hearing the question, the guide turned his head, looked at the
memorial tower dedicated to the late leader, and said, "For us in North Korea, the
thing that really matters is politics. The economy is nothing compared to politics.
We are ready to endure hunger and sacrifice our lives for politics if necessary."
Upon hearing this explanation, Byung-Ho Chung wished to say something back
to him but did not know how to articulate his thoughts. He could not find the
words to continue the conversation, which in any case was interrupted when a
North Korean official approached. Back at the hotel, he wondered what the mid-
dle-aged man meant by "politics" and how to make sense of this meaning within
the generally accepted meaning of politics in the outside world. He also pondered
the sudden change of tone and the look on the face of the guide when he spoke
of politics, wondering whether that abrupt change related in any way to a hidden
story about North Korean politics—its unspoken, unspeakable consequences for
human lives and relations.

The man in Pyongyang is not the only person who tells of a conceptual an-
tinomy of politics versus economy or a concept of politics that takes on such a
supreme moral value that the pain of hunger and the tragedy of mass death can be
justified. The same radical notion of moral politics is a familiar subject in North
Korea's official media and literary productions. Eminent South Korean anthropologist and veteran North Korea observer Lee Moon-Woong writes, "Anyone
who took interest in North Korean society would have observed the fact that poli-

tics is an essential element in daily lives in North Korea and in integrating these lives into a whole. Politics in North Korea is a vital mechanism of mobilization to link and tie members of society with the totality of its political system. What then are the meanings of this *politics*?"[3] The preeminence of politics also appears frequently in conversations with recent refugees now settled in China, South Korea, and elsewhere. Most of these refugees left their homes due to the food shortage and can be critical, some more so than others, of the North Korean administration for its failure to ensure the basic subsistence of the population.[4] However, it is relatively rare for these people, particularly recent arrivals, to criticize the politics of North Korea as such.[5] Some of these refugees underwent the harrowing experience of being forcibly sent back to North Korea after escaping to northeastern China in search of food. The returnees were liable to be fined, confined in reeducation camps, or even physically abused, sometimes severely, at the hands of the security forces.[6] In the view of the North Korean administration, placing economics, or anything else, before politics is a sign of selfishness and constitutes a serious and punishable weakness.[7] That escaping in search of food is a public crime relates to the fact that it is criminal to think of anything before politics in the hierarchy of civic virtues and human values—or "[to care] about one's mouth before ideology," as a North Korean refugee we recently met in Brussels put it. Many North Korean refugees are aware that the core element of citizenship in North Korea is to respect the supreme virtue of politics and that failing to do so can constitute an act of betrayal or even treason.[8] Another broadly related, recent example is the following remark made by South Korea's head of state on February 21, 2009: "I believe that a socialism that fails to provide daily meals to people is better to be abandoned." This offhand remark provoked some of the angriest reactions heard recently from North Korea, including the following: "We shall settle the scores with the band of traitors in most brutal and resolute manner."[9]

What, then, is this "politics"—a politics that transcends economy? Why is it so vital to the lives of North Koreans? How do we make sense of this transcendental moral politics that exists before and independently of economic well-being and basic subsistence?

These questions are at the heart of any attempt to come to terms with the so-called enigmatic state of North Korea.[10] The North Korean political system is unique in the world in that it has largely ignored the structural changes that have swept through most other former socialist states and societies since the late 1980s. Unlike other societies in the former Soviet bloc, North Korea did not experience the radical socioeconomic changes that observers of eastern and central Europe describe as postsocialist transition. Although there have recently been some limited, haphazard economic liberalization initiatives, mainly in relation to South Korea and China, North Korea is still a solidly single-party state (unlike former socialist countries in Europe) and still stubbornly adheres to a centrally planned and executed system of economic production and distribution (unlike other Asian socialist societies), be it functional or dysfunctional. Nor did North Korea follow the related yet different sets of changes associated with other Asian socialist polities, notably China and Vietnam. Unlike the latter, North Korea has not embraced a general move toward market economic reform, often called market socialism, and still less political reform toward a controlled social liberalization. In fact, its official media outlet sometimes accuses these streams of postsocialist transition of being treacherous. Because of its refusal (or inability) to embrace the predominant forms of postsocialist transition, North Korea has earned a reputation as a reclusive, isolated, and anachronistic polity not only among international actors in the liberal world but also among previous allies in the former Eastern bloc. North Korea itself seems clearly conscious of its public image in relation to the outside world. In the country's renowned public spectacle, the Arirang Festival, one of the most prominent recent messages sent to spectators (and the outside world) said, "Do not hope for any change in me!"[11]

Despite this disclaimer, however, North Korea is clearly in a state of transition, as are all the other former members of the Eastern bloc. In a way, the need itself for public disclaimers against change indicates that a change is in progress. This view is shared by contemporary observers of North Korea, some of whom highlight changes in North Korea's economic organization and trade relations, particularly in urban areas and industrial zones and in the country's relationship with South Korea and China.[12] Others emphasize the force of social change aris-

Figure 1.1. "Do not hope for any change in me!" (mass gymnastics performance). *Source: T'aeyanggwa ch'ŏngch'un* (Pyongyang: Geumsung Youth Press, 1999), 111.

ing from below in opposition to the reluctant, confused administration, particularly regarding the distribution of food and other basic subsistence goods.[13] If North Korea appears to be an unchanging, unchangeable actor on the international stage, it is probably because the changes the country is now undergoing are unfamiliar and therefore not easily perceptible to the outside world rather than because North Korea is truly defying change. In this sense, the declaration "Do not hope for any change in me" should probably be understood as "I am not going to change in the way you hope I will." The identity of this "you" to whom the statement is addressed is, of course, an interesting question. If North Korea is undergoing changes unlike those experienced by other former and existing socialist polities, an understanding of this change requires a more pluralistic understanding of the contemporary global processes and a departure from a perspective confined to the existing transitory forms, in light of which North Korea comes to stand as an outsider to the global process of postsocialist transition.

The inclusion of North Korea in any discussion of global postsocialist transition involves some conceptual difficulties, however. Of these difficulties, we would like to highlight the lack of attention to colonial and postcolonial histories in existing public and academic interests in postsocialist social and political transitions. Elsewhere, we have raised the point that the scholarship of postsocialist research is too narrowly focused on European examples and does not consider a broader comparative historical horizon.[14] The history of socialist revolution has different ramifications and varying significance across regions; in a large part of the world, this history is thematically inseparable from colonial and postcolonial politics, which differ in significant ways from those in Russian or European experiences. The narrow, Europe-focused understanding of socialism and what comes after hinders the existing postsocialist research from engaging the broad scholarship of international studies and a comparative understanding of Cold War history.

The Cold War was a global conflict, but it was hardly experienced in identical ways worldwide. Although closely interrelated in the geopolitical imaginations of the superpowers, the bipolar conflicts in the European theater and in non-Western postcolonial regions were radically different. The Cold War in Europe was primarily an "imaginary war," consisting of competition in economic development, political organization, and war preparedness that made it possible to thwart the outbreak of actual wars such as those that had destroyed Europe in two world wars.[15] In many postcolonial nations, however, the Cold War consisted of nonimaginary, actual wars, often following revolutionary upheavals and related domestic armed conflicts and other exceptional forms of organized political violence (often with heavy international intervention).[16] For example, Mark Bradley writes that the political history of Vietnam's socialist revolution is not to be considered separately from the experience of devastating wars as part of a postcolonial transition involving protracted fighting by French and then American (and also Korean) forces. Bradley defines the Vietnamese revolution as the pursuit of a postcolonial vision of a fully independent, prosperous nation-state in the era of the Cold War.[17]

It follows that the nation's contemporary social transition, after the initiation of the *doi moi* reform, involves much more than a shift from one economic form to another, just as Vietnam's past historical struggle was not merely about realizing a particular economic order.

A similar point may be made—and indeed has been—about the political history of North Korea.[18] In the view of the outside world, today's North Korea may appear to be a highly anachronistic political entity, unable to shake off the political ethos of the Cold War era and therefore incapable of joining postsocialist developmental streams.[19] Prominent in the domestic political arena of North Korea are, however, issues of colonial and postcolonial history rather than those of Cold War bipolar history.[20] North Korea stands out as unique among other existing or historical socialist polities, its political history having been shaped by a set of powerful postcolonial questions—questions that continue to shape the country's development today. In this book, we emphasize the fact that today's North Korea is a profoundly postcolonial polity—even more so now, after the breakdown of the Soviet empire, than in earlier years. The analytical significance of this argument is that, to understand modern North Korea, it is necessary to attend carefully to the political process in which colonial history and postcolonial rhetoric are being reinvented during the course of postsocialist transition.

The last point brings us back to the question of "politics" mentioned at the outset of this chapter and to the succession of power associated with this politics, that is, the political process after the death of Kim Il Sung in 1994 and, as we will show, the revitalization of colonial memory and postcolonial rhetoric that this process entailed. To consider this idea within the context of contemporary North Korea, it will be necessary to introduce briefly certain fundamentals of the North Korean political system. The idea of the preeminence of politics was invoked by the man in Pyongyang with specific reference to the town's monuments. Here, we focus the discussion on the country's public art and political aesthetics. From several recent scholarly attempts to define North Korean political culture, the concepts of the "partisan state" and "family state" stand out as having particular relevance to our discussion. Chapter 2 discusses another concept, the idea of a "theater state," which is meaningful for grasping how the partisan and family state ideas are interconnected.

First, however, a brief note on postcolonial history: In contemporary scholarship, postcolonial history or culture is frequently deployed in an analytically critical spirit (against the unequal global power structure) and as part of descriptive projects that interrogate the enduring effects of imperial and colonial rule upon developing societies beyond the formal colonial era. The idea of postcolonial historical experience, proposed by scholars like Dipesh Chakrabarty and Partha Chatterjee, is based on a conceptual separation of colonialism into two domains, an institutional order and a cultural schema, and the related premise that the latter, colonialism as culture, continues after the achievement of political self-rule, that is, the end of colonialism as an institutional order.[21] Chatterjee conceptualizes the predicate "post" in the postcolonial as a potent symbolic vitality in the present of the past experience of the actually existing colonialism. The idea of postcolonial experience suggested by the above scholars tends to project the historical epoch from the end of World War II to the present as an uninterrupted struggle to be free from the cultural and mental effects of colonialism, after this world is freed from the formal institutional grid of colonial subjugation in the late 1940s to the 1960s. This conceptual scheme does not consider the momentous shift in global power relations from a colonial to a bipolar Cold War formation during the period or the resultant complication in nation building in the decolonizing world.[22]

For an analysis of revolutionary postcolonial socialist polities, however, postcolonial criticism may take on a different significance. When a revolutionary anticolonial movement develops into revolutionary state politics, and when this state then mobilizes militant postcolonial rhetoric to bolster its legitimacy, the rhetoric can turn into a locally hegemonic force, thereby stamping out divergent voices and interpretations.[23] In such circumstances, postcolonial criticism ought to involve a critical look at the way in which the postcolonial perspective can turn into an instrument of power. North Korea is a radical example of the use and abuse of postcolonial rhetoric, and since Kim Il Sung's death in 1994, the rhetoric has been integrated with the powerful drama of commemoration and longing. It is in this drama of longing for the leader that we witness how memories of colonialism are reinvented to serve the purpose of political rule and succession, as part of and in reaction to the global postsocialist, post–Cold War transition.

The Partisan State

In a seminal study of North Korea's political history, eminent Japanese historian of modern Korea Wada Haruki proposes a definition of North Korea's political system as a "partisan state" (*yūgekitai kokka*, in Japanese).[24] The concept draws attention to the group of political actors who played a central role in the foundation of North Korea in the middle of the twentieth century (and the vigorous power struggles between the different political factions involved) and to the career backgrounds of these formative actors in colonial times as members of an armed resistance group based mainly in Japanese-occupied Manchuria.[25] One relatively small group of armed resistance fighters was led by the young Kim Il Sung and attracted considerable moral support from the large group of settlers of Korean origin in northeastern China.[26] As is well known, after 1945, these originally Manchurian-based armed revolutionaries were privileged against other nationalist groups in the early years of state building in North Korea after liberation from Japan's colonial rule, with strong support from the Soviet military, which occupied the northern half of postcolonial Korea (the southern half was occupied by US forces).[27] It is also well known that after the disastrous Korean War of 1950 to 1953 (disastrous for the people of Korea but also for the North Korean leadership because it failed to liberate the southern half of Korea as anticipated), Kim and his former partisan group from the Manchurian era succeeded in a power struggle against all other revolutionary groups and factions.[28] By the end of the 1960s, Kim's so-called Manchurian partisan faction had become an unchallenged, singular political force in North Korea, and it remains so to this day.[29] In this regard, Wada locates the establishment of North Korea as a partisan state at the Workers' Party Central Committee meeting in May 1967 and the party's general assembly in November 1970. By then, according to Wada, the internal power struggle within the party was over, and the story that "North Korea was established by Kim Il Sung and his Manchurian faction" became North Korea's official history and constitutional episode.[30] Observers of North Korea generally hold the view that this group of now-aged former guerilla fighters is the principal power base on which the so-called personality cult of Kim Il Sung advanced throughout the postwar years.[31] These people contributed to building North Korea's People's Army, in which they held key posts, into an increasingly vital political force after Kim's death, in support of his designated successor and, after this successor passed away in December 2011, his own chosen heir and defender of Kim's legacy. In proposing the idea of a partisan state, Wada describes how the above postwar political development of North Korea involved the sublimation of the history of the Kim Il Sung–led partisan group's armed anticolonial resistance activity in Manchuria into the single most important, most sacred, and all-encompassing saga of the nation's modern history. At the center of this powerful process of historical sublimation was what anthropologist Sonia Ryang calls "sovereign love"—the "boundless love of the nation" for their supreme hero, Kim Il Sung (and, in turn, the leader's immeasurable love for the people), who was, according to the countless cultural productions of the national saga, the nation's single hope for liberation from colonial misery.[32]

Wada's partisan state provides an effective way to think about North Korea's public culture as well as its political history. The concept's validity is amply demonstrated in recent official publications and, above all, through important public political events such as the Arirang Festival.[33] Here, we focus on the latter rather than on official literature (see chapter 3) because these theatrical performances have wider audiences and are more popular than books in North Korea. Accordingly, they are more significant in shaping domestic political processes. According to Charles Armstrong, musicals and films play important roles in North Korean politics in modeling the regime's emphasis on "the primacy of correct thought."[34] The recent article "The Songs from Our Leader," published in *Rodong Sinmun*, the official news organ of North Korea's Workers' Party, goes to the extent of claiming that the revolutionary state of North Korea was born out of songs—the songs that the country's founding leader sang in his Arduous March to national liberation—and that these songs are "the soul and pulse beats of the Kim Il Sung nation."[35] Films are widely used at schools and workplaces. In the regular study-cell meetings held in these places, films are frequently introduced as important study material (as are the leaders' writings and important newspaper articles and editorials) for updating and consolidating citizens' political literacy. After watching the films, people write reports about them and later discuss the written reports. The discussion groups are led by the leaders of local party cells, who are also in charge of reporting to the higher party organization the group members' commitment to studying.

The importance of thought in revolutionary politics and that of art and music in nurturing correct thought also explain why Kim Jong Il's accomplishments as the country's new political leader were closely associated with his purported interest and talent in the arts and musical production.[36] The prominence of correct thought also explains, as the next chapter demonstrates, why the first transition of power and authority from senior to junior Kim involved a proliferation of musical and theatrical production. Lee Woo-Young, a South Korean sociologist and acute observer of North Korean art history, makes a poignant point in this regard. Noting that "art and literature are an important political domain," Lee argues that Kim Jong Il's active involvement in cultural production should be seen as "the performance of his public duty as a leader of a socialist system rather than the expression of his personal taste."[37] Lee makes this point in part against the prevailing perception in South Korea and elsewhere that characterizes Kim's interest in music and art as an odd quality for a political leader and even a deviant obsession. Spectacles such as Arirang are also intended for the outside world. Carol Medlicott notes, "While symbol occupies a vital role in any country, in a reclusive state like North Korea—which eschews or is excluded from normal venues of diplomacy or international policymaking—symbol and symbolic performance collectively constitute a single grand mediating layer between the 'real' North Korean state and the world external to it."[38]

Arirang is a gigantic mass spectacle involving tens of thousands of highly trained citizen-actors (children, students, women, and soldiers) and well-choreographed mass performances. It incorporates key elements of other, smaller previous productions and, therefore, stands as the grand master of all major North Korean theatrical performances. Its details change each time, particularly the work of art called "background art" (*baekyŏngdae*) in North Korea, performed by thousands of spectator-actors who deliver important slogans and images by moving handheld multicolored pickets in carefully synchronized actions.[39]

Arirang depicts the country's revolutionary history as having originated in the communities of displaced Koreans in colonial Manchuria: their tragic lives are emblematic of the fate of the whole nation, displaced within and from its homeland by colonial occupation. The communities' sorrows are embraced by a heroic revolutionary leader, through whom the displaced people recover hope and passion for an honorable destiny and national liberation. In a strikingly biblical fashion, the story of Arirang highlights the redemptive aesthetics of exodus and illustrates the prophecy of truth emerging from life in exile. It is by virtue of being a partisan that one is able to glimpse the truth against the misery and despair of colonial displacement. For the partisans, seeing the truth is equal to nurturing an absolute belief in the infallible ability and pure spirituality of the leader they are following. Their sacrifice to the cause of national liberation is thanks for the priceless gift of discovering the truth of life made clear by the partisan leader. Their dedication to the leader is in return for the leader's boundless paternal love for all displaced children of the nation, who, thanks to the leader, found a place to belong as well as a purpose in life. An identical theme of a displaced child (often an orphan whose family has been lost to the brutality of the Japanese colonial power) awakening to truth along the revolutionary path paved by the "Single Star" (representing Kim Il Sung and embodying the nation's single hope for liberation) permeates other prominent North Korean cultural productions, including the highly celebrated musicals *The Flower-Selling Girl* (1972) and *The Sea of Blood* (1971). The story line of these productions is anchored in the revelatory power of adoptive kinship: The young patriot becomes a lonesome soul in the world, having lost her dearest blood relations to colonial violence. She finds substitute filial ties and a moral sense of belonging in the partisan leader, becomes enlightened, and finds the meaning of life thanks to the revolutionary family, which is the partisan group. The family's unbreakable solidarity and unconditional loyalty to the leader evolve into the mightiest resistance force against the colonial power.

As indicated, the concept of the partisan state involves another set of motives and values. The work of the partisans is depicted as militant in the face of powerful outside forces, while the partisans' internal solidarity is portrayed as resembling a family organization featuring the powerful values of paternal love and filial piety. The amity of kinship stands out, in contemporary rendering, as the core element of revolutionary activism and, by extension, as the constitutional virtue of the revolutionary state.

The Family State

Several observers have explored the position of kinship norms and idioms in the constitution of the North Korean political system. Armstrong notes that North Korea's early revolutionary politics "combined images of Confucian familialism with Stalinism," of which the virtue of collective filial piety (toward Kim Il Sung) was the most distinctive element.[40] South Korean anthropologist Lee Moon-Woong defines North Korea's political order as a "family state." He argues, "The ties between the masses and their supreme leader [in North Korea] are very much like kinship relations. It is therefore appropriate to call the political system of modern North Korea a family state. . . . The leader's role is akin to the role of a head of the household; he exercises an absolute authority and is the source of all wisdoms. [Thus] the destiny of the state resembles the fate of a family."[41] Indeed, it is claimed in today's North Korean media that "our people, looking up our Ŏbŏi-Janggunnim [parent-general], are all a single household [*hansiksol*], our country is everywhere a place of real kin [*ch'inhyŏlyuk*] and amicable large family [*daegajŏng*]."[42] Other South Korean observers frequently allude to a "[neo-] Confucian state."[43] These references are intended to highlight the relevance of considering North Korea's pronounced normative and ideological dispositions (often glossed over as "political culture") in coming to terms with the country's political structure and process. This perspective is shared by Bruce Cumings, one of the most insightful historians of modern Korea and the Korean War. Cumings's recent writings adopt a more cultural explanation for North Korea's political development, moving somewhat away from his earlier analysis of social revolution in postcolonial Korea, in which he emphasized land questions and rural class relations.[44] The analytical relationship between political culture and political economy is an important one.[45] For the purpose of this chapter, it suffices to mention a few conceptual issues raised by the idea of a family, or neo-Confucian, state with reference to North Korea.

The idea of the neo-Confucian state is widely referred to in the growing body of literature on North Korea published in South Korea and also in Japan.[46] The idea is useful for understanding many aspects of North Korean reality. For instance, the country's public media (e.g., books, broadcasts, political meetings, and public spectacles) hammer into the population the virtues of *ch'ung* (loyalty to the sovereign or to the country) and *hyo* (filial piety)—two of the preeminent human ethical dispositions highlighted in the Confucian tradition. In the second half of the 1990s, visitors to the Chosun Revolutionary Museum in Pyongyang were welcomed not only by the imposing, omnipresent statues and memorabilia of the nation's late Great Leader but also by tributes to the grandfather of the Chosun Dynasty's last king, Taewŏn'gun, who, in the face of threats from imperial powers, sought to protect the dynasty's Confucian political order through extreme defensive measures, including the purge of reformists, known as the "Closed-Door" policy.[47] South Korean historian Kim Seong-Bo advocates for conceptualizing North Korea as a neo-Confucian state based on the strong analogy he believes exists between the Closed-Door policy of the late Chosun Dynasty and the self-defensive isolation of today's North Korea.[48]

That the socialist revolution, while claiming to make a radical break with the political community's prerevolutionary past, is nevertheless affected by it is a well-studied topic. For China, North Korea, and Vietnam, the Confucian tradition constituted a major element of the past that the revolutionary movement sought hard to overcome. Armstrong details this process in the early state-building era of North Korea.[49] However, as Armstrong notes, the North Korean revolution's explicit negation of the defined feudal, exploitative, and backward tradition progressed in parallel with what may be called an invention of the Confucian tradition for the purposes of social integration and political consolidation.[50] In the Vietnamese context, intellectuals and party cadres discussed this ambiguous relationship between revolutionary politics and prerevolutionary social and cultural traditions in long-lasting debates about the compatibility of Marxism and Confucianism.[51] The issue has been addressed also in the domain of ancestor worship, a strong Vietnamese tradition. Although the postwar Vietnamese state authority strongly discouraged popular ancestor worship, it tried, at the same time, to appropriate the custom as an instrument of revolutionary mobilization and political integration by transforming the domestic and communal sites of ancestor worship into memorials for fallen revolutionary soldiers and party leaders.[52] The idea of a neo-Confucian state, addressed to North Korea, points to the political community's similar contradictory ties to the prerevolutionary, precolonial past, at once negated by the new order and assimilated into it. The idea is also based on the understanding that Korea traditionally harbored a stronger, more orthodox ideology of neo-Confucianism than China.[53] Interestingly, some observers use the last observation to explain China's and North Korea's different paths of social development since the 1980s, tracing Korea's less pragmatic and more conservative approach to political and social change to the deep heritage of the nation's neo-Confucian past.[54] Lee Moon-Woong poignantly notes, "The cultural process of North Korea may be described as a transformation towards a new Confucian society and a 'family state' united under the principle of filial piety which has become an expression of powerful political loyalty. In a way, perhaps we can conclude that the society dreamed by Zhu Xi [the most influential neo-Confucian thinker of twelfth-century China] has become reality in modern communist North Korea."[55] Similar arguments attracted South Korean intellectuals and students in the 1980s and early 1990s during their country's turbulent progression toward political democracy. The arguments appealed to nationalist sentiments, which at the time involved a growing sympathy for North Korea, which allegedly kept national culture and spirit more intact compared to South Korea, which was seen as dominated by foreign influences (this development was partly a reaction to South Korea's then prevailing anticommunist state ideology, which painted its northern neighbor as a hostile, alien entity to be resisted and negated).[56] This drastic change in South Korea's view of its northern neighbor is relevant to understanding the definition of North Korea as a neo-Confucian state. This formulation, framed mainly by a younger generation of South Korean historians, represents an effort to understand North Korea within Korea's national cultural tradition and therefore as part of national history, rather than as an alien, communist system.

The idea of a neo-Confucian state and a family state gained currency, however, not only due to the changes in South Korean society mentioned above but also because of broader changes in the region in the 1990s. These two sets of changes were of course interrelated and were both manifestations of the period's global upheaval, which we now habitually call the end of the Cold War. In North Korea, the upheaval resulted in an unprecedented economic and human crisis, which involved the collapse of trade and industrial activity, a rapid decline in agricultural output, and serious failures in public health and food distribution. The magnitude of these failures was such that the entire system of North Korea's production and distribution had become largely dysfunctional by the mid-1990s, and the combined effects of economic and administrative failures soon developed into a tragic famine and massive loss of human life.[57] These catastrophic social crises coincided with, and escalated after, the death of the country's revered founding leader, Kim Il Sung, which sank the entire nation of North Korea into a deep spiritual crisis and subsequently into a prolonged process of collective bereavement.

The impression that North Korea is a family or neo-Confucian state was greatly reinforced by these general structural crises, as well as by the way in which the country's leadership sought to avert them.

There is no doubt that the death of Kim Il Sung on July 8, 1994, induced a profound shock and rupture in North Korea. The event, called the Great National Bereavement in North Korea, brought the entire society to an abrupt halt. Hundreds of thousands of mourners crowded the public spaces of Pyongyang to participate in what, to an outside observer, looked like an intensely genuine, colossal, collective expression of grief. The scene of collective lamentation was at once familiar and deeply alien to South Koreans. It was familiar to the extent that the way in which individual mourners expressed their grief was akin to how Koreans would express grief at family funerals, according to the custom of public lamentation. The spectacle in Pyongyang's public squares appeared alien, however, because public lamentations in traditional Korean custom are usually for the loss of a close kinsman rather than a political leader (although there were also historical occasions in South Korea when people lamented the death of their state leaders publicly). Nevertheless, it is safe to say that the sorrow expressed by North Koreans was largely genuine (this was confirmed by the testimonies of recent North Korean refugees; see below) and that the citizens' grief was indeed very much akin to the shock felt by many on losing their dearest blood relation (although the contrary was probably also true—there were reports from peripheral areas that people participated in the public lamentation out of duty and that people who failed to take part in the national mourning were criticized and reprimanded).

People heard the news during their lunch hour on Saturday, July 9, 1994. Prior to the news announcement, workplaces and residential units were instructed to pay attention, at the appointed time, to TV or wired radio speakers. The latter is one of the North Korean state administration's principal instruments of policy dissemination and communication with the populace, a technology borrowed from the former Soviet Union. At a school in the country's northern region along the Chinese border, the teachers were assembled in the principal's office to listen to an "announcement of grave importance." Everyone was shocked to hear a single, repeated statement: "Our Great Leader Comrade Kim Il Sung has left our side." The principal let out a deep sigh; other, older members of the school's faculty remained silent, and a few young teachers shed tears. One teacher from a "soldier's family" (a family that contributed several of its members to the armed forces) reacted to the news with a particularly vigorous expression of sorrow. At another school, the headmaster took to loud wailing upon hearing the news; nearly all members of the staff gathered at his office joined in. The school's headmaster was from a prominent "war martyr's family," a status of considerable prestige and material benefits assigned to the families of the fallen soldiers of the Korean War. Teachers in this school followed the headmaster in their loud collective lamentation. Differences existed even within the close circle of a family. One refugee from North Korea told us how unresponsive her husband and his elder brother had been to the news, whereas her husband's youngest brother spent a long period crying and grieving deeply. Informants of North Korean origin who experienced the Great National Bereavement there commonly emphasized group dynamics and circumstantial conditions in explaining the variability in emotive reactions to the loss of the national leader. Several informants invoked the concept of *nunch'i* (side glances), a type of socioecological awareness and alertness that influences practical actions and behavioral choices. According to this scheme, the expression of feelings is a deeply social phenomenon, inseparable from where and with whom the feelings are expressed. Thus, the different reactions to the news of Kim Il Sung's death from the two groups of teachers related to the variant organizational cultures between the two schools and to the varying particular atmospheric conditions generated by the group and within the group's hierarchical order. In this context, therefore, it becomes nearly certain, as one informant insisted, that had a teacher who remained silent throughout the announcement been working in the other school, he would have actively joined in the collective lamentation. Indeed, when the two groups of teachers came together a few days later at the town's monument for Kim Jong Suk (deceased first wife of Kim Il Sung and his most trusted comrade, see chapters 2 and 4) to lay flowers as a tribute to the memory of Kim Il Sung, they were united in action, and all the teachers cried publicly over the country's loss of its guiding figure. Of course, some visitors to the monument still struggled silently with the disparity between their own relative unresponsiveness to the tragedy and the eruption of sorrow in the crowd they were part of. However, others experienced hysteria or fainting spells, overcome by the pain of loss. They grieved, as we heard from several informants, "more sorrowfully than they would grieve for the death of their own parent." Some brought a table of food offerings, such those people traditionally prepare for the departed in a funeral or ancestral death-day remembrance rite, and stood vigil at the monument throughout the night (also a familiar practice in Korea's traditional mortuary rite).

Despite the diversity of reactions, the evidence suggests that the death of Kim Il Sung was akin to the death of a father for many North Koreans and that the drama of collective bereavement and ensuing funerary proceedings (which nominally lasted one hundred days, including the ten days of prefuneral mourning, and later were extended to three years, but which actually continue to this day) were in fact, in an important sense, a *family* affair. A North Korean woman working in China said in her conversation with representatives of a South Korean humanitarian agency, "One most unforgettable event in my life was the shock I had when I heard about the death of our Supreme Leader in 1994. Until then, we thought 'Life in North Korea is much better than life in South Korea. Why is this? Because we have nothing to fear in the world, as we have the greatest human being as our leader.' We were educated as such and we believed what we were taught. Then we suddenly lost that virtuous human being; this deeply saddened all of us and we all cried over the loss."[58] According to a memorial speech delivered at Kim Il Sung University,

The businessmen and technicians from a capitalist foreign country who visited our country during the national bereavement commonly remarked that they had never seen people like us, a truly unique people in the world. The CNN network of the United States and the NHK of Japan broadcast broadly how our people so deeply grieved the loss of our Supreme Leader. CNN said, "The Supreme Leader Kim Il Sung once mentioned that North Korea was a single family, which it would not be easy for people in the West to comprehend clearly. The Funeral held on Tuesday showed in a most lucid way how this is true, how people in our country hold the Supreme Leader indeed as their dearest Parent [ŏbŏi]. The collective sorrow that our people expressed over the loss of the Supreme Leader Kim Il Sung was genuine, not a coerced expression." Our enemies witnessed the force of our solidarity demonstrated in our collective bereavement, the force of which is mightier than a nuclear bomb.[59]

According to a commemorative poem written for the tenth anniversary of Kim Il Sung's death and printed in the newspaper of the North Korea's Workers' Party on July 2, 2004,

Having lost Father,
On the Longevity Hill under the pouring, punishing rain,
Your children wailed and cried.
"How may we carry on living without Father?" we asked.
When the funeral car passed along the Victory Square,
We stood against it with our arms wide open,
To prevent the soldiers from taking you away.
We cried, "You can't go, you can't abandon us."[60]

This poem, titled "The Single Way to Victory along the General's Footsteps," is an extremely long epic narrative that depicts North Korea's Arduous March after Kim Il Sung's death. The general in the poem's title refers to the nation's new leader, Kim Jong Il, and the bulk of the poem is about this new leader's heroic efforts to keep the family (of the nation) together after the founding leader passed away. According to the epic narrative, the driving force behind these efforts was the successor's deep filial piety and unshakable spiritual ties to his predecessor. Through witnessing and appreciating the new leader's filial piety, the national family of North Korea overcomes its grief and embarks on a united advance toward the glorious future. Here, the political amity of kinship works in two domains—within Kim's family and between this family and the family of the nation—and Kim Jong Il's status as the country's new leader derives from his exemplary performance of his filial obligations to the nation's dead father. The new Kim is the leading "funeral host" or "funeral master" (*sangju*)—a role allocated to the deceased's eldest male descendent in traditional Korean custom—of a funerary event that involves the entire nation. Kim Jong Il's masterful execution of this role constitutes the post-1994 history of North Korea, according to the epic narrative, the message of which is in fact replicated in many other recent North Korean cultural productions.[61] We learn from the narrative that contemporary North Korean politics has been, in a crucial way, funerary and commemorative. Key to this commemorative politics was the challenge of replacing the irreplaceable Kim Il Sung at the country's exemplary center.

In considering the recent history of North Korea's family state, therefore, it is important to note that the idea of family in this context does not necessarily refer to a solidary community based on actual ties of consanguinity, although saying this does not necessarily mean either that the "family" in the family state can collapse into what is in anthropological literature called a fictive or metaphoric kinship. Kim Il Sung's political fatherhood, as noted earlier, abounds with stories of fostering and adoption. In contemporary renderings of early revolutionary history during anticolonial partisan activity, the actors who allegedly built kinship with Kim were mostly uprooted, displaced, and orphaned youth, through whom the larger population is depicted as entering into a relationship of kinship with the revolutionary leader.[62] The central role of the orphaned revolutionary youth in the construction of Kim's political fatherhood continued in subsequent eras. This was demonstrated by the establishment of Mankyŏngdae Revolutionary School, a very prestigious institution in North Korea established in 1947.[63] Mankyŏngdae

Figure 1.2. General Kim Jong Il as the nation's guardian (painting depicting the Great National Bereavement). *Source: Juch'e yesulŭi widaehan yŏllun* (Pyongyang: Art and Education Press, 2002), 212.

Figure 1.3. Mankyŏngdae Revolutionary School. *Source: Yŏnggwangŭi 50nyŏn* (Pyong-yang: Chosun Art Book Press, 1995), 309.

refers to Kim Il Sung's birthplace, a sacred location and prominent pilgrimage destination for North Koreans. Mankyŏngdae Revolutionary School (together with Kang Ban Sŏk [Kim Il Sung's mother] Revolutionary School and Heaju Revolutionary School, which opened in 1958) originally sheltered children who had lost parents to the revolutionary causes, and it is believed that the elite cadres most loyal to Kim Il Sung (including his son Kim Jong Il)—those who would make up the "spinal core of [North Korean] revolution"—were brought up in it.[64]

Therefore, the idea of a family state is closely bound up with the idea of a partisan state, as well as with the memory of colonial suffering and struggle the latter represents, and we can conclude that the two concepts are constitutive of each other. In our opinion, the same conclusion applies to Kim Il Sung's relationship to his political successors. Contrary to the perception held widely in the outside world, we do not think that North Korea's succession story justifies our calling the country's political system a "dynasty," or the nation a "dynastic state," or its late leader a "god-king."[65] Veteran North Korea observer Suh Dae-Sook rightly argues,

Kim Il Sung never considered himself as the lord of a feudal society. He was a pragmatic politician. It is without doubt that he decided to hand over his power to his son believing that, after carefully considering other options, this way it would be more likely for him to maintain his power in his late years and for his legacy and the political system he established to be guaranteed to last. He witnessed the de-Stalinization and the end of political life for numerous other state leaders; in this light he was certainly concerned about the implications of possible events after his death.[66]

The handover of absolute power from father to son was based not merely on a real, biological relationship of descent but rather, more significantly, on the historically constituted political kinship, which, as described earlier, originates in the heroic story of the partisan family in colonial Manchuria. In other words, the succession of power implemented in North Korea was not a family affair, in the sense of a genealogical continuity or a feudal dynastic order of succession, but instead a political event rooted in the modern history of political fatherhood, the constitution of a family state, and the national narrative of the Manchurian era that provided the origin myth for the patriarchal, familial-political order. Chapter 2 returns to this idea and considers it with reference to what Max Weber said about the transition from personal to hereditary charisma.

New Family State

Once again, the ideas of the partisan state and the family state are both instructive for understanding North Korea's political history and process. Regarding questions about North Korea's current state formation amid the ongoing crisis since Kim Il Sung's death, however, it is important to look afresh at these two concepts. Before 1994, there were no contradictions between them, as Kim Il Sung embodied both the leader of the nascent revolutionary partisan group and the father of the revolutionary workers' state. The national community of North Korea had had only one collective father, as it were, from its legendary inception throughout its political reality. After Kim's death in 1994, however, the symbolism of the partisan state had to be revised, as the country set out to celebrate the new leader. Kim Jong Il was born in 1942 and thus had no claim to the heroic, founding legend of anticolonial revolutionary partisan activity in colonial Manchuria. Therefore, it was necessary either to provide a place for Kim Jong Il in the founding legend or to reinvent the legend so that it could be played out with the young Kim assuming a formative role. Both of these blatant attempts at historical revision have occurred in the North Korean public media and official historical scholarship since the early 1980s.[67] The symbolic properties relating to the idea of the family state also had to undergo some major changes. The old leader, having been the country's single founding father for many decades, became an ancestral figure in 1994. North Korea had to make adjustments to accommodate the change in the condition of the country's supreme leader from the living political father to the founding ancestor (*sijo*).

The above-mentioned structural adjustments have indeed been vital issues in North Korea's political process since Kim Il Sung's death and even before then. These issues are both historical and genealogical. In the historical dimension, the most important measure of adjustment was probably to bring the old history of armed partisan resistance to a history of the present. The last point helps to explain Kim Jong Il's privileging of the People's Army under the so-called military-first politics, one of the most consistent policies of post-1994 North Korea (see chapter 3). The policy has been manifested not only in government and party documents but also strongly in public slogans and spectacles. These public forms make it clear that Kim Jong Il's manner of ruling the country derived directly (or was meant to) from Kim Il Sung's.

The epic poem "Single Path to Victory" claims, "The tradition of the Arduous March inherits the tradition of revolutionary anti-Japanese struggle." The poem also asserts, "Our Great Leader founded the shining free fatherland, crossing the sea of blood and the sea of fire in his heroic defiance against colonialism; remember that it is the highest virtue of patriotism to continue the struggle and to protect its legacy by the arms of military-first politics. It is no one but the Dear Leader [Kim Jong Il] who keeps that virtue so deeply in his heart." The mass spectacle Arirang begins with tragic scenes in colonial Manchuria and depicts how the tragedy was overcome by the leadership and military genius of Kim Il Sung. The story it tells culminates in the shining example of another military genius of the nation, Kim Jong Il, the only one who can lead the nation in the global crisis of socialist revolution. It is when the hundreds of soldiers of the People's Army appear on stage and perform their synchronized combat art that North Korean spectators begin their most enthusiastic cheers. The scenario stresses that the time of the Arduous March is a national crisis as grave as the era of colonial domination and that the power of the armed forces is vital for overcoming it, just as the power of the partisan forces was for ending colonial domination and displacement. Within this postcolonial scenario, the manifest destiny of Kim Jong Il, as the head of the country's armed forces, overlaps and merges with the historical destiny of his predecessor as the shining leader of the revolutionary partisan forces. As claimed in the epic poem, connecting the new tradition of the Arduous March to the old tradition of anticolonial struggle is the unchanging "revolutionary military spirit," which, inherited from Kim Il Sung's anti-Japanese partisan politics, is now being crystallized in Kim Jong Il's military-first, or "army as revolutionary vanguard," politics. The epic narrative "Single Path to Victory" shows what constitutes the primary duty of patriotic citizens in this transition: "Dear Leader, please do not worry! Ten million rifles are standing next to you! Should there be any soul who dares to betray you, our 10 million rifles will punish it in most merciless ways!"

The aesthetics of filial piety play a key role in connecting the two revolutionary traditions, past and present. The narrative "Single Path to Victory," as well as many other cultural productions, makes clear that Kim Jong Il's authority derives from his historical proximity to and demonstrated affinity with the late founding leader (that is, rather than his blood ties). On this matter, what stands out with particular significance is the North Korean leadership's tradition of "on-the-spot-guidance" trips or "field visits." This public political practice is in form opposite to the mass-performed collective spectacles such as Arirang. The spectacle constitutes an assembly of and performance by ordinary citizens at the country's political center (Arirang is always performed in Pyongyang, the country's capital), at which members of North Korea's political leadership stand as spectators (as well as the offstage choreographer); in on-the-spot-guidance performances, on the other hand, the country's sovereign leader goes out to the peripheral areas and performs intimate encounters with ordinary citizens. Medlicott, discussing North Korea's sovereignty symbols, proposes an interesting analogy between the pomp of early modern Europe and North Korea's symbolic political arena. She observes,

> But the most profound symbolic commonality between North Korea and early modern England in terms of performative practice has to do with the Elizabethan pattern of the monarch "going on progress," that is, performing a physical ceremonial circuit through the countryside. In this way the regime of Elizabeth transformed England's rural terrain into political territory. . . . This combination of pageantry with the physical embodiment of the state in the person of the monarch was essential to the process of constituting England as a national territory. In the North Korean case, surely one of the most commonly observed practices of Kim Il-sung during his lifetime was his "on-the-spot-guidance" tours, on which he travelled throughout the country to personally visit collective farms, factories and other sites of economic production. Images of Kim interacting with working-class North Koreans on these visits fill North Korean pictorial magazines, and the images convey powerfully and palpably the intent of the "on-the-spot-guidance" practice to embody state power and state authority.[68]

Medlicott could have mentioned the tradition of royal pageantry invented in Asian imperial politics to narrow the enormous gap between the art of politics in sixteenth-century Tudor England and that in a twentieth-century workers' state. Pageantry was an important element in Meiji Japan and Qing China, as well as in the last years of the Chosun Dynasty under Japan's informal colonial rule of Korea from 1905 to 1910.[69] However, she is absolutely right to note the "on-the-spot-guidance" tours and to highlight the importance of this practice in North Korea's political process.

The North Korean leadership's tradition of on-the-spot-guidance trips consists of countless encounters between the late leader Kim Il Sung and ordinary North Koreans—in the latter's workplaces, their residential compounds, and even their homes—involving the leader's caring attention to all the details of people's lives; in turn, the people turned the leader's visits into local historical episodes.[70] This tradition is certainly in line with the practice of pageantry in modern monarchical orders, as Medlicott says, but it is nevertheless distinguished from them in its emphasis on intimate contact between the ruler and the ruled as well as the obviation of the pomp that characterizes the modern monarchy's art of ruling. The North Korean media claim that on-the-spot guidance is a "new mode of popular leadership invented by Kim Il Sung, which led to the victory of our work of socialism in all spheres: the construction of the party and the state, the building of military power, and the transformation of society, nature, and human beings."[71] It is known that Kim Jong Il accompanied Kim Il Sung on these important journeys of popular leadership in the 1980s, and these joint trips were a crucial part of the preparation for the succession. The North Korean media assert that although this tradition was invented by Kim Il Sung, "today, it is practiced by Dear Leader [Kim Jong Il] at a higher level and significance, which provides the fundamental source for all the miracles of the military-first Chosun [North Korea] that makes the whole world marvel at us."[72]

After Kim Il Sung's death in 1994, as the last remark demonstrates, the tradition of field visits took on a yet more vital importance. The places where the late leader visited during his lifetime, particularly military installations, became pilgrimage sites for the new leader. The popular song "Twelve Months of Sŏn'gun Victory" (*sŏn'gun sŭngri yŏldudal*) depicts the untiring on-the-spot-guidance trips made by Kim Jong Il over the course of four seasons; his destinations are all army locations, including one along the militarized frontier with South Korea visited in December. Throughout the second half of the 1990s, Kim Jong Il made a number of trips to many places in order to "feel the Great Leader's spiritual traces" and because he greatly missed the Great Leader. Although the places that attracted the new leader were mostly military installations, his pilgrimages reportedly included viewing the "pond that keeps the memory of the Great Leader's footsteps, the gift of a refrigerator from the Great Leader, the steam rice cooker sent by the Great Leader, and the bunk bed where the Great Leader once gave his curious look."[73] It is said that Kim Jong Il wrote the song "The Great Leader Is Forever with Us" based on his pilgrimage experience, and the song has since become a most sacred song, together with another important popular song titled "Where Are You? We Miss You, General." Kim Jong Il is reported to have said, "The bloodline of our nation will not continue without our songs dedicated to the Father-Supreme Leader. Losing these songs will mean losing the nation's life force and its future. When the songs continue to be sung and heard, the blood genealogy of the Kim Il Sung nation will stay strong and prosper."[74] According to the epic narrative "Single Path to Victory," the people of North Korea deeply miss their late leader; yet, the entirety of their emotive dedication to the late leader remains humble compared to the intensity of longing and power of filial piety felt by the Dear Leader toward the Great Leader. The narrative says of the Dear Leader, "The military-first era is the landscape of longing. . . . The Dear Leader is the supreme embodiment of [our collective] longing."[75]

Politics of Longing

Building the landscape of longing was, of course, extremely costly for North Korea. The "landscape" was the *politicheskoe voobrazhaemoe* (political imaginary, in Russian), which is, according to Susan Buck-Morss, "a topographical concept in the strict sense, not a political logic but a political landscape, a concrete, visual field in which political actors are positioned."[76] The Russian word *obraz* signifies "shape" or "form," as in graphic representation, but, more specifically, an "icon."[77] In this political landscape of longing, the new leader's performance of exemplary filial piety and spectacular pilgrimage was not merely a family affair but rather everybody's affair, concerning all the "family" members of North Korea who owed their lives and spirits to the political fatherhood of Kim Il Sung. The landscape of longing required devotion from every member of the family state, and the devotion was both spiritual and material. On the spiritual side, the politics of longing was not to be affected by the economic crisis or the famine. The grief over the Great Leader's death was all that was to be visible in the spectacle of national funerary commemoration; there was no space in this collective bereavement for private, communal grief over the victims of the great famine. On the material side, the landscape of longing had to be manifested in the material culture of commemoration, and this required the mobilization of labor and resources from among the famine-stricken population. Most prominent was the transformation of Kim Il Sung's former office complex into a dazzlingly sumptuous memorial palace (Kŭmsusan Memorial Palace) for 1994 to 1998.[78] Also notable were the completion of a gigantic memorial to the Workers' Party in 1994 and 1995, various other large-scale historic monuments relating to the majesty of early Korean statehood, and an expressway built in 1996 and 1997 to link the city of Pyongyang to the Myohyangsan Kim Il Sung memorial complex.[79] The Myohyangsan memorial includes the prominent International Friendship Exhibition Hall (see chapter 5), which houses the numerous gifts to Kim Il Sung from state leaders and progressive groups the world over; the road was built exclusively to connect this eminent place of pilgrimage to Pyongyang and is unavailable for mundane public use. Other epitaphs and memorials emerged in the country's capital during the second half of the 1990s, and many more (such as the Eternal Life Tower) arose in peripheral regions and localities.

In the extreme hardship of 1995 to 1997, when the state distributive system completely collapsed and the shortage of food took a particularly devastating toll, ironically the famine-stricken population was eagerly drawn to the monumental projects. The state administration prioritized these projects, and the people who joined them thus were allocated scarce subsistence resources. Public spectacles and ceremonies also became more pompous and spectacular, putting enormous pressure on a society at the brink of collapse and facing an unprecedented economic crisis and food shortage. The political "landscape of longing" partly acknowledged this crisis, as shown by the idiom "Arduous March." Later, Kim Jong Il himself admitted the devastation of the time. He said to soldiers during his on-the-spot-guidance trip to an unidentified military installation, "The lives of our people still have difficulties, and we have not yet fulfilled the Great Leader's will. This makes me unable to rest or sleep comfortably."[80] In a speech welcoming international delegates to North Korea, he is reported to have said, "You must have pondered why the streets are unlit and so dark. No matter how bright and lively the streets in capitalist countries are, there is no future in those streets. We may have difficulties now, but we have hopes for the future. Our aim is to build perpetually lively streets, not ephemeral ones."[81] The North Korean song "We Shall Not Forget," released in 2000, says,

How many days of severe hardship has this land been seeing?
How many miles of arduous journey have we marched along?
We shall not forget,
The Arduous March our General embarked on from the hill of blood and sorrow.
We shall not forget,
The traces of hardship our General left behind while sharing a bowl of gruel with us.
Our Chosun would have stopped breathing without our General.
We have come to triumph only thanks to Him.
With our barrel of a gun ahead of us and as we have always done,
We shall trust and follow our General, and only Him.[82]

Yet, the morality of patriotic filial piety, presented in this landscape as the supreme virtue, also forcefully insisted that the subsistence crisis must not affect the process of commemoration. "Single Path to Victory" calls the pains of hunger "peevish cries [of children] for food," unsuitable for the soldiers of military-first politics and the heritage of the glorious partisans of colonial Manchuria. Although the regime recognized the "difficulties" and human sufferings of the Arduous March, it also averred that the fundamental obligation of all soldiers of the military-first-era partisan state and all members of the post-1994 family state was to endure the "difficulties" as heroically as the exemplary, ancestral partisans of the 1930s (see also chapter 6).

Figure 1.4. Eternal Life Tower, Pyongyang (built between 1995 and 1997). *Source: Chosun* 541 (May 2000): cover image.

Figure 1.5. The Foundation of the Workers' Party Tower, Pyongyang (built between 1994 and 1995). *Source:* Photo by Byung-Ho Chung (2006).

Figure 1.6. Three Principles of Fatherland Unification Tower, Pyongyang (built between 1999 and 2001). *Source:* Photo by Byung-Ho Chung (2006).

Military-first politics may have provided a solution to a crisis in the family state and to challenges to the partisan state. In advancing this solution, however, the new partisan state politics, called military-first politics, and the new family state politics, which created the landscape of longing, resulted in one of the most tragic events of death in modern history, in which the commemoration of one man's death contributed to the loss of innumerable human lives, the lives of people who were all categorically the deceased man's children.

The North Korean guide in Pyongyang said, "We are ready to endure hunger and sacrifice our lives for politics if necessary." While saying this, he gazed at the towering memorials dedicated to the living memory of the Great Leader, built after his death in 1994 and during the time of the Arduous March. The man was telling the truth: the politics of longing involved unimaginable sacrifice. The remaining question that confronts us is whether keeping the memory of the parent is worth the enormous sacrifice resulting in the loss of so many of his children's lives. How can people reconcile this radical moral failure of the family state and how its renewed claim for vitality violated the fundamental norms of familial unity? The subsequent chapters consider these critical questions faced by North Korea's political system today. They examine the crisis in North Korea's familial political order and the moral contradictions between this normative order and the country's partisan state historical paradigm. Before we proceed further, however, it is necessary to turn to the idea of the theater state mentioned earlier, which we believe is useful for understanding the political process of North Korea after the seismic rupture of 1994.

Notes

1. Byung-Ho Chung, "North Korean Famine and Relief Activities of the South Korean NGOs," in *Food Problems in North Korea: Current Situation and Possible Solutions*, ed. Gill-Chin Lim and Namsoo Chang (Seoul: Oruem Publishing House, 2003), 239–56; Ian Jeffries, *North Korea: A Guide to Economic and Political Developments* (New York: Routledge, 2006), 82–107; Stephan Haggard and Marcus Noland, *Famine in North Korea: Markets, Aid, and Reform* (New York: Columbia University Press, 2007); Andrew S. Natsios, *The Great North Korean Famine: Famine, Politics, and Foreign Policy* (Washington, DC: U.S. Institute of Peace Press, 2001).

2. Woori minjok sŏrodopgi bulkyo undong bonbu (Korean Buddhist sharing movement), *Bukhansigryangnanŭi silt'ae (Jaryojip)* [Reality of the North Korean food shortage] (Seoul: Joŭnbŏtdŭl, 1998); Byung-Ho Chung, "Bukhan kigŭnŭi inlyuhakjŏk yŏn'gu [An anthropological study on the North Korean famine]," *T'ongilmunjeyŏn'gu* [Korean journal of unification affairs] 16, no. 1 (2004): 109–40; W. Courtland Robinson et al., "Famine, Mortality, and Migration: A Study of North Korean Migrants in China," in *Forced Migration and Mortality*, ed. Holly E. Reed and Charles B. Keely (Washington, DC: National Academy Press, 2001), 69–85.

3. Moon-Woong Lee, *Bukhan jŏngch'imunhwaŭi hyŏngsŏnggwa gŭ t'ŭkjing* [The formation and characteristics of North Korean political culture] (Seoul: Institute of National Unification, 1976), 3 (original emphasis).

4. Byung-Ho Chung, Woo-Taek Jun, and Jean-Kyung Chung, eds., *Welkŏm tu koria: Bukjosŏn saramdŭlŭi namhan sali* [Welcome to Korea: North Koreans in South Korea] (Seoul: Hanyang University Press, 2006); Joŭnbŏtdŭl [Good friends], *Bukhansaramdŭli malhanŭn bukhaniyagi* [Tales of North Korea told by North Koreans] (Seoul: Jŏngto, 2000).

5. According to a twenty-three-year-old North Korean refugee in China, "I still cry when I think of the supreme leader. But for our general [Kim Jong Il] who is now doing politics as a heir to the supreme leader: I will surely worship him if he can make us live a slightly better life and without worries. In reality, however, our lives become more painful and less bearable as days pass—so I think this is too much really. It is probably the case that our general genuinely cares about us, whereas those in power who are supposed to support him are not doing their proper jobs." Cited from Kun-O Lim, "Baeksŏnghaebang—ŏnlonhaebangi ch'oiusŏnida [Liberation of people: Liberation of press is the first priority]," *Limjingang* [Imjin river], no. 3 (August 2008), 142–43.

6. Sun-Ho Choi, *T'albukja gŭdŭlŭi iyagi* [Defectors from North Korea, their stories] (Seoul: Sigongsa, 2008); Byung-Ho Chung, "Living Dangerously in Two Worlds: The Risks and Tactics of North Korean Refugee Children in China," *Korea Journal* 43, no. 3 (2003): 191–211; Mike Kim, *Escaping North Korea: Defiance and Hope in the World's Most Repressive Country* (Lanham, MD: Rowman & Littlefield, 2008); Katherine Moon, "Beyond Demonization: A Strategy for Human Rights in North Korea," *Current History* (September 2008): 264–66.

7. See the testimonies available online at "Bukhan sigryangnanminŭi saenghwalsang [Life conditions of North Korean food refugees]," CyberHumanRights.com, http://www.cyberhumanrights.com/media/material/5049_1.pdf (March 6, 2010).

8. See Joel R. Charny, *Acts of Betrayal: The Challenge of Protecting North Koreans in China* (Washington, DC: Refugees International, 2005); Chung, "Living Dangerously in Two Worlds," 191–211. According to a refugee from Ch'ungjin, who was interrogated by the North Korean border security after being arrested while trying to cross the Chinese border together with his seven-year-old son, he was, for his captors, "a traitor who was happy to abandon the fatherland" and "a traitor who would bring up treacherous children" (http://www .cyberhumanrights.com/media/material/5049_1.pdf [accessed March 6, 2010]). According to another refugee, "The most painful burden to today's [North Korean] refugees is the political entitlement 'crime of treason against the nation.' Those who come to cross the river for finding a way to survive have no will to betray the nation." Cited from Kun-O Lim, "Salgi wihan t'albukdo joiinga? [Is it a crime to try to leave North Korea to survive?]" *Limjingang* [Imjin river], no. 4 (March 2009): 27.

9. "Buk, 'kkŭtkkaji kyŏlp'an bol kŏt' [North, we will settle (the scores) till the end]," *Dong-A Ilbo*, February 23, 2009.

10. The expression "enigmatic state" is quoted from Marika Vicziany, David Wright-Neville, and Peter Lentini, eds., *Regional Security in the Asia Pacific: 9/11 and After* (Cheltenham, UK: Edward Elgar, 2004), 15. See also Jon Halliday, "The North Korean Enigma," *New Left Review* 127 (1981): 18–52.

11. This statement in Korean originates from Kim Jong Il and was made publicly known through an article titled "Urinŭn sŭngrihanda [We shall win]," published on June 3, 1996, in *Rodong Sinmun*, the news organ of North Korea's Workers' Party. It is reported that Kim Jong Il reiterated the statement once again in his public speech delivered on February 16, 2007, his sixty-fifth birthday. See also "Sŏngsŭrŏun 3nyŏn [The sacred three years]," *Rodong Sinmun*, July 2, 1997, and "Pulmyŏlŭi 5nyŏnŭl hoigohamyŏ [Remembering the unforgettable five years]," *Rodong Sinmun*, July 1, 1999.

12. Rudiger Frank, "The North Korean Economy," in *Handbook on the Northeast and Southeast Asian Economies*, ed. Anis Chowdhury (Cheltenham, UK: Edward Elgar, 2007), 298–316; James E. Hoare and Susan Pares, *North Korea in the 21st Century: An Interpretative Guide* (Folkestone, UK: Global Oriental, 2005), 46–64; John Larkin, "North Korea, Mysterious Reform," *Far Eastern Economic Review* 8 (August 2002): 18–19.

13. Joŭnbŏtdŭl [Good friends], *Bukhansahoe muŏti byŏnhago itnŭnga?* [What changes are taking place in North Korean society?] (Seoul: Jŏngto, 2001); Haggard and Noland, *Famine in North Korea*. See also Hyung-Min Joo, "Visualizing the Invisible Hands: The Shadow Economy in North Korea," *Economy and Society* 39, no. 1 (2010): 110–45.

14. Heonik Kwon, *Ghosts of War in Vietnam* (Cambridge: Cambridge University Press, 2008), 29–32.

15. Mary Kaldor, *The Imaginary War: Interpretation of East-West Conflict in Europe* (Oxford: Blackwell, 1990).

16. Odd Arne Westad, *The Global Cold War* (Cambridge: Cambridge University Press, 2005).

17. Mark P. Bradley, *Imagining Vietnam and America: The Making of Post-colonial Vietnam, 1919–1950* (Chapel Hill: University of North Carolina Press, 2000).

18. Charles K. Armstrong, *The North Korean Revolution, 1945–1950* (Ithaca, NY: Cornell University Press, 2003).

19. It is in fact common to hear from South Korean intellectuals the complaint that the entire Korean peninsula is the last "fortress" or "island" of the Cold War. This spatial perception generates the understandable yet illogical temporal perception that the Korean nation as a whole is lagging behind the outside world in the progression of history. Some of these issues and problems in contemporary perception of Cold War history are discussed in Heonik Kwon, *The Other Cold War* (New York: Columbia University Press, 2010).

20. See Charles K. Armstrong, "Socialism, Sovereignty, and the North Korean Exception," in *North Korea: Toward a Better Understanding*, ed. Sonia Ryang (Plymouth, MA: Lexington Books, 2009), 41–55.

21. Dipesh Chakrabarty, *Provincializing Europe: Postcolonial Thought and Historical Difference* (Princeton, NJ: Princeton University Press, 2000); Partha Chatterjee, *The Nation and Its Fragments: Colonial and Postcolonial Histories* (Princeton, NJ: Princeton University Press, 1993).

22. See Kwon, *The Other Cold War*, 121–38.

23. Heonik Kwon, *After the Massacre: Commemoration and Consolation in Ha My and My Lai* (Berkeley: University of California Press, 2006), 161.

24. Haruki Wada, *Kitachōsen: Yūgekitai kokka no genzai* [North Korea's partisan state today] (Tokyo: Iwanami shoten, 1998).

25. Dae-Sook Suh, *Kim Il Sung: The North Korean Leader* (New York: Columbia University Press, 1995), 123–36, 149–57. Also Balázs Szalontai, *Kim Il Sung in the Khrushchev Era: Soviet-DPRK Relations and the Roots of North Korean Despotism, 1953–1964* (Washington, DC: Woodrow Wilson Center Press, 2005), 85–112, 214–28.

26. Hyun Ok Park, *Two Dreams in One Bed: Empire, Social Life, and the Origins of the North Korean Revolution in Manchuria* (Durham, NC: Duke University Press, 2005). Also Charles K. Armstrong, "Centering the Periphery: Manchurian Exile(s) and the North Korean State," *Korean Studies* 19 (1995): 1–16, and Armstrong, *The North Korean Revolution*, 13–37.

27. Armstrong, *The North Korean Revolution*, 222–39. Also Andrei Lankov, *From Stalin to Kim Il Sung: The Formation of North Korea, 1945–1960* (London: C. Hurst, 2002).

28. Andrei Lankov, *Crisis in North Korea: The Failure of De-Stalinization, 1956* (Honolulu: University of Hawaii Press, 2005).

29. Suh, *Kim Il Sung*, 107–58; Lankov, *Crisis in North Korea*, 202–10.

30. Haruki Wada, *Kimuiruson to manshū kōnichisensō* [Kim Il Sung and anti-Japanese war in Manchuria] (Tokyo: Heibonsha, 1992), 377.

31. Dae-Sook Suh describes, "Just as the [former Manchurian] partisans supported Kim Il Sung in his early effort to uproot his competing political factions, the country's People's Army is behind the sustenance of Kim Il Sung regime. North Korean army focuses more on its political role than military functions. It lies on their shoulder rather than the party's that Kim's personality cult has developed to the extent of surpassing Stalin's or Mao's. . . . The People's Army provided major force to the realization of Kim Jong Il's rule after Kim Il Sung's death." Dae-Sook Suh, *Hyŭndae bukhanŭi jidoja: Kim Il Sunggwa Kim Jong Il* [Leaders of modern North Korea: Kim Il Sung and Kim Jong Il] (Seoul: Ŭlyu, 2000), 156–57.

32. Sonia Ryang, "Biopolitics, or the Logic of Sovereign Love: Love's Whereabouts in North Korea," in *North Korea: Toward a Better Understanding*, ed. Sonia Ryang (Plymouth, MA: Lexington Books, 2009), 57–84. The expression "boundless love of the nation" is quoted from the column "Widaehan

t'aeyang, jaaeroun ŏbŏi [The great sun, the loving parent]," *Rodong Sinmun*, July 8, 2009.

33. These publications include Chung-Hi Kang and Sung-Il Lee, *Yŏngwŏnhi inmingwa hamkke* [Eternally together with the people] (Pyongyang: Pyongyang Press, 2007), and U-Kyoung Kim, *Yŏngwŏnhan chuŏk* [Eternal memory] (Pyongyang: Pyongyang Culture and Art Press, 2003). See also Bradley K. Martin, *Under the Loving Care of the Fatherly Leader: North Korea and the Kim Dynasty* (New York: Thomas Dunne Books, 2004).

34. Charles K. Armstrong, *The Koreas* (New York: Routledge, 2007), 78.

35. "Suryŏngnim purŭsin norae [Song sung by the Supreme Leader]," *Rodong Sinmun*, April 6, 2007.

36. The North Korean book *The Veteran of Music* claims that although he had no formal education in music, Kim Jong Il showed a great talent in the composition of songs since a very early age. He wrote his first song, "The Bosom of the Fatherland" (*Jogukŭi p'um*), in 1952, during the Korean War, at the age of ten. The songs he wrote in his tender youth include also "Celebration [of Kim Il Sung]," "My Mother," "Sunrise in Daedong River," and "Chosun! I Will Bring You Glories." See Chosŏnmisulch'ulp'ansa (Pyongyang art press), *Ŭmakŭi wŏnlo, Kim Jong Il* [The veteran of music, Kim Jong Il] (Pyongyang: Pyongyang Art Press, 1998), and also Du-Il Kim, *Sŏn'gunsidae wiinŭi jongchi'wa norae* [The politics and songs of the hero of the military-first era] (Pyongyang: Literature and Arts Press, 2002). See chapter 4 for the importance of 1952 in Kim Jong Il's political career and the drama of his succession of power from Kim Il Sung.

37. Woo-Young Lee, "Munhakyesulŭl tonghaesŏ bon Kim Jol Il sidaeŭi bukhan [North Korea in the era of Kim Jong Il seen through its literature and art]," *Kyŏngjewa sahoi* [Economy and society], no. 49 (2001): 104.

38. Carol Medlicott, "Symbol and Sovereignty in North Korea," *SAIS Review* 25, no. 2 (2005): 70.

39. Sung-Mo Kim, Sung-Il Tak, and Chul-Man Kim, *Chosŏnŭi jip'danch'ejo* [Mass gymnastics of Chosun] (Pyongyang: Foreign Culture Press, 2002); Young-Sun Chun, "Bukhanŭi daejipdanch'ejoyaesulgongyŏn 'Arirang' ŭi jŭngch'ijŏk·munhakyesuljŏk ŭimi [The socio-political and literary-artistic meanings of North Korea's Arirang Festival]," *Jungsoyŏn'gu* [Sino-Soviet affairs] 26, no. 2 (August 2002): 131–58; Byung-Ho Chung, "Kŭkchangkukka bukhanŭi sangjingkwa ŭirye [Symbol and ritual in the theatre state of North Korea]," *T'ongilmunjaeyŏn'gu* [Korean journal of unification affairs] 22, no. 2 (2010): 1–42.

40. Armstrong, *The North Korean Revolution*, 223.

41. Lee, *Bukhan jŏngch'imunhwaŭi hyŏngsŏnggwa gŭ t'ŭkjing* [The formation and characteristics of North Korean political culture], 43.

42. "Urinŭn hansiksol [We are a single household]," *Rodong Sinmun*, October 3, 2007.

43. See Jin-Ung Kang, "Bukhanŭi gajokgukgach'ejeŭi hyŏngsŏng [The formation of North Korea's family state system]," *T'ongilmunjeyŏngu* [Unification

studies] 13, no. 2 (2001): 323–46; Seong-Bo Kim, Kwang-Su Kim, and Sin-Cheol Lee, *Bukhan hyŏndaesa* [Modern history of North Korea] (Seoul: Ungjin, 2006); Gwang-Oon Kim, "The Making of the North Korean State," *Journal of Korean Studies* 12, no. 1 (2007): 15–42; Seong-Bo Kim, "Bukhanŭi juch'esasang, yuilch'ejewa yugyojŏk jŏnt'ongŭi sanghogwangye [Confucian tradition, *juch'e* ideology, and personality cult in North Korea]," *Sahakyŏngu* [Journal of the historical society of Korea] 61 (2000): 234–52; Heon-Kyoung Lee, "Kim Il Sung, Kim Jong Il buja usanghwarŭl wihan yugyŏjŏk jŏngch'isahoihwa [The personality cults of Kim Il Sung and Kim Jong Il, and the confucianization of politics and society]," *Segyejiyŏkyŏngu* [Global area studies] 18 (2002): 89–104; Jong-Heun Lee, "Bukhan dodŏkgyŏyukesŏ yugyoyunliŭi bip'angwa suyong [The reception and the criticism of Confucian ethics in the moral education of North Korea]," *T'ongiljŏnlyak* [Unification strategy] 8, no. 1 (2008): 217–49.

44. Bruce Cumings, *Korea's Place in the Sun: A Modern History* (New York: W. W. Norton, 1997), 576–600. See also Bruce Cumings, *North Korea: Another Country* (New York: The New Press, 2004), 103–27.

45. The idea of culture in this context is, of course, an already political, politicized concept inseparable from the idea of power (of the state), as Sheila Fitzpatrick famously wrote in regard to 1920s Soviet Russia. Sheila Fitzpatrick, *The Cultural Front: Power and Culture in Revolutionary Russia* (Ithaca, NY: Cornell University Press, 1992), 5.

46. Minjok t'ongil yŏnguwŏn [Research institute for national unification], *Bukhan jŏngch'isahoiesŏ jŏnt'ongmunhwaŭi yŏkhwal* [The role of traditional culture in the formation of North Korea's political society] (Seoul: Minjokt'ongilyŏnguwon, 1997). See also Hiroshi Furuta, "Kitachōsenniokeru Jukyō no dentō to shutaishisō no tenkai [Confucian tradition in North Korea and the emergence of *juch'e* ideology]," *Shimonoseki City University Review* 34, no. 3 (1991): 29–71; Masayuki Suzuki, *Kitachōsen: Shakaishugi to dento no kyōmei* [North Korea: The resonance of socialism and tradition] (Tokyo: Tokyo University Press, 1992); Kizo Ogura, *Kankokujin no shikumi* [The composition of Koreans] (Tokyo: Kōdansha, 2001).

47. Although the "closed-door" policy was primarily a defensive reaction against the perceived yet real external threats to the monarchical order and lacked a vision for sustainable sovereignty in a highly versatile condition of the late nineteenth century, it was not entirely anachronistic or reactionary (in the sense of refusing an inevitable change). James Palais says, "The basic goals of the Taewŏngun were to preserve the country and the dynasty by removing the superficial causes of peasant discontent, restoring the power and prestige of the throne to earlier levels, increasing the central government's control over financial resources, eliminating subversive and heterodox doctrines, and building up military strength by traditional means. His approach was primarily pragmatic rather than programmatic or idealistic." Quoted from James B. Palais, *Politics and Policy in Traditional Korea* (Cambridge, MA: Harvard University Press, 1975), 3.

48. Kim, "Bukhanŭi juch'esasang, yuilch'ejewa yugyojŏk jŏnt'ongŭi sang-hogwangye [Confucian tradition, *juch'e* ideology, and personality cult in North Korea]."

49. Armstrong, *The North Korean Revolution*, 215–29.

50. Armstrong, *The North Korean Revolution*, 215–29. See also Kim, Kim, and Lee, *Bukhan hyŏndaesa* [Modern history of North Korea], 203–13.

51. David G. Marr, *Vietnamese Tradition on Trial, 1920–1945* (Berkeley: University of California Press, 1981).

52. Shaun K. Malarney, *Culture, Ritual, and Revolution in Vietnam* (New York: RoutledgeCurzon, 2002).

53. See James B. Palais, *Confucian Statecraft and Korean Institutions* (Seattle: University of Washington Press, 1996). We thank Professor Hung-Youn Cho and Martina Deuchler for bringing this point to our attention.

54. Kim, "Bukhanŭi juch'esasang, yuilch'ejewa yugyojŏk jŏnt'ongŭi sang-hogwangye [Confucian tradition, *juch'e* ideology, and personality cult in North Korea]." See also the T'ongilbu [Ministry of unification], *Bukhan ihae* [Understanding North Korea] (Seoul: Ministry of Unification, 1995).

55. Lee, *Bukhan jŏngch'imunhwaŭi hyŏngsŏnggwa gŭ t'ŭkjing* [The formation and characteristics of North Korean political culture], 44. See chapter 2 of the present volume on the interplay between the ethic of filial piety and the norm of political loyalty.

56. Among the most influential publications of the time in this respect are Bruce Cumings, *The Origins of the Korean War: Liberation and the Emergence of Separate Regimes, 1945–1947* (Princeton, NJ: Princeton University Press, 1981), which was translated into Korean in 1986; Man-Kil Kang, *T'ongilundongsidaeŭi yŏksainsik* [Historical awareness in the era of unification movement] (Seoul: Ch'ŏngsa, 1990); Young-Hee Rhee, *Saenŭn jwauŭi nalgaero nanda* [Birds need both left and right wings to fly] (Seoul: Dure, 1994); and Young-Hee Rhee, *Bansegiŭi sinhwa: Hyujŏnsŏn nambukenŭn ch'ŏnsado akmado ŏpta* [A half-century-long myth: No angel or devil across the armistice line] (Seoul: Samin, 1999). See the excellent discussion of this era in Namhee Lee, *The Making of Minjung: Democracy and the Politics of Representation in South Korea* (Ithaca, NY: Cornell University Press, 2007), 131–44. Also Sheila Miyoshi Jager, *Narratives of Nation Building in Korea: A Genealogy of Patriotism* (Armonk, NY: M. E. Sharpe, 2003), 97–116.

57. Haggard and Noland, *Famine in North Korea*, 21–50.

58. Joŭnbŏtdŭl [Good friends], *Bukhansaramdŭli malhanŭn bukhaniyagi* [Tales of North Korea told by North Koreans], 60–61.

59. Memorial speech delivered in the Kim Il Sung University, April 23, 2009, http://www.ournation-school.com/Radio_lecture/w2-72/w2-72.htm (accessed December 19, 2009).

60. "Changgunnimddara sŭngriŭi han'gillo [Following the general towards the road of victory]," *Rodong Sinmun*, July 2, 2004.

61. It is argued that Kim Jong Il's exemplary performance of filial piety included making these cultural products available for the people of North Korea, who would, through them, be able to preserve the memory of Kim Il Sung deep in their hearts. "T'aeyangŭi noraenŭn yŏngwŏnhamnida [The song of the sun is forever]," *Rodong Sinmun*, April 17, 2008. See also Woo-Kyung Kim, Ki-Chun Dong, and Jong-Suk Kim, *Kŭmsusan'ginyŏmgungjŏn chŏnsŏlchip* [Legends of Kŭmsusan memorial palace], Vols. 1–4 (Pyongyang: Literature and Arts Press, 1999).

62. There is considerable historical falsification in this rendering. Kim Il Sung was not the only leader of armed resistance movements in colonial Manchuria; nor was he the most influential one. Moreover, equalitarian comradeship, rather than mystical kinship, held these movements together.

63. Keun-Cho Kang, *Chosŏnkyoyuksa* [History of North Korean education], Vol. 4 (Pyongyang: Social Science Press, 1991), 356–71.

64. The expression "spinal core of revolution" is quoted from "Hyŏkmyŏngga yujanyŏdŭlŭn paekduŭi sŏn'gunjŏnt'ongŭl iŏnagal haeksimgolgandŭlida [The orphans of revolutionary fighters are the spinal cord who will lead Paekdu's military-first (politics) tradition]," *Rodong Sinmun*, October 12, 2007. See also Hiroshi Furuta, "Chūsei to kōsei: Kitachōsen ideorogi kyōkashijo no nidai kakkiten, 1967, 1987 [Loyalty and filial piety: 1967, 1987 as two major turning points in the history of indoctrination in North Korea]," *Shimonoseki City University Review* 36, nos. 1–2 (1992): 1–94; Pyongyang ch'ulpansa [Pyongyang press], *Sŏn'gunt'aeyang Kim Jong Il janggun* [The sun of military-first (politics), General Kim Jong Il], Vol. 1 (Pyongyang: Pyongyang Press, 2006), 87–101.

65. For instance, Tai Sung An, *North Korea in Transition: From Dictatorship to Dynasty* (Westport, CT: Greenwood Press, 1983); Adrian Buzo, *Guerrilla Dynasty: Politics and Leadership* (London: I. B. Tauris, 1999).

66. Suh, *Hyŭndae bukhanŭi jidoja* [Leaders of modern North Korea], 170. A similar point was raised by the astute South Korean observer of North Korean society Park Hyun-Sun, who notes that "the origin of North Korea's 'socialist great family' theory should be found, rather than in the Confucian tradition, in the organizing principles of classical socialist polity." See Hyun-Sun Park, *Hyundae bukhansahoiwa gajok* [Contemporary North Korean society and family] (Seoul: Hanul Academy, 2003), 44.

67. Armstrong, *The Koreas*, 78–79. See also Furuta, "Kitachōsenniokeru Jukyō no dentō to shutaishisō no tenkai [Confucian tradition in North Korea and the emergence of *juch'e* ideology]," 29–71.

68. Medlicott, "Symbol and Sovereignty in North Korea," 77–78.

69. See Christine Kim, "Politics and Pageantry in Protectorate Korea (1905–10): The Imperial Progresses of Sunjong," *Journal of Asian Studies* 68, no. 3 (2009): 835–59. Also see Takashi Fujitani, *Splendid Monarchy: Power and Pageantry in Modern Japan* (Berkeley: University of California Press, 1998).

70. The North Korean literary journals for children or workers abound with stories of local experience of the leader's visit. A schoolchild's poem published

in a recent edition of the journal *Children's Literature*, entitled "She Smiled; She Cried," reads.

> The youth workroom at the edge of the rice field,
> The day Father-General came to see us in this place.
> As if she had the happiness of owning the world,
> Our Manager-Mother couldn't stop smiling and laughing.
> Listening to the proud stories of our rice fields,
> Father-General smiled brightly.
> Overjoyed with General's smiles,
> She too kept smiling like a child.
> Inspecting her beautifully made bedroom,
> Father-General smiled brightly.
> Overjoyed with General's smiles,
> She too kept smiling like a child.
> Happy with a flood of smiles,
> Our Manager-Mother cried when General left.
> She had forgotten it was past lunchtime,
> "Where would he have a meal in his long way ahead?"

Cited from Su-Won Park, "She Smiled; She Cried," *Adong munhak* [Children's literature] 4 (2009): 27.

71. Chosun jungang t'ongsin [North Korean central broadcast], April 13, 2002.

72. Cited from "Jŏngryŏkjŏkin hyŏnjijido kanghaenggun [The passionate on-the-spot-guidance marches]," *Rodong Sinmun*, June 18, 2009.

73. "Changgunnimddara sŭngriŭi han'gillo [Following the general toward the road of victory]," *Rodong Sinmun*, July 2, 2004.

74. "T'aeyangŭi noraenŭn yŏngwŏnhamnida [The song of the sun is forever]," *Rodong Sinmun*, April 17, 2008.

75. "Changgunnimddara sŭngriŭi han'gillo [Following the general toward the road of victory]," *Rodong Sinmun*, July 2, 2004.

76. Susan Buck-Morss, *Dreamworld and Catastrophe: The Passing of Mass Utopiain East and West* (Boston: MIT Press, 2002), 12.

77. Mark Neocleous, *Imagining the State* (Maidenhead, UK: Open University Press, 2003), 1–2.

78. Kŭmsusan Palace is where Kim Il Sung's embalmed body is kept. Some critics claim that the renovation of this memorial complex cost US$300 million—an amount that could have purchased 2 million tons of dried corn, North Korea's main staple food. *Daily NK*, May 11, 2009, http://www.dailynk.com/korean/read.php?cataId=nk01300&num=71175 (November 5, 2009).

79. Pyongyang ch'ulpansa [Pyongyang press], *Minjokŭi wŏnsijo dan'gun* [National founding ancestor, Dangun] (Pyongyang: Pyongyang Press, 1994); Eun-Duk Kim, *Koryŏ t'aejo wanggŏn* [The founder king of Koryo, Wanggŏn] (Pyongyang: Science Encyclopedia Press, 1996).

80. See "Nanŭn Kangyejŏngsinŭl yŏngwŏnhi itjianŭl gŏsipnida [I will never forget the spirit of Kangye]," *Rodong Sinmun*, May 8, 2000.

81. "Nanŭn Kangyejŏngsinŭl yŏngwŏnhi itjianŭl gŏsipnida [I will never forget the spirit of Kangye]," *Rodong Sinmun*, May 8, 2000. See also Chang-Un Oh, "Sŏngunsidae bukhan nongch'on yŏsŏngŭi hyŏngsanghwa yŏn'gu [Representation of rural women in the military-first era]," *Hyŏndaebukhanyŏn'gu* [North Korean studies review] 13, no. 2 (2010): 84–117.

82. Cited from "Changgunnim saranghasinŭn norae [Song the general cherishes]," *Rodong Sinmun*, July 25, 2000.

2

The Modern Theater State

Kim Il Sung's death in 1994 was a critical event in modern North Korea. Since then, the North Korean state has struggled to reinvent itself, confronting the challenging task of turning the country's founding hero and supreme leader into a physically absent, yet spiritually omnipresent ancestral figure, on the one hand, and to replace the irreplaceable authority of Kim Il Sung, on the other.

This process broadly relates to what Max Weber calls the "routinization of the charismatic focus of the structure" and, more specifically, the "process of routinization of revolutionary charisma."[1] According to Weber, social actions are framed and shaped by a belief held generally among the members of a society that a legitimate social order exists. The possibility that social behavior will be directed in terms of that order constitutes the basis for its authority. Weber postulated that there were several ways to convert power into legitimate authority and that each type of authority was validated differently. As is well known, Weber was particularly interested in charismatic authority among the three ideal-typical forms of political authority he set out to compare: charismatic authority, traditional authority, and rational-bureaucratic authority. He saw charismatic authority as a dynamic form of moral and political power with creative and revolutionary potential (the potential power to make a radical break with the past), unlike modern bureaucratic authority, which he believed was static and ultimately alienating, and traditional authority, which he considered stagnant and conservative. Charismatic authority is also related to a crisis in the other two types of authority, due to which a charismatic personality arises to attract followers and eventually create a new legitimate order.[2] However, Weber was doubtful about charismatic authority as a durable form of social and political order, considering it to be an inherently precarious form of authority. Rule by an inspirational leader, with the legitimacy of the rule grounded in the leader's magnetic appeal to the followers, could rarely be maintained for more than a limited period, he believed, and would eventually have to adjust to the inevitable fading of the leader's magnetism and charm as a spellbinder.[3] The problem is particularly daunting in the inevitable process of succession in which the inspirational quality of the founder must be vested in another. Weber expressed these doubts about the sustainability of charismatic political authority with the expression "routinization of revolutionary charisma." He also had doubts about whether societies and collectives based on charismatic authority would be able to reconcile "the conflict between the charisma of office or of hereditary status with personal charisma."[4] The problem is basically about reconciling a highly personalized charismatic authority with the imperative to reproduce the authority in the absence of the exemplary person. The routinization of charisma is fundamentally a self-contradictory (if not self-defeating) process, for Weber, and a liminal process in which charismatic authority in transition would eventually have to give way to some other basis of authority—either reverting back to traditional authority or developing into a form of rationalized bureaucratic structure. In this light, Weber observed that the common empirical trend in the beginning of the twentieth century was for charismatic authority to replace traditional authority temporarily (and often by violent means) and to be replaced in turn by rational-bureaucratic-legal authority.

North Korea faced a similar kind of problem in the transfer of power from the country's prophetic founding leader to its new leader; in this sense, Weber's thoughts on the historicity of charismatic authority are instructive for comprehending the contemporary North Korean political process. Weber's insights into the nature of charismatic authority also shed light on the preeminence of "politics" over economy introduced in the previous chapter. For Weber, charisma is pitted against socioeconomic forces: it has to be dismissive of everyday economic concerns and matters because, by its very nature, charismatic authority strives to be extraordinary and enchanting, to go beyond and ultimately transcend ordinary, routine, everyday life.[5] We return later to the relationship between charismatic politics and economy in relation to the painful, radical subsistence crisis that the people of North Korea have endured since the mid-1990s (see chapter 6). For the purposes of this chapter, it is necessary to mention that a different legacy of Weberian historical sociology is found in the existing literature on North Korea's political history and culture.

The previous chapter discussed the useful idea of the North Korean polity as a partisan state. The concept of the partisan state proposed by Wada Haruki draws attention to the founding episode of North Korea's political genesis, the Kim Il Sung–led Manchurian-based armed-resistance activity in the 1930s against Japan's colonial occupation. Toward the end of his careful analysis of North Korea's political history, Wada proposes another idea about the country's political formation, the concept of the theater state, which relates particularly to the drama of the power transfer from the country's founding leader, Kim Il Sung, to his eldest son and the country's former leader, Kim Jong Il. According to Wada, North Korea's stateliness changed considerably in the process of political succession, becoming much more ritualized in Kim Jong Il's era and relying more on symbolic and theatrical means to demonstrate the power and authority of the partisan state. A similar idea is proposed by other close observers of North Korea, including Carol Medlicott, who argues that state rituals and state-instituted mass spectacles take on central importance in contemporary North Korean political processes.[6] Unlike Wada, however, Medlicott starts with the premise that the North Korean political order is fundamentally Confucian—a premise widely shared by other observers of North Korea, who maintain that the self-consciously revolutionary, apparently modern regime in North Korea relentlessly appropriates the traditional norms and values of premodern Korea in its rule. In highlighting the role of political spectacles, moreover, Medlicott draws liberally on diverse historical material, including the politics of Tudor England as well as the Confucian political ethics of traditional Korea and China.

Both Wada and Medlicott emphasize the supremacy of symbols and metaphors in the contemporary North Korean political process; in doing so, they commonly introduce as their primary reference material a work written by one of the most influential social anthropologists of the past century, Clifford Geertz. In *Negara: The Theatre State in Nineteenth-Century Bali*, published in 1979, Geertz advances a semiotic theory of culture and a rhetoric-based theory of power.[7] We come back to Geertz's notion of symbolic power later in this chapter; for now, it suffices to say that Geertz's professed theoretical interest in *Negara* is to challenge the classical Weberian definition of state power as the monopoly of coercive forces (bureaucracy, army, and police) and to pluralize the concept of political power. To this end, Geertz argues that the political authority of the Negara kingship in precolonial Bali was built on periodic ritualized demonstrations of the king's social and cosmological centrality rather than a control of coercive capabilities.

This chapter considers whether the idea of the theater state, developed mainly in the analysis of a traditional polity, can be meaningfully extended to an understanding of modern revolutionary states such as North Korea. We also intend to reflect on the somewhat contradictory situation that the idea, which Geertz advanced as a critique of Weber's notion of political power, is applied by the above scholars to a context of charismatic political authority in transition, which is, as mentioned, very much a Weberian theme. We argue that the theater state idea is useful for grasping North Korea's contemporary political process. However, we also argue that in order to further the idea's descriptive and analytical value in the context of North Korean studies, it is necessary to think of symbolic politics in a more dynamic way than Geertz conceptualizes them and to situate the idea more squarely in the context of what Weber calls conflicts between personal and hereditary charisma.

Power as Display

Referring to Geertz's idea that political power can be a question of the display of power and "the ordering force of display, regard, and drama," Wada argues, "The partisan state of North Korea, directed and designed by Kim Jong Il, takes on, partly but evidently, some characteristics of what Geertz calls the theatre state."[8] Medlicott writes, "[Symbol] and symbolic performance collectively constitute a single grand mediating layer between the 'real' North Korean state and the world external to it."[9]

On this matter, as mentioned in chapter 1, one of North Korea's most important public events is the periodic Arirang Festival, a gigantic, well-choreographed mass spectacle involving more than one hundred thousand schoolchildren, women, and soldiers annually, who participate as immaculately trained citizen-actors. As such, it is much more than a public performance and indeed constitutes a "grand mediating layer" between the reclusive state and the rest of the world (although it must be mentioned that Medlicott's notion of the "real" North Korean state goes somewhat against Geertz's idea of the theater state, which is intended to challenge such political realism conceived in distinction to political symbolism). The spectacle delivers formative moral and political slogans to the domestic population and key diplomatic messages to the international community. In this sense, Arirang says what the North Korean state thinks about itself and its relationship to the outside world. The Arirang Festival delivers these important messages on the basis of children's athletic labor and ordinary citizens' dramatic labor, which together narrate the political community's historical genesis and future aspirations in a theatrical form.[10]

However, Arirang is relatively new, with its first performance taking place in 2002. It was briefly discontinued in 2009, then reinstituted in 2010. It is under-

Figure 2.1. The rising sun performance, Arirang Festival, 2005. *Source:* Photo by Jae Soo Liu (2005; permission granted).

stood among many observers of North Korea that the temporary discontinuation of Arirang was closely connected to the question of political succession in the country's leadership, which North Korea is currently facing. It is also understood that the content of Arirang may undergo substantial change in the run-up to the important year 2012, the one hundredth anniversary of the birth of Kim Il Sung. The current North Korean administration has long earmarked 2012 as the time when North Korea would become a "mighty and prosperous great country" (*kangsôngdaekuk*). The situation provoked prolific speculation about the "problem of succession"—about who would inherit after the time of Kim Jong Il, and whether that person will be a member of his biological family (see conclusion to this volume). The succession undoubtedly has huge implications for the future of North Korea and thus understandably attracts intense public interest in neighboring countries. South Korean policy and academic specialists in North Korean affairs generally believe that when a new Arirang opens in 2012, it will send clear messages about what the new leadership hopes to achieve and how it plans to relate to the outside world.

Although Arirang did not exist until 2002, its major constitutive elements did, having been invented around the time of Kim Il Sung's sixtieth birthday in 1972. At that time, the question of the succession of power after Kim Il Sung was being settled.[11] The Arirang theater of the 2000s draws upon some key theatrical, musical productions of the 1970s, all of which, it is claimed, have been made possible by the artistic genius and efforts of Kim Jong Il, and it incorporates these conventional elements with the more contemporary inventions of the latter half of the 1990s, after Kim Il Sung's death in 1994. We may call the latter a commemorative, or

Figure 2.2. Kim Jong Il and his son and designated successor Kim Jong Un, together with top party and military elite, at the Kŭmsusan Kim Il Sung Memorial Palace. *Source:* Yonhap News (September 30, 2010).

"legacy," art (*yuhun yesul*) in the North Korean language. In comparison, the political art of the 1970s and 1980s can be called "succession" art, considering that the central objective of the era's artistic production was to sublimate Kim Il Sung's authority in preparation for transforming his personal charisma into a historical, hereditary charisma. Kim Jong Il's artistic genius is often associated with the invention of the so-called seed theory (*jongjaron*; see below).[12] Much more than a theory of art, it was a theory of political authority and succession, containing the seed for future legacy politics in which the inventor of the theory would be the main beneficiary of the fruits from the seed he had sown. Weber's doubts about the sustainability of charismatic authority notwithstanding, this theory of art turned out to be crucial to a spectacularly successful achievement in this sphere—what some observers call "the communist world's first hereditary transfer of power."[13]

It is worth reemphasizing that the Arirang mass theater performance of the 2000s culminated a longer history of political art production since the early 1970s. Kim Jong Il was formally announced as the successor to the Great Leader in 1974, two years after North Korea celebrated Kim Il Sung's sixtieth birthday. In the run-up to the sixtieth anniversary, it is argued, an important "musical revolution" took place under the guidance of the would-be successor.[14] Among the most notable results of this musical revolution are the highly celebrated productions *The Sea of Blood* and *The Party's True Daughter*, released in 1971, and 1972's *The Flower-Selling Girl*. Included among the acclaimed Five Revolutionary Musicals in North Korea today, these three dramas are recognized as gifts of exemplary filial piety from Kim Jong Il toward the country's founding hero and singular political father, Kim Il Sung. *The Party's True Daughter* takes as its background the Korean War; based on the story of a real female war martyr, this musical is considered an excellent artifact of the military-first political era.[15] *The Sea of Blood* and *The Flower-Selling Girl* also center on heroic female revolutionary figures, but they are set in the 1930s in colonial Manchuria.[16] We consider the meanings of the Korean War as demonstrated in North Korean dramas and monumental art in chapter 4, especially in relation to the premises of military-first politics as well as with regard to the memory of Kim Jong Suk, the birth mother of Kim Jong Il and powerful maternal icon in contemporary North Korea referred to as the "mother of military-first politics."[17] This chapter focuses on the two musical productions dealing with the Manchurian partisan era as we consider, through their narrative order and symbolic structure, issues relating to the Weberian question introduced earlier—that is, the question of how the structural problem of maintaining personal charisma in the absence of the exemplary person has been dealt with in the North Korean context. Weber believes that the end of a personal charismatic authority must involve either recourse to traditional authority or a progression to rational-bureaucratic authority. Related issues include the modifications to traditional and bureaucratic authority involved in the efforts to bring Kim Il Sung's personal charisma to the next generations. In short, we examine how North Korea achieved a political transition that no other former or existing socialist polities have been able to accomplish. We explore this question with reference to two formative musicals made in the early 1970s; however, it is instructive to look first at the epochal significance of the early 1970s not only for North Korea but also in the world at large during the Cold War era.

Earlier we pointed out problems in applying the chronological scheme of "after 1989," referring to the fall of the Berlin Wall in November of that year, uncritically to Asian socialist polities. The idea may be meaningful in grasping the historical upheaval that we commonly call the end of the Cold War in European and Western contexts, but it comes up against serious conceptual problems in the context of East Asian history and, more specifically, in understanding the post–Cold War social and political development of revolutionary postcolonial states such as North Korea. The end of the Cold War in Europe and the collapse of the Soviet political order between 1989 and 1991 unquestionably had a seismic impact on North Korea. The advancement of North Korea's military-first politics from the mid-1990s, as we shall see in the next chapter, was largely a reaction to the momentous changes taking place in Europe and Russia, which contemporary scholarship calls postsocialist transitions. However, changes in the international environment of North Korea cannot be properly understood according to the post-1989 scheme only. To come to terms with these changes, it is necessary to move out of the Europe-centered temporality of the Cold War and to attend to the specificity of Cold War development in an Asian context. Only through this effort to decenter and diversify Cold War history will we be able to understand why North Korea came to defy the stream of global postsocialist transition and, for that matter, why the Cold War has not ended in the Korean peninsula.

In this respect, it is notable that "the week that changed the world"—Richard Nixon's description of his 1972 visit to China—and the related "long 1970s," which led to the onset of economic reform in China toward the end of that decade and the normalization of diplomatic ties between China and the United States in 1979, have received fresh attention in recent scholarship on East Asian regional history and studies of contemporary global political economy.[18] These studies typically view the rise of China as a global economic power (and its resurgence as a regional superpower) and the related tectonic shift in global power relations in the post–Cold War world as having originated in the momentous bilateral détente between the United States and China from 1970 to 1972. This historic event involved complex geopolitical questions, including the conflicts between China and the Soviet Union since the 1960s, which Nixon and his chief advisor Henry Kissinger sought to exploit by bringing China closer as a power friendly to the United States, and the debacle of the war in Vietnam, from which the United States sought to have China disengage. For China, the initiative was highly meaningful for outstripping Taiwan in the competitive diplomatic war for international recognition, for finding solutions to domestic economic problems of the time, and for surpassing the Soviet state in the competition for leadership of international socialism. In retrospect, there is some truth to what several contemporary world-system theorists argue about the event—that 1972, rather than 1989, actually marked the beginning of the formation of the post–Cold War global political and economic order.[19] There is also some truth to what former president Nixon claims in his memoir about his career as a pragmatic politician—that a man who started his high political career in the 1950s with a strong anticommunist position was able to take an apparently contrary position two decades later and thereby change the face of the world.[20] In this respect, perhaps we should give similar credit to the Chinese leadership of the time.

The events of 1970 to 1972 had quite different meanings for other Asian revolutionary socialist states, however. For Vietnam, they were deplorably disappointing, almost constituting an act of betrayal on the part of China. In his recent memoir, Kissinger writes, "Confrontation made no sense for either side; that is why we were in Beijing. Nixon was eager to raise American sights beyond Vietnam. Mao's decision had been for a move that might force the Soviets to hesitate before taking on China militarily. Neither side could afford failure. Each side knew the stakes."[21] The hopeful desire to "raise American sights beyond Vietnam" notwithstanding, in actuality, American hearts and minds were still very much in the Vietnam conflict at the time. It was the apex of violence in Vietnam; communist North Vietnam was fighting the last stage of one of the longest wars in the twentieth century against the United States and its southern ally. Understandably, China's collusion with the United States at this critical juncture deeply disappointed the North Vietnamese leadership. The consequences of these events were indeed manifested in the outbreak of political and military conflicts between Vietnam, China, and Cambodia (the Third Indochina War) in the later part of the 1970s, and they continue to mar the prospect of friendly relations between Vietnam and China today, despite rapidly growing economic ties between the two countries.[22]

China's reception of Nixon "caused serious apprehension in Pyongyang" as well, although China made a great effort to persuade North Korea to accept its change of course in foreign relations with the United States and provided substantial aid to North Korea for the purpose.[23] North Korea had a strong interest in the unfolding of the Vietnam War, which caused Pyongyang considerable anxiety and fear of war for itself. It was also disturbed by South Korea's active participation in the war as a key military ally of South Vietnam and the United States from 1967 to 1973. This was manifested in the aborted attempt by the North to assassinate South Korea's head of state, Park Chung-Hee, on January 21, 1968, by sending a group of commandoes across the Demilitarized Zone (at the same time, North Korea captured the US Navy intelligence ship USS *Pueblo* near its eastern coastal waters on January 23, 1968). As for South Korea, its participation in the Vietnam War proved a vital springboard for its speedy economic growth in the 1970s. However, Park Chung-Hee was very much disturbed by the orientation of the Nixon administration, particularly by its lukewarm and increasingly apathetic attitude toward South Korea's security questions despite Seoul's having sent many tens of thousands of soldiers to the most precarious combat zones in America's war with Vietnam.

The détente between China and the United States, therefore, came as a stern warning to both North and South Korea. Leaders in each country felt that a powerful ally since the time of the Korean War, China or the United States, respectively, was becoming selfish and untrustworthy, forgetting the trust relations based on international revolutionary solidarity, on the one hand, and the international solidarity of anticommunism, on the other. Following "the week that changed the world," many events of great importance occurred in and between the Koreas. Most notably, disillusionment with great ally powers brought the two Koreas to a brief yet crucial period of rapprochement, the first of its kind since the division of the nation in 1945. In his speech on August 15, 1970, marking the anniversary of national liberation from colonial occupation, South Korean president Park proposed embarking on an era of peaceful coexistence between the two Koreas. A year later, the South Korean Red Cross met with its North Korean counterpart to discuss, among other things, the humanitarian issue of helping families divided between the two countries resume contact. This was followed by a secret visit of the South Korean state security chief, Lee Hu-Rak, to Pyongyang, which eventually led to the historic joint statement about the prospect for reconciliation and national reunification between the governments on July 4, 1972.

According to recently released sources in South Korea, Lee Hu-Rak sent a confidential message to his North Korean counterpart, Kim Young-Ju, a younger brother of Kim Il Sung, on October 18, 1972: "Situations in Asia have radically changed in coming to the 1970s. Notable changes have taken place in the US-USSR bipolar system as well as in the relations among four powers—US, USSR, China and Japan. In this circumstance, we have come to the conclusion that we must solve matters that concern our state by our own means rather than relying on the United States or Japan."[24] According to sources on North Korean diplomacy made recently available in eastern European state archives, North Korea believed that "the Nixon doctrine conspired to perpetuate the national partition [on the Korean peninsula] by instigating conflicts among Asian states and between North Korea and South Korea."[25] While these views were being communicated across the Demilitarized Zone, as well as to North Korea's European allies, the two states of Korea were coming to a reciprocal recognition of the imperative that they solve the national question by themselves, without the big powers; however, important changes were also taking place in the domestic political order in both states. In South Korea, Park formally declared a political dictatorship (*yusin* system) in October 1972, through a constitutional change that enabled him to hold lifetime power and abolished the direct ballot for presidential office. Two months later, North Korea passed its own constitutional amendment, which established an absolutist political system (*jusŏk* system) and gave Kim Il Sung a position of power that transcended the power of the party. By the end of 1972, therefore, a system of dictatorship had been established in each of the two Koreas amid the first-ever initiative for dialogue between the two national states and in reaction to the beginning of détente between China and the United States.[26]

The détente in Korea did not last. The Red Cross initiative for reunion of separated families did not materialize until the end of the 1980s. Soon after the constitutional changes were accomplished, radical revolutionary and anticommunist politics were brought back by the two strengthened dictatorial orders. In South Korea, the dictatorship advanced a textbook case of Walt Rostow's anticommunist developmental economy with considerable success.[27] It also provoked a strong societal resistance against political dictatorship, which eventually culminated in the democratic revolution in the second half of the 1980s. Meanwhile, the North Korean economy began to show worrying signs and, later, to fall visibly behind its southern antagonist. The country's political dictatorship faced no systematic challenges from the society, however, and continued magnifying and radicalizing the aesthetics of revolutionary dictatorship. Ultimately, the North Korean state advanced from domestic dictatorship to create a self-image as a global revolutionary imperial power on equal footing with its powerful guardians, the Soviet Union and China (see chapter 5). In the development of this radical political dictatorship during and after the momentous détente of 1970 to 1972, North Korea's nascent future leader, Kim Jong Il, emerged as a central actor and played a spectacular role.

The Flower-Selling Girl

Kim Jong Il's long political career began as an artistic career in the early 1970s. A recent article featured in the Chinese magazine *Global People* argues that the people of North Korea view Kim not merely as a political leader but also as a great artist and art theorist.[28] His *Theory of Art and Cinema*, which first appeared in 1973, is indeed regarded in North Korean art history as a masterpiece that revolutionized the philosophy of socialist art.[29] Kim Jong Il is also the inventor of the so-called seed theory, which advances an analogy between human artistic creativity and horticultural organic production. It argues that the most vital element in the artist's creative work is starting with the right kind of seed for thought, which determines the finished work's aesthetic value and creative quality. Kim Jong Il not only wrote about theory of art but also brought his seed theory into practice.

In 1971, as part of preparation for his father's sixtieth birthday celebration, the young Kim created a distinguished theater group consisting of 150 of North Korea's best actors and actresses. Named after its first important production, 1971's *The Sea of Blood*, this national theater troupe staged in the following year what is considered the greatest, most popular revolutionary musical of all times, *The Flower-Selling Girl*. The musical was soon made into a film, and these two productions together, according to North Korea's official national art history, opened up a brand-new era of revolutionary art in the country and the world over. *The*

Figure 2.3. Kim Jong Il
looking at a roll camera.
*Source: Yŏnggwangŭi
50nyŏn* (Pyongyang:
Chosun Art Book Press,
1995), 168.

Flower-Selling Girl was an immediate success in China as well as domestically. Emerging out of the drab era of the Cultural Revolution, numerous Chinese viewers fell for the powerful, moving, and heartwarming sentimental aesthetics and musicality of North Korean musicals and cinema. Some contemporary observers even call *The Flower-Selling Girl* the first "Korea wave" (*hallyu*), referring to the immense popularity of (South) Korean romantic and family dramas in China, Japan, Vietnam, and elsewhere in Northeast and Southeast Asia. Since then, *The Flower-Selling Girl* has been performed more than fourteen hundred times around the world and has become the best-known, representative modern cultural product of North Korea. Its storyline and dramaturgical elements also make up a crucial part of the contemporary Arirang mass spectacle.

The story of *The Flower-Selling Girl* centers on a teenage girl named Flower (Kkotbuni) from a poor, landless, and fatherless family of four in colonial Manchuria. Her mother works as a servant laborer for a landholding family, which causes misery to Flower and her helpless family as they struggle both with exploitation by the community's landholding elite and with repression by the Japanese colonial authority with which the elite collaborate. Flower tries to help her family survive the double exploitation by collecting wildflowers and selling them on the street, while singing the beautiful and most celebrated song of the musical, "Please Buy My Flowers." Despite her efforts, her family falls apart due to cunning manipulations by the landowner family. Flower's mother does not recover from exhaustion and passes away, her little blinded sister is lost, and her elder brother goes missing. Flower believes he has been killed by the colonial police but later discovers that he has actually escaped from prison and become a member of the local partisan group. Learning what the landowners have done to his family, he returns to the village and mobilizes the villagers to punish the exploiter. Flower reunites with her brother and learns from him the virtue of the partisan struggle. Discovering that the true meaning of life is available only along the glorious path of partisan revolution, Flower goes back to the street to sell flowers—this time, to support her new family, the family of partisan fighters. Now she has a new song: "Spread the Seeds of Flowers of Revolution." Her earlier song, "Please Buy My Flowers," says, "Please buy my beautiful flowers, flowers I grew with care that will buy medicine for my sick mother. Please buy these flowers so that my sorrowful heart can receive the light of a new spring." Her new flower song celebrates true flowers and the true meaning of flowers:

> Each spring beautiful flowers blossom in mountains and fields.
> For us who have lost our country,
> When will spring flowers blossom in our hearts?
> No matter how ferocious the winter frost and the cold wind are,
> They cannot resist the coming of flowers in a new spring.
> As the sun shines over the world with its blessing lights,
> The red flowers of revolution are maturing to full blossom.

In the closing scene of the musical (in the North Korean domestic version; the overseas versions are slightly different), Flower and other people of her village welcome the leader of the glorious partisan group. When the leader slowly emerges onto the stage, he does so against the background of the rising sun. The gathered villagers are overjoyed to encounter the legendary leader of national liberation and class struggle, and Flower joins in the climax by graciously offering her gift of a wildflower to the honored visitor.

The production of *The Flower-Selling Girl* in 1972 under the direction of Kim Jong Il was not a creation but a recreation of tradition. The drama was originally invented by Kim Il Sung in one of his partisan group's bases in Manchuria, Ogaza, in 1930, in celebration of the thirteenth anniversary of the 1917 Bolshevik revolution. The story line of this musical drama also closely resembles the plot of an important, early feature film, *My Home Village* (1949), although the story of this film is based in colonial-era Korea rather than Manchuria. Another masterful production of Kim Jong Il in the early 1970s was *The Sea of Blood*. Released in 1971 as a musical and later as a film and novel, this award-winning production, also depicting life in colonial Manchuria, is said to be based on the cultural performance of Kim Il Sung's partisan troops in August 1936 at their Manchurian base, Mangang. While the historical origin of *The Flower-Selling Girl* is associated with the Bolshevik revolution in Russia (offering a gift of flowers to the leader

Figure 2.4. The Flower-Selling Girl (from the revolutionary film *The Flower-Selling Girl*). *Source: Yŏnggwangŭi 50nyŏn* (Pyongyang: Chosun Art Book Press, 1995), 169.

Figure 2.5. A still from the revolutionary musical *The Sea of Blood. Source: Kim Il Sung Jusŭkkwa onŭlŭi Chosun* (Pyongyang: Chosun Art Book Press, 1992), 216.

was a very prominent activity in Stalin's Russia; see chapter 4), it is interesting to note that *The Sea of Blood* draws on the preexisting revolutionary art of Chinese partisan forces with similar content and titles (although this Chinese origin is not acknowledged in contemporary North Korean art history).

The Sea of Blood

The Sea of Blood shares many common elements with *The Flower-Selling Girl*. It also centers on a poverty-stricken, fatherless family of four struggling with harsh living conditions in colonized northeastern China. The difference, however, is that the story concentrates on the military and political oppression of colonialism, unlike *The Flower-Selling Girl*, in which class conflicts between landless settlers and landowning collaborators with colonial power are highlighted.[30] In addition, *The Sea of Blood* presents the widowed mother of three children as the main character instead of a daughter and (eventually) orphaned young revolutionary, as in *The Flower-Selling Girl*. In *The Sea of Blood*, the woman's husband died as a fighter for national liberation, although not as part of the Kim Il Sung–led militia, which her eldest, teenage son joins instead of his father (to advance his father's way of resistance). Her family suffers from poverty and exploitation but more bitterly from intimidation by the colonial security apparatus due to its association with the national independence movement. One of the most dramatic scenes takes place in the family's home after a fugitive partisan takes shelter with the family. A Japanese policeman interrogates the widowed mother, pointing his gun at her youngest son and threatening to shoot him unless she tells the truth about the fugitive. Having refused to reveal the secret, she is in agony, and her resolve begins to weaken. She looks at her son and sees in his eyes the silent plea, "Mother, please don't give in." After she loses her son, she and her daughter move to the base camp of Kim Il Sung's partisan army, where she is reunited with her eldest son. There, her daughter joins the youth propaganda group (like the protagonist of *The Flower-Selling Girl*), and the mother becomes a dedicated member of the partisan army's female seamstresses unit, making warm clothes for her many new children in her new, true family of partisan fighters.

It is not difficult to see that the central features of Arirang, described in chapter 1 as an artistic production representative of the current military-first political era, had already been formulated to a great extent in the structure of the aforementioned musicals made in the beginning of the 1970s. As discussed in the previous chapter, the epic narrative of Arirang begins with a history of displacement, depicting North Korea's revolutionary history as originating in the communities of displaced Koreans in colonial Manchuria. Their tragic lives are emblematic of the fate of the whole nation. They have been dislocated from their homeland by colonial occupation and subjected to inhumane living conditions by the exploitative feudal-agrarian elite collaborators with colonial politics. Only by becoming partisans can they overcome their humiliating conditions and find a true path out of the despair of colonial displacement to the recovery of a meaningful life and moral selfhood. *The Sea of Blood* and *The Flower-Selling Girl* both manifest this powerful aesthetic of revolutionary redemption and advocate for the transformation of a consanguine familial unity into a higher political familial solidarity centered on the partisan leader from whom the hope for virtuous rebirth emanates. The two stories disclose the common message from variant structural positions and related moral-affective perspectives within the consanguine family. *The Flower-Selling Girl* presents the perspective of a filial daughter and her ties of affection to her revolutionary brother, whereas *The Sea of Blood* brings to the fore a maternal figure embracing political relations of filiation in extension of and substitution for her biological children. Although the stories differ from each other in this respect, they both relate to a powerful national icon invented in North Korea during the political artistic development that began in the 1970s and reflect what Weber calls the routinization of the charismatic focus of the political structure.

Particularly notable in this matter is the life story of Kim Jong Suk, the "Mother of Chosun" and the birth mother of Kim Jong Il. Kim Jong Suk's biography, as it is presented in the North Korean media, encapsulates all the key elements of the aesthetics of revolutionary redemption mentioned above. Kim Jong Suk was born in 1917 in Hoiryŏng, a northernmost Korean settlement bordering China, to a poor, landless family. Her family migrated to Manchuria in 1922 in the hope of escaping poverty and colonial exploitation in their homeland. Life in Japanese-dominated Manchuria was hardly better, however. After losing her father and brother to the brutality of colonial power, she joined the Kim Il Sung–led partisan group in 1935, which changed her life. Kim Jong Suk subsequently became, according to North Korea's official biography of her life, the most loyal follower of Kim Il Sung and the most dedicated defender of the leader's safety and authority.[31]

The epic history of the Manchurian partisan era depicted in the two stories introduced above highlights the revelatory power of adoptive kinship. This power is elicited from two different standpoints. *The Flower-Selling Girl* approaches the power of the partisan family from the perspective of a daughter. The young patriot becomes a lonesome and destitute soul in a bleak world after her family is broken by the forces of colonial class exploitation. She finds substitute filial ties and a moral sense of belonging in the partisan leader, and she discovers the meaning of life thanks to the revolutionary family, which is the partisan group. *The Sea of Blood* depicts the same dynamics from the perspective of a caring, protective mother. Having lost her child to colonial violence, she reclaims her identity within the true family of revolutionary unity and becomes a devoted mother figure for all the partisan youth. Kim Jong Suk's life history brings these two different perspectives on the partisan family together in a single, organic whole. She joined the Kim Il Sung partisan's group, like Flower in *The Flower-Selling Girl*, at a tender age and as a lonesome child of a poor family broken by colonial violence. Like Flower, she undertook the hazardous task of proselytizing behind enemy lines and within the communities under colonial occupation. Like Mother in

The Sea of Blood, however, she also led the partisan army's seamstress group in the army's secret bases and was a benevolent, protective mother figure for the partisan youth, whom she clothed and deeply cared for. Kim Jong Suk's biography is slightly more complicated than the stories of Flower and Mother combined, of course, for her relationship with the leader developed into real ties of kinship through marriage, not merely an adoptive filial relationship or adoptive motherhood for partisan children. North Korea's literary and theatrical productions tend to understate the aspect of real family ties between Kim Jong Suk and Kim Il Sung, choosing to highlight instead her pivotal role in the constitution of the revolutionary family. In these renderings, Kim Jong Suk appears, on the one hand, as an exemplary partisan fighter whose loyalty and dedication to the leader were absolute and unchallenged and, on the other, as a caring maternal figure for other young partisans as well as a benevolent adoptive mother for the orphaned children of martyred partisans.

The symbolism of Kim Jong Suk's political motherhood is fascinating and important for understanding today's North Korea, particularly the succession of absolute power from Kim Il Sung to Kim Jong Il, and we will have a chance to pursue it in more depth later (see chapter 4). The sublimation of Kim Jong Suk's maternal iconic status advanced in parallel with the apotheosis of Kim Jong Il as the sole legitimate heir to the senior Kim. The process involved, most importantly, the renovation of the Graves of Revolutionary Martyrs in the mid-1970s and again in the mid-1980s, which Kim Jong Il personally oversaw. The cemetery contains the graves of the most revered heroes of the early North Korean revolution (members of the so-called First Revolutionary Generation referring to the Kim Il Sung–led Manchurian partisan group); as such, it is one of North Korea's most sacred national monuments. The grave of Kim Jong Suk is located at the top center of this sacred place and surrounded by concentric circles of graves of other First Revolutionary Generation heroes. In this place, as well as in North Korea's official publication, Kim Jong Suk was referred to as the Mother of Chosun in the 1980s and, after Kim Jong Il took power, as the Mother of Sŏn'gun, or military-first politics. Military-first politics, as mentioned, has been Kim Jong Il's trademark ideology and his most consistent policy since 1994 (see chapters 1 and 3).

The new identity of Kim Jong Suk was also crystallized in the epic narrative of Arirang. The form and content of this dramatized national narrative supports Wada's characterization of the North Korean political order as a partisan state; the legend of colonial-era Manchuria is indeed pivotal to the moral foundation of the North Korean polity. In proposing the idea of a partisan state, Wada highlights the power struggle in the early state-building era of North Korea, that is, how Kim Il Sung's partisan group from the Manchurian era emerged as a prominent political force in the second half of the 1940s and, after the Korean War, succeeded in winning over all other revolutionary factions. By the end of the 1950s, Kim's so-called Manchurian faction had risen as an unchallenged, singular political force in North Korea, and it remains so to this day. This group of now-aged former guerrilla fighters was the principal power base on which the so-called personality cult of Kim Il Sung advanced in the postwar years. These people also contributed to building North Korea's People's Army, in which they held key posts, into an increasingly vital political force after Kim's death in July 1994 in support of Kim's designated successor. Wada's idea of the partisan state points to the way in which the above postwar political development generated the sublimation of the history of the Kim Il Sung–led partisan group's armed resistance activity in Manchuria into the single most important, all-encompassing saga of the nation's modern history. In broader terms, this process of sublimation speaks of the fact that modern North Korea is a profoundly postcolonial polity, drawing its moral and political legitimacy from the perpetually reproduced collective memory of colonialism and resistance against it. In this process, Kim Jong Suk represents the most virtuous partisan, the one who is closest and most loyal to the partisan leader, and being the mother of military-first politics, she provides the bridge between the old and the new partisan politics and spirit.

This point helps to explain the conceptual relationship between the paradigm of the partisan state and the idea of the theater state. Within the formation of the partisan state, the history and myth of the Manchurian era cannot be relegated to a thing of the past but must be brought into actuality, time and again, as a living history of the present. Kim Il Sung's heroism in the 1930s cannot be a legacy from the past but should be a reenacted, reexperienced living heritage. In this sense, the concept of the theater state helps to explain the way in which the old heroism of the Manchurian partisans becomes an ever-new glory of the polity's contemporary life—that is, how North Korea's political history transforms into its political culture. Thus, we can conclude that the scheme of the partisan state and that of the theater state are constitutive of each other: the partisan state provides the content for the art of the theater state, and the theater state gives form to the virtue of the partisan state legend and sovereignty paradigm.

Wada associates the empowerment of the paradigm of the partisan state particularly with the transfer of power from Kim Il Sung to Kim Jong Il and with North Korea in the era of Kim Jong Il. Medlicott, also advancing the idea of North Korea as a theater state, makes an important observation regarding North Korea's stateliness. She does so with reference to the tradition of "on-the-spot guidance" trips described earlier: "Through the visits, the state was transformed from a distant impersonal dictatorial authority to a parental figure, whose authority is often distant but just as often interceding into daily life. The national territory then becomes a father's household 'writ large,' and the 'Great Leader' is the father passing throughout the household giving benevolent instruction, inspecting conditions and suggesting corrections, and reaching out to physically touch and embrace the members of the nation."[32]

The conception that the country as a whole constitutes an organic unity and a household writ large indeed appears prominently in the literature about North Korean political history as well as in North Korea's official literature. North

Korea's contemporary public media hammer into the population the virtues of *ch'ung* (loyalty to the sovereign or to the country) and *hyo* (filial piety)—two of the preeminent human ethical dispositions highlighted in the Confucian tradition. According to Wada, "In the 1990s, Kim Jong Il coined the new concept, 'Unity of One Heart.' This concept is alien to traditional Korean culture. Subsequently, a more familiar concept was necessary and 'Unity of Ch'ung and Hyo' was invented. The latter is from the premodern tradition of Confucian ethics. This latest statehood of North Korea, in conclusion, follows the image of a traditional, premodern state."[33]

Wada's remark that the civic ethics emphasized in today's post-1994 North Korea follows the premodern Confucian moral codes opens up an important yet controversial point. The idea that North Korea is a Confucian state also features prominently in the growing body of literature published in South Korea, as noted in the previous chapter, and the related impression that North Korea resembles a feudal dynastic state is widely mentioned in the policy and academic communication about North Korea in South Korea and elsewhere.[34] The North Korean regime's relentless emphasis on the unity of loyalty and filial piety, as Wada notes, is much responsible for the growing impression that North Korea is a revived neo-Confucian state (as well as the country's chosen mode of succession). Bruce Cumings observes, "Loyalty and filial piety form the deepest wellsprings of Korean virtue, nurtured over thousands of years, just as myriad Korean tales of the rare powers, magnificent ethics, and bottomless omniscience of the very long list of kings who presided over a millennium of dynasties form the subjective basis of the Korean identity and its love of exemplary leaders."[35] Be this as it may, however, it is important to recognize that the virtues of *ch'ung* and *hyo* are separate in Confucian tradition and that the effort to collapse the distinction between these prime ethical principles is very much a modern political practice. Although it is true that in traditional Confucian societies, the two virtues conceptually formed an ethical, ideological whole, it is important to recognize that filial piety, unlike loyalty to the sovereign, constituted an absolute ethical principle. Anthropologist Lee Moon-Woong rightly notes, "In traditional Korean society, the filial relations were considered to be the primary backbone of all human relations; by comparison, the relations between the ruler and the ruled were secondary in significance and were not an all-encompassing, powerful element."[36] Even in a highly dogmatic Confucian society such as pre-eighteenth-century Korea, the subjects of the sovereign, be they indignant mandarin scholars or angry peasant rebels, had the right to withhold their loyalty to a particular sovereign order if they felt that it violated the virtue of politics (e.g., the heavenly mandate or the principle of filial continuity within the dynastic succession). Another telling example is a famous story of a peasant soldier, told by Kim Si-Sup, the eminent scholar and literary genius of the fifteenth-century Korea: a young soldier joins the army not out of loyalty to the sovereign but because of his filial obligation to his conscripted father—in the hope of staying close to the latter to protect his life. The principle of *hyo*, in contrast to *ch'ung*, was an absolute virtue, as Lee mentions and as the story of the soldier also testifies, and its supremacy was unaffected by historical circumstances and contingencies.

About what he calls a patricentric modern political order (e.g., Nicolae Ceausescu's Romania or Erich Honecker's East Germany), John Borneman writes, "These regimes were patricentric in that they attempted to unify their subjects and create a modern subjectivity through identification with a leader who becomes the general equivalent of his subjects, the standard of all value, but who himself operates outside measurement."[37] In the North Korean context, the conceptual interplay between the moralities of *ch'ung* and *hyo* makes up an important difference between modern "patricentric" order and premodern dynastic order. We emphasize again that in traditional Confucianism, these two normative principles belong to separate spheres and dimensions of life: *ch'ung* to the public relationship to the sovereign and *hyo* to domestic kinship relations. We may think of this separation in light of the distinction between political life (participation in the polis) and biological or private life (household economy) in the Aristotelian philosophical legacy. North Korea's modern familial political order is distinct from Korea's traditional Confucian dynastic order in that its claim on people's loyalty and fidelity to the sovereign power appropriates the morality of *hyo*, thereby blurring and dismantling the existing boundary between the political and the domestic. The last is, according to Hannah Arendt, a principal feature of modern politics as well as the origin of totalitarianism.[38]

Arendt's notion of modern politics is anchored in the conceptual distinction between the domestic and the political and in how, she observes, the state in modern times draws its legitimacy from taking on the role of a gigantic household manager, whether this role is expressed in the form of a liberal welfare state or in that of an authoritarian polity harboring charismatic paternalism. In the history of revolutionary state politics, too, the blurring of the domestic and the political has been prominent. In chapter 1 we briefly mentioned, in the postwar Vietnamese context, how the state intruded into the domestic ritual realm, turning the household's space of ancestor worship, traditionally a sovereign space for the family, into a political shrine meant exclusively for state-chosen war heroes and party leaders. In the context of the Chinese revolution, likewise, we can think of many corresponding examples, such as the one-child policy or the institution of the communal dining hall invented during the Great Leap Forward.[39] For an understanding of North Korea, it is instructive to think of the issue along a different comparative trajectory. In his classical work on the logic and psychology of the political organism in imperial Japan, Masao Maruyama examines the interpenetration of the private and the public and the process by which the ethics of domestic life are being spatially turned inside out, displaced from the interiority of kinship and identified with the public political values of the state.[40] Maruyama focuses on the conceptualization of the state in the image of an extended family consisting of the imperial house as the main family and the people as branch families.[41] As Cumings notes, this was not merely an analogical reasoning but had substantial meanings.[42] Emiko Ohnki-Tierney also probes the Meiji government's attempts, partly following the proposition of the government's German advisor Lorenz von Stein, to sublimate the emperor as the father of the people of Japan and to reach a conceptual equivalence between the ethics of filial piety and the virtue of loyalty to the sovereign. She argues that the invented state ritual of royal pageantry was an important instrument in the making of the imperial political household in modern Japan: "If one of the state's strategies for equating loyalty to parents with loyalty to the emperor was to mandate the teaching of the Rescript in the schools, another strategy was the practice of *jungyo*—the tour of the country by the emperor to build up his image as the merciful father. The emperor visited the aged and the poor. He watched peasants in the field in order to demonstrate his appreciation of their toils. The Meiji emperor toured the country ninety-six times during his forty-five-year reign, from Hokkaido to Kyushu and from the Pacific to the Japan Sea coast."[43]

On the basis of the above discussion, we can conclude that the unity of loyalty and filial piety is an expression and instrument of modern politics, not a regression to norms of the traditional political order.[44] The unity appropriates the ethics of *hyo*, an absolute ethical principle, as the political morality of *ch'ung*, loyalty and fidelity to the political order. In the North Korean context, this process of appropriation is integral to the succession and the critical structural adjustments that it involves. The memory of the Manchurian heroism fades with each generation; the collapse of the Soviet empire and the disintegration of the socialist interna-

Figure 2.6. Schoolchildren's musical performance, Mankyŏngdae Children's Palace, Pyongyang. *Source:* Photo by Byung-Ho Chung (2006).

tional order brought an unprecedented moral and political crisis to North Korea; the death of Kim Il Sung induced a crisis in the scheme of the partisan state; and the ensuing economic collapse and tragic famine raised questions about the very sustainability and moral legitimacy of the country's entire political system. This challenging, generalized social crisis required the invention of a new definition of political loyalty in order to keep the suffering population and confused public as loyal citizens and defenders of the country's revolutionary tradition. The new loyalty invented in this process was, on the one hand, a militaristic one, in which every citizen of North Korea stands as a loyal soldier of military-first politics (see chapter 3), but it was also a familial one, in which every soldier of military-first politics defends the country and its leadership in the spirit and absolute morality of filial piety—that is, true to the invented tradition of the Manchurian legend that Arirang performs.

Invention of Tradition

The unity of loyalty and filial piety commands that the citizen-soldiers of the military-first era act in the political arena as if it were a sphere of domestic life—that they keep and protect the founding heritage of their political community in the same manner as they would their own family ancestral memory and that they be loyal to the state with deep filial dedication to the state's exemplary center according to the glorious tradition of the Manchurian partisans and the revolutionary family they formed. The norm of loyalty and the virtue of filial piety in action in this context are undoubtedly in line with Korea's premodern, traditional Confucian culture. However, this aspect of continuity should not blind us to the important differences, in the words of Eric Hobsbawm and Terence Ranger, "between invented and old traditional practices."[45] The principle of filial piety advocated in today's North Korea constitutes an invented tradition, being a political and radically politicized ethical principle. It represents the propensity of the body politic to appropriate traditional cultural norms and ethical values as a new instrument of political loyalty and solidarity in an increasingly precarious international and domestic environment.

On a closing note, let us return to Geertz's idea of the theater state and its relevance for understanding contemporary North Korea. After introducing Geertz, Wada expresses some reservation about the utility of Geertz's ideas in the context of North Korean studies. He does so following his discussion of the unity of loyalty and filial piety in the era of Kim Jong Il: "The premodern, traditional kingdom of Bali could have existed as a 'theater state.' However, states in the modern world may not exist as an absolute 'theater state.' For the 'theater state' presumes a static order and is not congenial to dynamic changes. Here we find a fundamental contradiction of the partisan state. There are no fixed norms or rules in guerrilla warfare. Ritualistic formalism is not in harmony with guerrilla politics. When the performance of the partisan state becomes a formalized ritual and spectacle of a 'theater state,' therefore, the state will lose the dynamism necessary for its survival."[46] Although Wada finds Geertz's theater state idea fascinating and useful, he doubts whether it can be extended to an analysis of a modern political system. This is because, as he says, that the premise of a theater state assumes that the world it governs has a stable, static order of things and ideas.

At the end of the 1970s, Geertz wrote about royal rituals in a precolonial Balinese state, Negara, in which, he argued, power worked as "systems of interacting symbols, as patterns of interworking meanings."[47] *Negara* is a traditional Balinese word referring to a polity or realm (of power and authority); in his book, Geertz sets out to elucidate the meaning of this elusive, indigenous concept. He does so, on the one hand, with reference to a body of historical sources on premodern, precolonial state formations—"the intrinsic structure of the classic polity"—in Bali and elsewhere in the Indonesian archipelago and, on the other, in critical engagement with concepts of sovereignty and political ruling developed in modern European political tradition and thought.[48] Geertz's masterful handling of this ambitious task is anchored in what he calls "the doctrine of the exemplary center" and in the related observation that court ceremonialism, in the pre-nineteenth-century Balinese kingdom, was "paradigmatic, not merely reflective, of social order."[49] Geertz's assertion that the symbolic, demonstratively ritual and theatrical dimension of state power is constitutive rather than merely representative of the political order must be understood, of course, in the context of the rich details of Balinese state rituals—most prominently, the royal funeral and cremation of the deceased king's body and those of his concubines. For the purpose of our discussion, it suffices to emphasize the relevance of Balinese Negara, in Geertz's terms, for political theory. He writes,

> And so far as political theory is concerned, it is there, in exposing the symbolic dimensions of state power, that the use of attending to decaying rank, dispersed prerogative, ritualized water control, alien-managed trade, and exemplary cremation lies. Such study restores our sense of the ordering force of display, regard, and drama. Each of the leading notions of what the state "is" that has developed in the West since the sixteenth century—monopolist of violence within a territory, executive committee of the ruling class, delegated agent of popular will, pragmatic device for conciliating interests—has had its own sort of difficulty assimilating the fact that this force exists. None has produced a workable account of its nature.[50]

Weber's characterization of state power as a monopoly of coercive force is, for Geertz, part of the "difficulty" and limitation of political theory. Geertz's professed theoretical interest in this work is to challenge the classical Weberian definition of state power as the monopoly of coercive forces and to pluralize the concept of political power.

However, *Negara* was not the only place where Geertz advanced his idea of the theater state. In his essay "Ideology as Cultural System," Geertz discusses extensively the nationalist politics of Sukarno's Indonesia as an exemplary case for symbolic coercion, partly drawing upon George Kahin's classical work on the topic.[51] In the essay, Geertz writes about "a polity as a concentrated center of pomp and power"—the theme that he later develops in an analysis of the public power of a precolonial theater state in Bali as "the ordering force of display, regard, and drama."[52] Here Geertz is trying to establish continuity between precolonial, traditional local states in Bali and Java and the postcolonial, centralized nation-state of Indonesia in terms of the aesthetics of power. Just as the power of the traditional state was performative rather than institutional in nature, based as it was on pompous religious rituals, so, too, is that of the modern secular state, in contrast to the conventional wisdom drawn from Weberian sociological tradition, and based primarily on ritualized symbols of power, such as the spectacles of military might and public speeches of secular political leaders made according to the order of traditional religious oratory.

Geertz's objective here is to make a case for the cultural continuity of state formation in Indonesian history and to bring the idea of the theater state to a critique of the Weberian theory of state power as the monopoly of coercive institutions. In other words, Geertz intends to present Indonesia's modern political history as an "Indonesian history," that is, in terms that, he believes, show how politics are created in a culturally distinctive way. For Geertz, the fundamental problem with postcolonial Indonesian politics is that Sukarno's charismatic rule under the slogans of "guided democracy" and "socialism à la Indonesia" was based on the traditional politics of spectacle, which failed to consolidate the complex, secular, and modern Indonesian society of the postcolonial era. What Geertz has in mind with his phrase "ideology as cultural system" is in fact that the *ideology* of Sukarno's guided democracy is intelligible only if it is seen within the context of a *cultural system* such as the ritualized universe of Negara.

Thus, we can conclude that the idea of the theater state formulated by Geertz did not merely stem from his historical interest in a premodern political system. Instead, it represents Geertz's deep interest in modern political development in a postcolonial region and his commitment to understanding this development in ways that are true, in his belief, to the region's deep history and culture, rather than through the prism of Western political theories. In this sense, Geertz's professed interest demonstrated in his pursuit of the theater state idea, despite his claimed distance from the Weberian theory of politics, falls very much squarely within the broad spectrum of Weber's historical sociology and, in particular, within Weber's topology of political and moral authority. Above all, the two scholars share common interest in the place and fate of charismatic authority in modern politics, and this interest, as mentioned, ultimately led Geertz to invent the idea of the theater state in regard to traditional Balinese polities. It is therefore not entirely correct to say, as Wada does, that the paradigm of the theater state has no conceptual ties with modern politics. On the contrary, the paradigm was invented out of concerns about the turbulent modern history of decolonization and the onset of the early Cold War. Geertz's interest in the politics of display, despite his stated criticism of Weber's definition of political power, is, in origin, fundamentally a Weberian question, rooted in his observation of problems of charismatic authority in modern politics.

The important analytical question that remains is, then, how to render the modern dimension of the theater state idea more explicitly. In the context of North Korean studies, the question at stake is how to come to terms with the state's forceful politics of display (and politics as display) as a fundamentally modern political practice (rather than as a symptom of premodern, feudal thinking) and to elicit in the performance of this theater state the elements of improvisation and innovation. The transformation of filial piety into a principle of political loyalty is one formative element of North Korea's contemporary theater state and of its ongoing effort to resolve the conflict between Kim Il Sung's irreplaceable personified charisma and the need to perpetuate it in the form of hereditary charismatic authority. How the state has handled the difficult task of transforming personal charisma into hereditary charisma must be understood as the work of modern politics and as the innovation of a modern theater state. This is the case no matter how traditional the result of the innovation appears to be and no matter how anachronistic the intention to reinvent the traditional concepts may have been.

The innovation was not limited to the invention of traditional moral concepts. In the careful, focused attempt to transfer Kim Il Sung's personal charisma to a powerful form of hereditary charisma, a series of structural reforms were made in the hierarchical order of North Korea's state bureaucracy as well as in the concentric order that defines the relationship between the country's exemplary center and its outer circles. Pivotal to these reforms and to the effort to legitimize them in the eyes of the people was the invention of two key symbols, which together masterfully conjoined the revolutionary partisan legacy with the morality of the political family. One of the two key symbols of North Korea's new theater state in the transition from the era of Kim Il Sung is a familial figure, the exemplary maternal icon of the family state, Kim Jong Suk. The other is a combative one, the universal material symbol from the partisan legend called "the barrel of a gun."

Notes

1. Max Weber, *The Theory of Social and Economic Organization*, edited by Talcott Parsons (New York: The Free Press, 1947), 371, 389.

2. Stephan Feuchtwang and Mingming Wang, *Grassroots Charisma: Four Local Leaders in China* (London: Routledge, 2001), 11.

3. Ann R. Willner, *The Spellbinders: Charismatic Political Leadership* (New Haven, CT: Yale University Press, 1984).

4. Weber, *The Theory of Social and Economic Organization*, 370.

5. Weber, *The Theory of Social and Economic Organization*, 329.

6. Carol Medlicott, "Symbol and Sovereignty in North Korea," *SAIS Review* 25, no. 2 (2005): 70.

7. Clifford Geertz, *Negara: The Theatre State in Nineteenth-Century Bali* (Princeton, NJ: Princeton University Press, 1980).

8. Haruki Wada, *Kitachōsen: Yūgekitai kokka no genzai* [North Korea's partisan state today] (Tokyo: Iwanami shoten, 1998), 160.

9. Medlicott, "Symbol and Sovereignty in North Korea," 70.

10. The Arirang performance, in recent versions, is frequently spiced up with demonstrations of gymnastic fitness performed mostly by schoolchildren. See the brilliant documentary *A State of Mind*, directed by Daniel Gordon (Sheffield, UK: VeryMuchSo Productions, 2004). About the preparation and performance of the Arirang spectacles, see Byung-Ho Chung, "Kŭkchangkukka bukhanŭi sangjingkwa ŭirye [Symbol and ritual in the theater state of North Korea]," *T'ongilmunjaeyŏn'gu* [Korean journal of unification affairs] 22, no. 2 (2010): 25–32.

11. The most important document for this event is Kim Jong Il's speech in his meeting with the cadres in the party's propaganda department on October 29, 1971. See Kim Jong Il, *Kim Jong Il sŏnjip* [Collection of essays by Kim Jong Il], Vol. 4 (Pyongyang: Workers' Party Press, 2010), 190–208. Bradley Martin observes, "In the early 1970s the regime dropped a very clear official hint that a close relative would become Kim Il-sung's successor. The 1970 edition of North Korea's *Dictionary of Political Terminologies* had included this critical definition: 'Hereditary succession is a reactionary custom of exploitative societies whereby certain positions or riches may be legally inherited. Originally a product of slave societies, it was later adopted by feudal lords as a means to perpetuate dictatorial rule.' The definition failed to appear in the 1972 edition of the dictionary." Cited from Bradley K. Martin, *Under the Loving Care of the Fatherly Leader: North Korea and the Kim Dynasty* (New York: Thomas Dunne, 2004), 194.

12. See Kim Jong Il, *Kim Jong Il sŏnjip* [Collection of essays by Kim Jong Il], Vol. 3 (Pyongyang: Workers' Party Press, 2010), 255–62. Also Kwahak paekkwa sajŏn ch'ulpansa [Science encyclopedia press], *Jŏngjaronae gwanhan ch'ŏlhakronmunjip* [Philosophical anthology of seed theory] (Pyongyang: Science Encyclopedia Press, 2002).

13. The quote is from "North Korea Confirms Kim Jong-Il's Son Will Take Over as Leader," *Guardian*, October 8, 2010.

14. Ji-Ni Kim, "Bukhansik jonghapgongyŏnyesulŭi jŏngch'akgwa jŏngae [The establishment and development of North Korea's synthetic performance art]," *Hyundaebukhanyŏngu* [North Korean studies review] 11, no. 2 (2008): 144.

15. Kim Jong Il, *Kim Jong Il sŏnjip* [Collection of essays by Kim Jong Il], Vol. 4, 221–30.

16. Young-Jung Pak, *Bukhan yŏn'gŭk/hŭigogŭi bunsŏkkwa chŏnmang* [Analysis and prospect of North Korean theater/play] (Seoul: Yŏn'gŭkkwa in'gan, 2007). Also Kim Jong Il, *Kim Jong Il sŏnjip* [Collection of essays by Kim Jong Il], Vol. 4, 1–15, 98–105, 131–36.

17. Pyongyang ch'ulpansa [Pyongyang press], *Sŏn'gunŭi ŏmŏni Kim Jong Suk nyŏjanggun* [The mother of military-first, Female-General Kim Jong Suk] (Pyongyang: Pyongyang Press, 2007).

18. Margaret MacMillan, *Nixon and Mao: The Week That Changed the World* (New York: Random House, 2008). The expression "the long 1970s" is quoted from Chen Jian, "The Great Transformation: How China Changed in the Long 1970s," a public lecture delivered at the London School of Economics (LSE) on January 22, 2009. A similar idea was presented by Niall Ferguson in his public lecture given at the LSE IDEAS, "The Political Economy of the Cold War," on October 18, 2010. See Chen Jian, "China's Changing Politics toward the Third World and the End of the Global Cold War," in *The End of the Cold War and the Third World: New Perspectives on Regional Conflict*, ed. Artemy M. Kalinovsky and Sergey Radchenko (London: Routledge, 2011), 101–2, 119.

19. See, for instance, Mark Selden, "East Asian Regionalism and Its Enemies in Three Epochs: Political Economy and Geopolitics, 16th to 21st Centuries," *Asia-Pacific Journal*, February 25, 2009, http://www.japanfocus.org/-Mark-Selden/3061 (accessed March 8, 2009); Giovanni Arrighi, Takeshi Hamashita, and Mark Selden, eds., *The Resurgency of East Asia: 500, 150 and 50 Year Perspectives* (London: Routledge, 2003); Giovanni Arrighi, *The Long Twentieth Century: Money, Power, and the Origins of Our Times* (London: Verso, 2010).

20. Richard Nixon, *The Memoirs of Richard Nixon* (New York: Grosset and Dunlap, 1978), 559–80.

21. Henry Kissinger, *On China* (New York: Allen Lane, 2011), 240.

22. Odd Arne Westad and Sophie Quinn-Judge, eds., *The Third Indochina War: Conflict between China, Vietnam and Cambodia, 1972–1979* (London: Routledge, 2006).

23. See Yongho Kim, *North Korean Foreign Policy: Security Dilemma and Succession* (Lanham, MD: Lexington Books, 2011), 35–52. Also Chin O. Chung, *Pyŏngyang between Peking and Moscow: North Korea's Involvement in the Sino-Soviet Dispute, 1958–1975* (Tuscaloosa, AL: University of Alabama Press, 1978).

24. Sok-Ho Shin, "1970nyŏndaech'o nambukjŏnggwŏn 'jŏkdaejŏk kong-saenggwangye' ipjŭng [The establishment of dictatorship and antagonistic coexistence]," *Dong-A Ilbo*, October 13, 2009. Also "7.4 Sŏngmyŏngŭn daenamhyŏkmyŏngŭl wihan p'yŏnghwa kongse [July 4th communique is a peace offensive aimed at instigating a revolution in the south]," *Dong-A Ilbo*, September 24, 2009.

25. "7.4 Sŏngmyŏngŭn daenamhyŏkmyŏngŭl wihan p'yŏnghwa kongse [July 4th communique is a peace offensive aimed at instigating a revolution in the South]," *Dong-A Ilbo*, September 24, 2009.

26. Don Oberdorfer, *The Two Koreas: A Contemporary History* (London: Warner Books, 1999).

27. W. W. Rostow, *The Stages of Economic Growth: A Non-Communist Manifesto* (Cambridge: Cambridge University Press, 1960). See also Michael E. Latham, *The Right Kind of Revolution: Modernization, Development, and U.S. Foreign Policy from the Cold War to the Present* (Ithaca, NY: Cornell University Press, 2011), 44–53.

28. *Global People*, no. 127, May 16, 2010.

29. This work was later published in a book: Kim Jong Il, *Yŏnghwa yesullon* [Theory of art and cinema] (Pyongyang: Workers' Party Press, 1984).

30. On questions of interplay between anticolonial nationalism and class conflicts in colonial Manchuria, see Hyun Ok Park, *Two Dreams in One Bed: Empire, Social Life, and the Origins of the North Korean Revolution in Manchuria* (Durham, NC: Duke University Press, 2005), 64–95.

31. See Kim Il Sung Jonghap Daehak ch'ulpansa [Kim Il Sung university press], *Kim Jong Suk dongchi hyŏkmyŏnglyŏksa* [Comrade Kim Jong Suk's revolutionary history] (Pyongyang: Kim Il Sung University Press, 2005), and Pyongyang ch'ulpansa [Pyongyang press], *Sŏn'gunŭi ŏmŏni Kim Jong Suk nyŏjanggun* [The mother of military-first (politics), Female-General Kim Jong Suk] (Pyongyang: Pyongyang Press 2007).

32. Medlicott, "Symbol and Sovereignty in North Korea," 77.

33. Haruki Wada, *Bukjosŏn: Yugyŏkdaegugkaesŏ jŏnggyukungugkaro* [North Korea: From partisan state to a military state] (Seoul: Dolbegae, 2002), 300.

34. Wada, *Kitachōsen:Yūgekitai kokka no genzai* [North Korea's partisan state today] (Tokyo: Iwanami shoten, 1998), 309–10; Masayuki Suzuki, *Kitachōsen: Shakaishugi to dento no kyōmei* [North Korea: The resonance of socialism and tradition] (Tokyo: Tokyo University Press, 1992), 119–39; Bruce Cumings, *Korea's Place in the Sun: A Modern History* (New York: W. W. Norton, 1997), 403–4; Hiroshi Furuta, "Kitachōsenniokeru shūkyōkokka no keisei [The formation of religious state in North Korea]," *Tsukuba Review of Law and Politics* 20 (1996): 51–87.

35. Bruce Cumings, *North Korea: Another Country* (New York: The New Press, 2004), 107.

36. Moon-Woong Lee, *Bukhan jŏngch'imunhwaŭi hyŏngsŏnggwa gŭ t'ŭkjing* [The formation and characteristics of North Korean political culture] (Seoul: Institute of National Unification, 1976), 39.

37. John Borneman, "Introduction: Theorizing Regime Ends," in *Death of the Father: An Anthropology of the End in Political Authority*, ed. John Borneman (Oxford: Berghahn, 2004), 3.

38. Hannah Arendt, *The Human Condition* (Chicago: University of Chicago Press, 1958).

39. See the gripping, moving depiction of China's Great Leap Forward and its devastating consequences in Stephan Feuchtwang, *After the Event: The Transmission of Grievous Loss in Germany, China and Taiwan* (Oxford: Berghahn, 2011), part II.

40. Masao Maruyama, *Thought and Behavior in Modern Japanese Politics*, edited by Ivan Morris (New York: Oxford University Press, 1969), 6–7.

41. Cumings, *Korea's Place in the Sun*, 402.

42. Cumings, *Korea's Place in the Sun*, 402.

43. Emiko Ohnuki-Tierney, *Kamikaze, Cherry Blossoms, and Nationalisms* (Chicago: University of Chicago Press, 2002), 78–79.

44. Byung-Chun Lee, ed., *Kebaldokjewa Pak Chung Hee sidae: Urisidaeŭi jŏngch'ikyŏngjejŏk kiwon* [Developmental dictatorship and Park Chung Hee era: Political economic origin of our time] (Seoul: Ch'angbi, 2003).

45. Eric Hobsbawm and Terence Ranger, Introduction to *The Invention of Tradition*, ed. Eric Hobsbawm and Terence Ranger (Cambridge: Cambridge University Press, 1983), 10.

46. Wada, *Bukjosŏn* [North Korea], 301.

47. Clifford Geertz, *The Interpretation of Cultures* (New York: Basic Books, 1973), 207.

48. Geertz, *Negara*, 9.

49. Geertz, *Negara*, 1.

50. Geertz, *Negara*, 111–12.

51. Geertz, *The Interpretation of Cultures*, 225.

52. Geertz, *Negara,* 121.

3

The Barrel of a Gun

North Korea's post-1994 commemorative politics advanced the moral unity of *ch'ung* and *hyo*—the imperative of political loyalty according to an ethic of filial piety. These concepts traditionally belonged to separate domains of life and value—*ch'ung* to the public's relationship with the sovereign and *hyo* to the domestic sphere and rules of kinship and descent. The merging of these traditionally distinct concepts into an undifferentiated, organic conceptual whole was intended to safeguard the survival of the political system at a time of radical domestic and international crisis involving political isolation and economic collapse. In particular, it aimed to perpetuate the charismatic authority at the center of the political order by transforming the authority from a personal into a hereditary form.

The transformation involved not only the appropriation of traditional concepts but also measures of crucial readjustment in the sphere that Max Weber would associate with legal-bureaucratic authority. Most notable in this matter was the institutional structural renovation referred to broadly as military-first (party-second, *sŏn'gunhuro*) politics, which reversed the hierarchical relationship between the party and the army in conventional socialist state politics. Of equal importance was the constitutional amendment following Kim Il Sung's death in 1994 that created an extraordinary position for the deceased leader as a supra, perpetual, and transcendental head of state. These two extraordinary institutional changes were closely interrelated and together were intended to cope with the profound structural crisis in North Korea's political order caused by the loss of the country's founding father and supreme charismatic leader.

When the three-year-long mourning period ended in July 1997, North Korea's party and army central committees revealed their joint decision to nominate Kim Il Sung's birthday as the "Day of Sun" and the "greatest national holiday." The decision included the inauguration of a new calendar, subsequently known as the *juch'e* national calendar, which takes the late leader's birth year of 1912 as the origin of North Korea's historical timeline. This was followed by the election of the new leader, Kim Jong Il, in October 1997, to the position of the general secretary of North Korea's Workers' Party. In September 1998, Kim Jong Il was elected by North Korea's Supreme People's Assembly also to the highest position in the country's armed forces, the chair of the National Defense Commission, an extension of the post as supreme commander of the People's Army that Kim had held since 1991. At the same time, the Supreme People's Assembly announced the decision to change the *gukga jusŏk* (paramount leader of state), which Kim Il Sung had held until his death in July 1994, to a position of perpetuity assigned exclusively to the late leader. In addition to this astonishing constitutional initiative to elect a deceased person as a permanent head of state (*yŏnggu jusŏk*), the Supreme People's Assembly named the new constitution the "Kim Il Sung Constitution" and defined "Kim Il Sung ideology" as the constitution's foundational principles.[1]

These legal-institutional reforms concerning the status of the defunct leader correlated closely with other decisions made during the national mourning period—notably, the decision to embalm the dead leader's body and the related mass campaign for an immortal Kim Il Sung. The embalming was intended, as in the Soviet Union and elsewhere in the socialist world with regard to the bodies of deceased state leaders, to preserve the memory and spirit of the defunct leader in a demonstratively materialistic way. This was done in part to distinguish memorial practices in socialist politics from the largely symbolic, idealistic conception of memory observed in bourgeois societies.[2] It was also intended to demonstrate the power of scientific knowledge and technology to defy nature—in this case, the natural process of bodily decay and decomposition.

Kim Il Sung's enduring presence in the polity and society was made real not only via the display of his embalmed body but also through a concerted mass campaign for the immortal Kim Il Sung that became a central element in North Korea's public culture in the second half of the 1990s. A number of songs were written in this regard, including "The Great Leader Will Be Forever with Us," and numerous "eternal life towers"—monuments inscribed with epitaphs dedicated to the living memory of Kim Il Sung—were erected throughout the country. The act of electing a *persona mortem* as head of state in perpetuity will probably become a revolutionary episode in modern political and constitutional history; for our discussion, the drama is relevant for understanding how North Korea sought to circumvent the critical structural problems involved in the continuity of charismatic authority. The post-1994 political process advanced an institutional renovation that transformed Kim Il Sung's historical charismatic authority into a constitutionally transcendental and conceptually transhistorical authority. Only after achieving this was Kim Jong Il elected to a supreme position in the Workers' Party in place of the deceased leader. The result was not a succession of office. Rather than a new head of state replacing the old, the constitutional change created a new office that the new and old leader could occupy together as a physical and a metaphysical head of state, respectively.

The above institutional reform and its result are aptly referred to, in contemporary North Korean language, as *yuhun jŏngch'i*, or "legacy politics." That this legacy entails a materially embodied bequest rather than merely an abstract conceptual principle is made clear both by the decision to embalm the deceased leader's body and by the location of his embalmed, immortalized body. Kim Il Sung is reported to have died in his office in Myohyangsan due to a cardiac stroke suffered while busy at work. According to the famous North Korean song "We Celebrate Our Supreme Leader's Longevity and Health" released in the wake of Kim Il Sung's sixtieth birthday in 1972, "Our Supreme Leader dedicates his entire life to the single purpose of bringing happiness to the people." The leader's other personal office and larger personal palace in Kŭmsusan later became, after a major renovation, the mausoleum for Kim Il Sung's body, which, preserved in an air-tight glass casket surrounded by flowers, receives a stream of mourners and pilgrims daily. The organization of this mortuary art is meant to convey the message that the country's founding father passed away while performing his sacred duty in his office and to reflect his lifelong dedication to the happiness of the North Korean people. It is also meant to give the sense that the country's supreme political father continues to be present in his office and to receive people there; that is, he continues to meet his sacred purpose in life even after death and in a quasi-material reality, while holding the immortal, perpetual sovereign power attributed to him by the constitutional change (Kim's death, in official North Korean language, is expressed as the end of the leader's physical life only, meaning that his political life continues). In an artful geometric feat characteristic of North Korean public memorial art in the era of Kim Jong Il, the chamber where Kim's physically dead yet politically alive body is kept has been made to face, in the distance, the tomb of Kim Jong Suk, the Mother of Sŏn'gun (military-first politics) and birth mother of Kim Jong Il buried at the top center of the Graves of Revolutionary Martyrs (see chapter 4). Both memorials are on the outskirts of Pyongyang; from the grave of Kim Jong Suk, visitors can see a prominent building in the distance, which is the office complex of the immortal leader.

The new constitutional order was also manifested forcefully in North Korea's public art of the 1990s. The period saw, amid and despite economic devastation and an extreme subsistence crisis, a number of large-scale construction projects in memory of Kim Il Sung, as well as the production of a multitude of new visual and musical artifacts celebrating the Great Leader's immortal life in the capacity of a perpetual, transcendental head of the North Korean state.[3] The development of these commemorative arts in the second half of the 1990s, together with the legacy of the partisan state art that had advanced since the early 1970s, culminated in the mass spectacle of Arirang in the beginning of the 2000s.

We have mentioned that the Arirang spectacle is a powerful combination of art and politics. Arirang tells the story of North Korea's political genesis in theatrical form; it also communicates what the North Korean state wishes to say to the people and to the outside world based on the mobilized performance labor of schoolchildren, women, and soldiers. In Arirang, therefore, North Korean citizens and their state become dramatically united in the act of speech, in which the citizens stand as the parole for the langue of the state. This demonstrated unity also has an aspect that goes beyond questions of language and representation. The citizens' collective performing bodies, in Arirang, do not merely communicate what the sovereign body of the revolutionary state wishes to say; they also, more importantly, participate in making and renewing, through their labor of drama, the very sovereign body as a vital historical and moral entity. We may add a further notion of participation, developed in the theory of rituals, and say that in this mass spectacle, not only do the performing masses participate in actualizing the imagery of the state, but, at the same time, their performed images and voices of the state affect the collective consciousness of the performing citizens, taking root in it as a meaningful, vital entity. As Émile Durkheim observed long ago, the power of a ritual performance consists of these two different yet simultaneous participatory dynamics: the performing individual bodies participate in the making of a collective social form, and an ideal image of collective unity participates in the spirit and consciousness of the rite-performing bodies.[4]

Arirang has a clear narrative order, which we earlier characterized as a postcolonial epic (see chapter 1); it depicts this narrative in a multidimensional way, involving both musical and visual media, as well as the carefully choreographed performance of numerous citizen-actors. The spectators (apart from the few foreign tourists and visitors) also play a vital role in this state theater through coordinated cheering and by operating their handheld multicolor pickets to draw key slogans and symbols. Some of these displayed symbols are intelligible to all spectators, including those from the outside world (i.e., the portrait of the late leader surrounded by thousands of flowers), whereas others are not, and an understanding of them requires what Jeffrey Brooks calls "political literacy."[5] The latter include scenes of specific historical events, such as exemplary heroic episodes from the time of the Korean War. The battle on Wŏlmi Island, west of Inchon, and that on 1211 Hill, Kangwŏn Province, are among the most prominent heroic episodes of the war of liberation in today's North Korean public history, and they have been frequent entries in the epic history exhibited in Arirang in recent years (see chapter 4). Other symbols that appear in Arirang relate to important labor heroes or scenes of construction projects of significant national value from the postwar years. Later we will have occasion to explore the place of labor heroism and miracles in North Korea's political and moral economy (see chapter 6). For now, it suffices to mention that among the most prominent visual symbols displayed in Arirang recently is the image of two pistols. In the Arirang performance of 2005 and 2008, this image, drawn by twenty thousand mobilized schoolchildren using their handheld pickets, appeared at the crucial juncture of the epic narrative between the Kim Il Sung–led national genesis and Kim Jong Il's military-first era.

The symbolism of the two pistols refers to a formative, legendary episode in Kim Il Sung's biographical history and thus has been a vital element in the efforts to bring Kim's historical legacy, after his death in 1994, into the moral and spiritual foundation of North Korea's constitutional order. These guns have therefore been given enormous historical and moral value in today's North Korea under the rule of his successors. The story associated with these eminent objects is of great importance for understanding this rule's claimed historical and genealogical ties to the founding episode of the North Korean revolution. Therefore, the symbolism of the two pistols has much to offer for an understanding of the progression of Kim Il Sung's personal charisma to the present-day form of hereditary charisma. The meaning of these pistols is important also for grasping military-first politics as a political culture—that is, how this political doctrine is understood and cognized by the country's ordinary citizens. *Sŏn'gun*, the Sino-Korean word for military-first or army-first politics and ideology, has another, more popular expression: *ch'ongdae*, or "the barrel of a gun." Although these expressions are sometimes used interchangeably, they nevertheless have a set of subtle yet important semantic differences; grasping the meaning of what is today referred to as "the barrel-of-a-gun philosophy" (*ch'ongdae ch'ŏlhak*) in North Korean public media and political literacy will be important for understanding how the guiding principles of military-first politics are understood at a grassroots level and how these politics are realized in the sphere of mass mobilization and civic participation.

The Political Theory of *Sŏn'gun*

A conference of North Korea's prominent political theorists was held in Pyongyang in August 2006 to discuss the genesis and theoretical premise of the military-first political idea. The conference concluded, according to a report, that "the Dear Leader's [Kim Jong Il] passionate ideological-theoretical activity advanced the Great Leader's *sŏn'gun* ideology to a theoretical principle of revolutionary politics and to a great guiding principle for our times."[6] This is an interesting statement, considering the fact that in the 1990s, the North Korean media tended to present military-first politics primarily as an original invention by Kim Jong Il. The claimed originality was meant to highlight the fact that Kim Jong Il's mode of rule, while inheriting principal elements from the Kim Il Sung era, was nevertheless distinct from the earlier era. This changed in the subsequent decade. The North Korean documents on the theory of military-first politics published in the 2000s typically claim a joint, hereditary authorship for the theory between Kim Il Sung and Kim Jong Il. An authoritative book published in 2004, *Understanding Sŏn'gun Politics*, for instance, carefully maneuvers between a genealogical explanation for the origin of *sŏn'gun* and a situational analysis of the idea's evolution. While locating the origin of military-first politics in the distant history of the Kim Il Sung–led anticolonial resistance in 1930s Manchuria, it argues that the idea took concrete form during the long interaction between the Great Leader and the Dear Leader. It also claims that although the military-first political idea has a deep historical origin, its full theoretical force has only been realized in the Kim Jong Il era, thanks to the Dear Leader's vigorous intellectual efforts to protect North Korea's revolutionary heritage at a time of grave crisis in international socialism in the 1990s.

Understanding Sŏn'gun Politics starts, as do many other contemporary North Korean social science publications, with a quote from Kim Jong Il: "Entering the last decade of the twentieth century, socialism collapsed in the Soviet Union and in countries of eastern Europe; this has resulted in great changes in the global political structure and relations of power."[7] A few pages later, the book introduces another quote from the Dear Leader: "Due to the imperialist reactionaries' plot against the Republic [Democratic People's Republic of Korea] that sought to isolate the Republic and to press it to death, our revolution came to confront cruel challenges and obstacles, unprecedented in history. We became a lone fighter against American imperialism and against the concerted aggression from the imperialist forces."[8] Based on these primary citations (featured in a bold script distinct from the rest of the text, according to the established printing tradition in contemporary North Korea), the first part of the book presents a readable, interesting analysis of the implications of the "collapse of socialism" for North Korea. Later, the analysis moves on to the main conceptual premises of military-first politics, arguing that this politics, spearheaded by the genius of Kim Jong Il, was the only possible philosophical thesis and the best theory of the North Korean socialist revolution in the hostile global environment of the 1990s.

About the collapse of international socialist political order in Russia and Europe and the consequent end of the Cold War as a geopolitical order, *Understanding Sŏn'gun Politics* has the following things to say. It argues that the bipolar world order of the Cold War era, after the end of the global conflict in 1989 to 1991, has not evolved into a peaceful, multipolar international order. Instead, the world has degenerated into a unipolar world order, dominated by American power and rife with political conflicts and threats of war: "Conflicts during the Cold War were mostly provoked and radicalized by the reciprocal enmity between the era's two superpowers, the Soviets and the Americans. After the end of the Cold War, by contrast, conflicts have arisen between nations, ethnic groups and political factions, and these were ignited by the contradictions resulting from the uncurbed preponderance of American power."[9] Emboldened after the end of the Cold War and with no countervailing forces provided by the international socialist order, United States, according to *Understanding Sŏn'gun Politics*, concentrates its aggression against anti-imperialist forces in the Third World seeking self-determination. Given this versatile condition, which poses a grave challenge to the global revolutionary forces, the book concludes that "after the breakdown of socialism in some countries and the end of the Cold War, the global political order has changed from the formation centered on the Soviet-US confrontation to one that is based on the contest of power between North Korea and the United States."[10] *Rodong Sinmun* also asserts that thanks to Kim Jong Il's military-first politics, "northeast Asia and the world at large now benefit from having a new pole of justice [North Korea] that can confront the power of super-empire in the unipolar world."[11]

The last assertions may sound astonishingly self-centered and like gross exaggerations of North Korea's power; yet, they are based on the following assessment of North Korea's place in the post–Cold War world order: "The flag of socialism was taken down in the former Soviet Union and eastern European countries. In the broader international sphere, people who long for socialism are thrown into confusion and left with no guidance. During this time of great trial, we refused to make any change. Instead, we raised our red flag of socialism even higher than before. This way, our country became the only remaining bastion of socialism and was illuminated with the esteemed honor of doing so."[12] At the same time, according to *Understanding Sŏn'gun Politics*, North Korea became the sole vanguard of the Third World revolution and a leader among developing nations in their collective struggle against coerced incorporation into the "new world order" orchestrated by American imperial power, and thus it is "the only source of light that can ignite the fire of self-determination among peoples in the Third World."[13] This singular, vanguard position of North Korea in the post–Cold War world explains, the book argues, why the United States feels so threatened by the existence of North Korea and, likewise, why the news media in the United States (such as the *New York Times*) call North Korea "the world's most dangerous country."[14]

A set of intriguing issues arises from the above rendering of contemporary world politics as the background for the rise of North Korea's military-first politics. Notable is the interpretation of the disintegration of Soviet political unity. *Understanding Sŏn'gun Politics* argues that North Korea took over the former Soviet Union's position as a main contender with American power in the post–Cold War world order. North Korea's substitution for the Soviet Union as the leader of a global socialist revolution was not North Korea's willful choice; rather, it was forced upon the nation as the only existing revolutionary polity in the new world order that keeps intact the proud flag of socialism. The book discusses what it takes to keep holding the flag of socialism high based on a strong assertion that

Figure 3.1. "Nobody in the world can beat us!" Arirang Festival, 2002. *Source: Chosun* 542 (June 2002): 20.

the most fundamental reason for the disintegration of the Soviet order was the depoliticization of the Soviet armed forces. In this light, *Understanding Sŏn'gun Politics* presents a highly negative view of the reform measures taken by former Soviet leader Mikhail Gorbachev in the second half of the 1980s, which it argues were aimed at separating the Soviet army from Soviet politics. This view conflicts directly with the conclusion reached by many Western observers, who typically present a positive assessment of Gorbachev's role in ending the Cold War in Europe, citing particularly his refusal to intervene militarily in the political crisis that the Soviet Union's European allies were undergoing at the end of the 1980s. Melvyn Leffler's recent authoritative history of the Cold War, for instance, assigns the most pivotal role in ending the long US-Soviet conflict to Gorbachev's exemplary efforts toward denuclearization and his search for nonmilitary solutions to international conflicts and crisis in eastern and central Europe, as well as in Afghanistan.[15] *Understanding Sŏn'gun Politics*'s assessment of this critical period draws a very different conclusion, arguing that Gorbachev's military reform and his opting for a nonmilitary solution to the crisis in international socialism resulted in "the fall of the Soviet army from the status of the Party's army and the army's loss of its fundamental character as the army of socialism and the [proletarian] class, which opened the door for the dissolution of the Communist Party, the collapse of the Soviet rule, and the return of capitalism."[16] Based on this assessment, the book asserts,

> The tragic fate of the former Soviet power shows that the army cannot retain its class-based character if it is separated from the Party's leadership. It shows that the Party will fail in its task and collapse itself unless it holds the army under its grip. From this analysis comes the principle that a victory in revolutionary struggle is viable only when the Party of the proletarian class holds the army within its power and when the army devotes its strength solely to defending the party. The principle is according to the law of revolution that the Army is the Party and that the Party is the Army.[17]

Also notable is North Korea's self-definition as an alternative world leader, after the collapse of the Soviet empire, in place of the former Soviet Union. The book advances this highly debatable, self-centered understanding of the contemporary global political order focused on the power nexus of North Korea versus the United States, drawing on supporting evidence from a number of selected Western sources. These sources include the Voice of America, which allegedly asserts, "North Korea is recognized as *the most influential basis*, in northeast Asia as well as in the broader global terrain, for the revival of socialism."[18] This and other references to foreign sources interact, within *Understanding Sŏn'gun Politics*, with extracts from the authoritative discourse of Kim Jong Il. The former are surely meant to generate the impression that the book's argument is a reasoned, scientific analysis based on knowledge of world opinions and trends. Like most other referential practices in contemporary knowledge production, the references to foreign sources introduced in this and other North Korean texts about military-first politics are meant also to strengthen the authority of the text's arguments. However, it is clear that the ultimate authority for the argument, within the textual reality, lies in the occasional bolded citations from the works and speeches of the country's leader rather than in sources from the outside world. Concerning this particular referential strategy, it is worth adding that the text's allusion to the leader's authoritative voice and knowledge goes beyond in meaning what we would normally understand with citational practice. In *Understanding Sŏn'gun Politics* as well as other analytical literature about military-first politics, it is apparent that the references to Kim Jong Il's spoken or written words are not merely meant to draw authority from the latter in support of the presented argument; more importantly, they are intended to augment the authority and esteem of the cited discourse. For example, the statement that North Korea has been brought to confront American imperialism all alone—which Kim Jong Il is quoted as saying about the destiny of North Korea after the collapse of the international socialist alliance—evolves in the narrative presented in the book into the somewhat astonishing conclusion mentioned above that North Korea has replaced the Soviet Union in the new global order after the end of the Cold War as the only capable opponent of American power. And the book employs the series of references to foreign sources for the specific purpose of justifying the argument intended to magnify the stately status of North Korea and thereby the prestige of the country's leader. The act of citing what the leader has said about the world, therefore, is aimed primarily at raising the honor and authority of the speaker, which may involve amplifying and even radicalizing his meanings.

In relation to the idea that North Korea and the United States make up a new bipolar world order after the collapse of the old bipolar geopolitical order, it is interesting to observe that the book's analysis of the post–Cold War, postsocialist world order focuses singularly on one particular stream of global change as against another equally important developmental stream. Earlier we noted two separate processes of postsocialist social development—one of them mainly associated with the former Soviet Union and eastern Europe and the other with Asian socialist polities, notably China and Vietnam. The latter is typically referred to as market socialism, or socialism with a market orientation, and characterized as a mode of social development combining a centralized political rule with a controlled market economic decentralization and liberalization. This mode of development, in ideological terms, involves the idea that the merits of socialism and the legacy of socialist revolution are to be more effectively defended and possibly increased only through economic growth, which requires, in practical reality, an engagement with global markets. Interestingly, *Understanding Sŏn'gun Politics* and other North Korean analytical literature published in the last ten years about world affairs and North Korea's place in the world are virtually silent about the theory of market socialism and the related idea of protecting socialist revolution through engagement with the global economy.[19] The absence of any mention of

this important politico-economic trend is understandable, considering the fact that
the theory of market socialism goes head-on against the military-centered theory
of socialist revolution in the post–Cold War world postulated by North Korea's
sŏn'gun politics. Nevertheless, this absence makes it an unsettling experience to
read North Korea's recent political literature, particularly because market socialism concerns developments in countries that are historically and culturally closest to North Korea and remains a haunting element in its discourses about North
Korea's vanguard role in global socialist revolution.

More can be said about the incongruity between North Korea's military-first
socialism and the economy-first socialism pursued by other Asian socialist polities, especially China, which is North Korea's close neighbor and traditional ally.
Important in this matter is the book's allusion to North Korea's esteemed status
in the Third World movement for political independence and self-determination.
After the Korean War, North Korea's political development was complicated not
only by the aggravated hostile relations with South Korea and the United States
but also, after the late 1950s, by the increasing mutual hostilities between the
country's two principal allies and supporters in the war effort, China and the Soviet Union. In this turbulent milieu, North Korea sought to confront both of these
separate hostile international environments by actively joining in the nonaligned
movement among the newly independent Third World nations, with the ambition
of becoming a leader in the movement. It is observed that the regional disputes
between China and the USSR and their rivalry in the 1960s for global leadership
in the socialist revolution played a major part in the rise of North Korea's strongly
nationalist, postcolonial state ideology, called *juch'e*.[20] This ideology replaced
the largely Soviet-style, Soviet-allied political orientation of the earlier state-
building era. According to Don Oberdorfer, "Beyond its sanctification of Kim
[Il Sung's] decisions, *juch'e* was a declaration of political independence from his
two communist sponsors. Although it was originally called 'a creative application
of Marxism-Leninism,' eventually all reference to Marxist connections was abandoned."[21] Subsequently, in the 1970s, North Korea made a considerable effort to
elaborate on this ideology and also to export it to other developing nations in the
Third World as a guiding ideology for national liberation and self-determination
whose global relevance would be superior to that of its Leninist or Maoist prec-
edents. North Korea's vigorous engagement with the nonaligned movement and
its related ambition to become a global revolutionary power in the postcolonial
world, equal to China or the Soviet Union in esteem and authority if not in military or economic power, are vividly demonstrated, as we shall see in chapter 5,
in one of North Korea's cherished public memorials, the International Friendship
Exhibition Hall, which displays gifts to Kim Il Sung brought from all corners of
the world.

In this regard, we may understand the idea of North Korea being the only
remaining "bastion of socialism," alluded to in the theory of military-first politics,
as having a deeper historical background than the implosion of the Soviet political

order in the early 1990s and the subsequent increased isolation of North Korea in the international community. Tatiana Gabroussenko notes in her careful reading of changes in early North Korean literature, "[From the late 1950s], North Korean policy makers started to position the D.P.R.K. as a self-sufficient state, equipped with a potentially world-dominating ideology. There emerged an image of North Korea as the sole, independent center of all the truly progressive forces of the globe. This image was strongly reminiscent of the image of the U.S.S.R. in old Soviet propaganda, with Pyongyang replacing Moscow as the center of the inhabited universe."[22] Gabroussenko explores this image of a global North Korea based on a dramatic shift in North Korea's literary production from a strong dependence on Soviet literature during the earlier postcolonial era of the 1940s and 1950s to a strong nationalist assertion of autonomy and authenticity beginning in the 1960s. Gabroussenko aptly terms this development North Korea's "national Stalinism," highlighting the fact that the development was prompted by the North Korean leadership's discontent with the dynamics of de-Stalinization in the Soviet Union in the later part of the 1950s. As we will see in more detail in chapter 5, the assault against Stalin's personality cult legacy in the Soviet Union posed a grave threat to the authority and esteem of North Korea's exemplary personality, Kim Il Sung. Thus, we may say that the contemporary idea of North Korea as the single leader of the progressive world is rooted in North Korea's long-held ambition to be distinct from, and treated as equal to, its powerful neighbors, the Soviet Union and China.[23] Just as the ideology of *juch'e* was supposed to mark North Korea as an original, independent player in the global socialist and postcolonial politics during the earlier era, so the theory of military-first politics is meant to set today's North Korea against the former Soviet Union, which North Korea sees as a failed guardian of global revolutionary ideals. It also works to distinguish North Korea from China, which concentrates on generating national economic growth rather than on sustaining the socialist and postcolonial revolutionary ideals, although this distinction is expressed much more implicitly than is the case with the former Soviet Union.[24]

The difference between North Korea's military-focused revolutionary socialist politics and China's economy-focused market-socialist politics points to other important issues. In his seminal work on early political and social revolution in North Korea, Charles Armstrong makes the important observation that North Korea's socialist revolution, as compared to those in other socialist societies, was unique in its strong emphasis on correct thoughts and ideological dispositions as the driving force of revolution (rather than appropriate material conditions and an apt economic basis, as is the case in orthodox Marxism). Armstrong associates the idealistic, "neotraditionalist" orientation of the North Korean socialist revolution partly with Korea's long, strong neo-Confucian tradition, which is considered to put supreme value on programmatic ritual propriety and nominal moral and ethical principles (see chapter 1).[25] North Korean literature on the origin of military-first politics indeed tends to stress strongly the moral imperative to continue the socialist revolution and to maintain the revolutionary heritage, privileging this imperative over questions of economic welfare and growth. In this respect, it is interesting to note that the term "preceding theories" appears frequently in North Korea's recent political and philosophical discourse. This term is intended to explain the originality and inventiveness of the country's guiding principles in relation to the traditional Marxist and Leninist philosophical heritages. Kim Jong Il said in his speech delivered at the Workers' Party Central Committee meeting on October 10, 1990,

> The historical materialism of Marxism divided society into infrastructure and superstructure, assigning the determining meanings to the former. This historical-materialist view is unable to establish a proper theory about the *juch'e* [meaning "subjectivity" in this context] of revolution. . . . The Workers' Party is a political organization assembled by people, who are also the object of this organization's work. Therefore, the Party's organizational principles must be based on scientific understandings about the nature of human beings. All human activities are determined by thoughts and ideologies; therefore, we must follow the principle of idealism [or "ideologism," *sasangron* in Korean] in the construction of the Party.[26]

The self-conscious disassociation of North Korea's state ideology from the established socialist intellectual and revolutionary ideology was already in motion, according to Oberdorfer, in the earlier advancement of the *juch'e* ideology in the 1960s.[27] The *juch'e* ideology advocates, as mentioned in the above quote, the centrality of human subjectivity in revolution—the idea that the collective human will is the main motor of historical progression—and accordingly makes claims against the existing theories of socialism and socialist revolution that privilege material forces and economic relations over ideational human moral and spiritual qualities. The idea of *juch'e* purports to have the history-making power of human collective subjectivity; it also centers this power on an extraordinary, exceptional, and exemplary human subjectivity.[28] Kim Jong Il says, referring tacitly to the critique of personality cults in Marx's writings, "The preceding theories approached the question of supreme leadership [*suryŏng*] merely as matters concerning the role of a superior individual [in revolution]. This problem also relates to the way in which preceding theories understood the role of a supreme leader mainly as questions of leadership. Questions about the supreme leader's status and role are not merely about his leadership. Instead, these are about the center of the sociopolitical organism, about this organism's highest cerebral organ."[29]

Later we will return to the theory of a political organism and how the advancement of this theory, which was part of the transition of power from Kim Il Sung to Kim Jong Il, shaped North Korea's early critique of "preceding theories." For now it is noteworthy that in the contemporary drive to advance the premises of military-first politics to a globally meaningful vanguard ideology, the claimed limitation and error of preceding theories refer specifically to how these theories conceptualize the relationship between military and economic forces in socialist revolution and state politics. *Understanding Sŏn'gun Politics* explains, "The preceding theories prioritized relations of production and economic development, thereby advancing the idea that socialism and the socialist army can be built and strengthened in a country only when this country has a proper economic basis. By contrast, the military-first politics provides a new formula for revolution, based on the principles of *juch'e* ideology, which prioritizes the empowerment of armed forces."[30] Based on this assertion that military-first politics and ideology constitute a decisive conceptual break with existing theories of socialist revolution, the book proceeds to an audacious assault on the premises of historical materialism and the primacy of material condition in relation to ideological representation, turning the order practically upside down: "The preceding theories advanced the working class as the principal army [of socialist revolution] based on socioeconomic relations and conditions. . . . These relations and conditions do not determine the principal forces of revolutionary movement; the determining force of socialist revolution is, rather than economic conditions, the people's ideological-mental qualities and their collective will and force. The military-first politics defines the revolutionary army as the core, primary power for the advancement of socialism and people's self-determination."[31]

The theory of military-first politics privileges the power of ideology and the power of the army over the forces of production and, therefore, turns the principles of historical materialism and Marxism on their head. As is noticeable in the last quotation, however, this self-acclaimed new theory of revolution does not explain the theoretical relationship between ideological unity and the power of revolutionary violence. We need to turn to the language of *ch'ongdae* in order to understand the conceptual relationship between the foundational power of thought and the constitutional power of the means of violence in contemporary North Korean sovereignty discourse.

The Gift of a Gun

In June 1926, the then fourteen-year-old Kim Il Sung received from his mother an important gift left by his father, which, in North Korea's contemporary official historical narrative, subsequently became the most meaningful object throughout Kim's turbulent life of exile on the frontier of anticolonial resistance in Manchuria and later during his career as the leader of a proud state on the frontier against American imperialism. His father's gift, a pair of pistols wrapped in red cloth, came with an explanation about the meaning of the object from the donor, Kim Hyung Jik, who said, "When you fight with an enemy who happens to have a knife in his hand, you need a knife yourself to fight and win the duel." The two pistols represented a profound, visionary thought on the part of Kim Hyung Jik, according to the North Korean press, who believed that "armed struggle was the supreme form of struggle for national independence." It also represented Kim Hyung Jik's hope that "the toiling masses will rise in an armed struggle against

Figure 3.2. Kim Il Sung
receiving two guns. *Source:
Sŏn'gun, sŭngliŭi kich'i*
(Pyongyang: Chosun Art
Book Press, 2003), 12.

imperialists to recover their country and to build a new world without exploitation and repression."[32] Upon receiving this gift of guns, according to the story, Kim Il Sung began, holding deep in his heart his father's teachings about the meaning of the gift, to nurture his unshakable revolutionary resolve to restore national independence through armed struggle.

The above story appears in many political and moral education materials distributed universally today in North Korea, and it is introduced in them as the historical origin (*siwŏn*) of military-first politics. The story includes another historical episode in which the young Kim Il Sung shows the guns that he has received from his father to his schoolmates in a Manchurian town, where Kim settled after leaving home in 1926, following his father's arrest by the Japanese colonial police. These pivotal episodes are widely available in other forms, including paintings, murals, and posters. The way these foundational stories are told marks a subtle yet important change in the cultural politics of North Korea in recent years. In the mid-1990s, as mentioned earlier, the North Korean literature and media tended to emphasize the inventiveness of military-first politics as associated with the genius of Kim Jong Il and his distinctive style of rule. The emphasis has shifted from originality to heritage since the mid-2000s, however, and the argument has since focused on military-first politics' deep historical and genealogical connections to the origin of the North Korean revolution and the early biographical history of Kim Il Sung. In parallel with this development to present the idea of military-first politics as a historically rooted theory, moreover, Kim Il Sung's revolutionary historical career has increasingly become more of a family genealogical history, departing from the singularly personalized charismatic history that had been prevalent in the previous decades and becoming increasingly a part of an extensive historical genealogical background for a continuously evolving, hereditary revolutionary political commitment. The revolutionary filial tie between Kim Il Sung and his father, Kim Hyung Jik, is one notable element in this development, and so is, as we shall see shortly, the political familial relationship between Kim Jong Il and his mother, Kim Jong Suk. Broadly speaking, the contemporary narrative aims to situate the idea of military-first politics in a sublime family heritage of supremely exemplary revolutionary merit, the progression of which is being crystallized in the persona of Kim Jong Il.[33] In today's North Korean political literacy, this family-based political heritage is referred to as "the barrel-of-a-gun family genealogy" (*ch'ongdae gamun*).

The Kim family heritage involves another story about the gift of a gun. In the Arirang spectacle, the image of a single pistol often follows that of a pair of pistols. The latter refers to the gift that Kim Il Sung received from his father in 1926 and thus represents the origin of the North Korean revolution in the colonial era; the story of the single pistol relates to the Korean War, a time of great trial for the North Korean revolution, and tells of a father-son encounter on an important battlefield during this three-year-long Victorious Fatherland Liberation War, the official name for the Korean War in North Korea.

In the summer of 1952, Kim Jong Il met his father in his father's field command office along the frontier of the Korean War in the mountainous Kangwŏn province. According to the story, featured in the book *The Father of Sŏn'gun, General Kim Il Sung*, the then ten-year-old Kim Jong Il had volunteered to visit the place (it is known that the young Kim was evacuated to northeastern China, possibly to the city of Jilin, during the time of the Korean War), hoping to be near his father, who was, as the supreme commander of North Korea's People's Army, personally leading the important defense line along the hills.[34] The young Kim stayed on the battlefield for two months, learning and witnessing how the people of North Korea were heroically struggling against superior American firepower with "a singular, unshakable belief in the Great Leader." On July 10, 1952, he was called to the office of the supreme commander. The Great Leader asked the young Kim what the day was; the boy replied that it was the birthday of his late grandfather. Pleased to hear this, the Great Leader handed his son a gift wrapped in red cloth and said, "I give this to you today. You should take it as a baton in the relay race of our revolution. This gun keeps the will of our Mankyungdae family genealogy. You must take good care of it for all your life." Mankyungdae, the name for Kim Il Sung's birthplace, is today preserved as a national monument and a sacred pilgrimage site. After offering the revolver to the boy, the supreme commander of the People's Army reportedly said to his ten-year-old son, "A revolutionary should never part with his gun throughout his life. You must remember this: guns are your closest friend along the way toward a victorious revolution." Introducing this episode, *The Father of Sŏn'gun* presents the following interpretation of the meaning of the gift: "The Great Leader passed over to his son the heritage of our revolution through this revolver, following what the honorable Kim Hyung Jik had done in earlier times. Contained in the gun was the Great Leader's dearest wish for a continuous Korean revolution across the generations and according to the glorious tradition of the Mankyungdae revolutionary family."[35]

The story of the revolver may sound too perfect to be true. Indeed, it has several incredulous elements. The expression "Mankyungdae family revolutionary genealogy" is fairly new to the North Korean political vocabulary; it is hard to imagine that Kim Il Sung was actually able to use this expression as early as 1952. In addition, it is difficult to imagine that a ten-year-old Korean child, no matter how exceptionally intelligent and virtuous, would remember his deceased grandfather's date of birth. It would be more acceptable if the remembered date were his death day, considering that death-day commemorative ceremonies for family ancestors are an important element of traditional Korean culture. The celebration of an ancestor's birthday is alien to this tradition. Although it is true that North Korea invented a custom to celebrate the birthdays of national leaders and to commemorate the deceased national leader using the latter's birthday, this was in a much later period, when the cult of personality for Kim Il Sung was in full swing. The presented scenario is therefore very likely to be the result of a latter-day narrative invention projected onto a distant historical event (assuming that the event actually happened). We note this point not necessarily to devalue the relative liberty observed widely in North Korean historical-narrative practice to modify and fabricate factual historical details. The dominant theory of art in North Korea puts the highest emphasis on an artifact's capacity to represent history in an ideologically correct and morally spirited way and, when the representation concerns the biographical histories of the country's leaders, in ways that enliven the genius and moral authority of the subject. In this historical art, political spirituality has a higher hand than commitment to empirical historical knowledge, and the value of creative work is judged on the basis of its capacity to perform a meaningful social function in the contemporaneous reality—that is, to raise the moral and political consciousness of the masses and to dedicate the wealth of honor to the polity's exemplary center. Modification of factual details, in this context, may not necessarily be understood as a historical revision or falsification of facts; rather, it represents a profoundly pragmatist and instrumentalist approach to history, seeking freedom to select elements from history (or to add elements to it) according to the needs and imperatives of the lived political and social reality. Although the North Korean case is probably an extreme example of this, similar constructivist approaches to history and historical memory are hardly unfamiliar to modern history, as French sociologist Maurice Halbwachs lucidly shows.[36]

The really interesting question about the incredulous elements lodged in the story of the revolver is, rather than whether and how far the story reflects truth, why these elements are introduced into the story and what the story intends to tell with these possibly imaginary narrative elements. Seen from this perspective, the story of the revolver raises important issues concerning North Korea's heritage politics in relation to the three analytical ideas discussed in the previous chapters: the idea of the partisan state, the constitution of the family state, and the question of hereditary charismatic authority. To understand how three handheld guns of relatively humble firepower have become the most powerful symbolic objects for the mighty question of state sovereignty, it is necessary to consider first the conceptual relationship between military-first politics and its twin popular ideology, the "barrel-of-a-gun philosophy."

The Barrel-of-a-Gun Philosophy

Military-first politics, which has been North Korea's hallmark state ideology in the era of Kim Jong Il, is more popularly known in North Korea as *ch'ongdae* thought or philosophy, meaning "the philosophy of the barrel of a gun" or "barrel-of-a-gunnism."[37] North Korean literature on this philosophical idea presents, without exception, the authoritative definition of the idea provided by Kim Jong Il: "Our Party's Military-First Politics is founded on the philosophy of the gun barrel, which advocates that revolution is pioneered, advanced, and completed by the barrel of a gun." We noted earlier that there is a strong tendency in North Korea today to extend the origin of the military-first political idea to a greater historical genealogical depth, departing from the trend in the 1990s in which the idea was presented as the unique invention of Kim Jong Il. The barrel-of-a-gun philosophy functions to facilitate this process of historical reconstruction through its close association with the stories about guns inherited within the Kim family. The first episode concerning the two revolvers (which Kim Il Sung received from his father at the age of fourteen) extends the origin of the barrel-of-a-gun philosophy to the era of Kim Il Sung's rule and even further to his early introduction to the quest for national liberation and armed revolution. As this so-called philosophical idea is paired with *sŏn'gun*, the military-first political form, in contemporary discourse, the extended historical origin also applies to the latter political form. In this regard, we can say that the barrel-of-a-gun idea is an instrument for North Korea's political succession process: the *sŏn'gun* idea facilitated distinguishing Kim Jong Il's rule from his predecessor's, and after the consolidation of that rule, the *ch'ongdae* idea was brought in to revamp the dimension of continuity between the old and new regimes.

The fact that these two ideas are closely associated, however, does not mean that *ch'ongdae* is merely an alternative expression of *sŏn'gun*. Rather, the former is intended to deliver the premises and meanings of military-first politics in a more historically grounded way and as part of a continuum from the founding legend of the North Korean revolution. In this sense, we may say that the barrel-of-a-gun idea functions to bridge the old and new forms of partisan politics discussed earlier, that is, the Manchurian-based, anticolonial partisan activity and the contemporary, post-1994 partisan state politics of North Korea. As mentioned, the two stories about handguns—the gifts of arms in 1926 and 1952—constitute an important element in the production of historicity in the constitution of the partisan state. In addition, the barrel-of-a-gun idea is distinct from the military-first idea in that its relevance is intended to go beyond the narrowly defined sphere of the army and the institutional structure of the military in relation to the party. In her thoughtful article on North Korea's political aesthetics, anthropologist Sonia Ryang argues that North Korean political society, contrary to how it is perceived in the outside world, is highly individuated. She writes, "The concepts of self and the individual are crucial in North Korea, unlike what is usually assumed to be the case in a totalitarian society. Not as elements of a collective or group, but individuals as individuals are each responsible for their own moral-ideological purity, discipline, and perfection. This includes bodily perfection. Thus, often, even one's own family members are irrelevant. The most valued and exclusive human connection in North Korean society is that between individuals (each isolated and in separation from the other) and the sovereign Leader."[38] There is truth in this bold assertion, although we should point out that the associative unity these "individuals" make up is far from a gesellschaft but takes on powerful idioms of family values and familial moral unity, as discussed earlier with reference to the idea of the family or neo-Confucian state (see chapters 1 and 2). The barrel-of-a-gun doctrine aims to speak to these individuals in a political gemeinschaft about their roles in military-first politics as well as about the centrality of the army in socialist revolution—that is to say, the place of individuals in a societal unity constituted in the image of an army. In this respect, the barrel-of-a-gun "philosophical" doctrine is actually more radical in its implications than the military-first political doctrine. *Sŏn'gun* is principally about privileging the role of military power and institutions in revolution at a time of general international crisis for socialist revolution. By contrast, *ch'ongdae* is principally about creating a moral and practical unity between the army and society, which involves reforming society in the model of a military organization as well as subordinating society's needs to the needs of the army. Furthermore, it also makes a radical postulation about how individuals should conceptualize their existential status within the wider political society and in relation to the sovereign order—that is, these individuals should see themselves as the barrel of a gun. If military-first politics is a political theory anchored in the idea of the army as the vanguard of revolution, then the barrel-of-a-gun doctrine is a social theory advocating an absolute moral unity between the army and the people, as well as a practical and spiritual unity between the person and the gun. In this sense, there is a reason why the barrel-of-a-gun idea is referred to as a philosophy (*chŏlhak*) in contemporary North Korean political literacy, whereas its twin idea, military-first politics, takes on the status of an ideology (*sasang*) instead. The North Korean song "Peace Lies on the Tip of Our *Ch'ongdae*," says, "No matter how precious peace is, we shall never beg for peace. Peace lies on the tip of our *ch'ongdae*." In this rhetorical context, *ch'ongdae* may mean a number of things: it can refer to the mock wooden rifles stored in workplaces used for civil military drills or to the old colonial-era arms displayed at important pilgrimage sites along the Chinese border that are associated with the heroism of Manchurian partisans; it can also refer to the obligation of cooperative farmworkers to hand over their grain harvest to the local army units or to the country's proud, successful development of nuclear arms. The last has contributed to further isolation of North Korea from the international community and the curbing of humanitarian aid, aggravating the country's food-shortage problem and the population's suffering. In this context, *ch'ongdae* speaks of the popular will to hold fast to the spirit of *ch'ongdae* no matter what physical pains and social sufferings the practice of *ch'ongdae*, in the national and international spheres, may bring to the people. It also speaks of the moral and structural relationship between two forms of *ch'ongdae*, the popular and the exemplary. The most exemplary *ch'ongdae* consists, of course, of the glorious heritage of armed revolutionary struggle against imperialism in colonial and postcolonial forms. This is crystallized in the biographical history of Kim Il Sung and the hereditary politics of Kim Jong Il, and it is symbolized by the guns inherited within the Kim family. The popular *ch'ongdae* refers to the entirety of North Korea's social forces, which, in the North Korean idiom, are united in the sacred task of "defending the core of revolution [i.e., the exemplary *ch'ongdae*] with our lives." These forces encompass inanimate as well as animate forces, including both nuclear capability and collective human commitment. In this scheme, each soldier and every citizen of North Korea becomes a gun in defense of the exemplary heritage guns and within the vast concentric circles comprising "10 million guns [citizens]" poised to protect the latter. The relationship between the 10 million popular guns and the set of three exemplary guns corresponds to the classic slogan of socialist revolution, "All for one, one for all," and thus takes on a concentric though not necessarily hierarchical form. The logic is that the exemplary *ch'ongdae* find their raison d'être in protecting the popular entirety, whereas the popular *ch'ongdae* exist for the purpose of protecting the integrity of the exemplary center. The connectedness between these two types of "guns" is organic and symbiotic; each provides life force to the other. In conclusion, the claimed philosophical character of the *ch'ongdae* idea refers to the metaphysical aspects of the military-first political form regarding the origins and meanings of life—that the truly meaningful political life originates in the vital heritage of the exemplary revolutionary violence and the related tautological idea that the meaning of true political life lies in keeping and protecting the vital heritage. The semantics of the gun barrel, therefore, go beyond questions of revolutionary sovereignty or national security manifest in the military-first doctrine. Instead, it reaches out to more fundamental questions about what makes a moral person, what constitutes an ethical life, and how to live a meaningful political life.

We saw earlier how questions similar to those raised by North Korea's barrel-of-a-gun public doctrine were already integral to North Korea's public culture in the early 1970s, as demonstrated by our discussion of a few important epic accounts of Manchurian heroism that underwent forceful revival and reconstruction at that time. The next chapter shows how some of the *ch'ongdae* doctrine's formative moral and ethical principles are manifested in epic historical dramas that unfolded against the background of the Korean War. For now, we wish to extend the horizon of our discussion and look briefly at the doctrine's broad comparative historical background. Military-first politics advocates the unity of the army and the people; this is far from a unique North Korean invention but rather has a long background in the history of progressive thought and the theory of revolutionary violence. The political form of *sŏn'gun* goes a step further. It not only advocates that "the army is the people, the state, and the party" but also prioritizes, in practice, the military over society.[39] For Wada Haruki, this total fusion of the people and the army entails a radical militarization of society, and the fusion of the army and the party points to a militarization of the state machinery.[40] Interestingly, Wada observes that the process of fusion also involves a paradoxical development that the army becomes increasingly a non-army-like organization,

Figure 3.3. "Honor to the great victory of military-first politics!" (North Korean poster). *Source: Juch'e yesulŭi bitnanŭn hwapok* (Pyongyang: Literature and Art Press, 2001), 116.

losing its military characteristics. This is a poignant point, although Wada does not elaborate on it. It suggests that the unity of the army and the people affects the army as much as the society.

None of the recent North Korean literature about military-first politics shows much interest in offering a broad historical background for the paradigm of the unity of the army and the people. The genealogy of this idea, in contemporary North Korean political discourse, is strictly confined to national history; it is attributed exclusively to the genius of Kim Jong Il with a genealogical origin in Kim Il Sung's career. However, the idea plainly has a deeper origin and broader historical background. Most obvious is the famous dictum by Mao Zedong with regard to the paradigm of the people's war: "Power comes from the barrel of a gun." The idea's genealogical origin surely goes much deeper in time—to Lenin's theory of revolutionary violence and even further, as Carl Schmitt argues, to the theory of the partisan that emerged during the Napoleonic Wars and the American Revolution.[41] Conceptually, the idea is traced to early-nineteenth-century Prussian military theorist Carl von Clausewitz, who, in the words of Schmitt, discovered the partisan as a theoretical concept.[42] Observing that Mao's concept of the partisan was much more concrete and "telluric" than Lenin's, which remained relatively abstract and intellectual, Schmitt further argues, "The ideological conflict between Moscow and Peking, which has become increasingly stronger since 1962, has its deepest roots in this concrete and dissimilar reality of the true partisan. Also here, the theory of the partisan proves to be the key to knowledge of political reality."[43]

Schmitt's last comment rings true in the political genesis of North Korea and its divergence from the routes taken by China and Russia. Like Mao's philosophy of the people's war, North Korea's *sŏn'gun* and *ch'ongdae* doctrines advocate a radically relativist view of war and violence. These doctrines divide war into popular, revolutionary, and just wars, on the one hand, and unpopular, counterrevolutionary, and unjustified wars, on the other. Accordingly, they divide violence into two contrasting kinds in moral terms: progressive and revolutionary violence versus reactionary and counterrevolutionary violence. The claimed moral purity of revolutionary violence in the dual conception of violence and war derives from the popular nature of revolutionary violence. North Korea's *ch'ongdae* philosophy postulates that the barrel of a gun in this context refers exclusively to the means of revolutionary violence, not the means of violence in general. The means of justified violence are held and used by the popular masses in the service of the ideal of political self-determination. This postulation is clearly in accordance with Mao's definition of virtuous violence based on the moral and practical integration of the people and the army, as shown in his famous adage "People are the water, and the army the fish." However, the similarity between Mao's military philosophy and North Korea's *sŏn'gun* and *ch'ongdae* ideas probably ends here. The latter borrow some key elements from existing theories of the people's war; yet, they also claim to offer an entirely new theory of revolutionary violence.

One claimed innovation of North Korea's *ch'ongdae* philosophy is the permanent importance of the means and force of justified violence in revolutionary politics. This contrasts with orthodox Marxist theories, as Hannah Arendt mentions in her critique of Mao's theory of violence, which limit the role of revolutionary violence to only exceptional, extraordinary events in history, such as the revolutionary seizure of political power.[44] Another self-claimed theoretical invention relates to the definition of what constitutes the means of violence. In the *ch'ongdae* theory, the means and force of revolutionary violence are moral and ideological, not merely physical and mechanical; they can be a mechanical device of great destructive capacity (e.g., nuclear arms) or a state of absolute spiritual and moral loyalty (e.g., that of the *ch'ongdae* citizens to the heritage of the exemplary revolutionary *ch'ongdae*). Hence, here again, as with the *juch'e* ideology discussed earlier, North Korean political theory inverts the conceptual hierarchy between material forces and ideological phenomena found in what it refers to as "preceding theories" and defines ideological and moral power as the driving force of historical transformation.

The Power of the Gun and the Power of Love

We mentioned earlier that although the military-first political paradigm and the barrel-of-a-gun philosophical paradigm are frequently used in reference to each other and thus appear interchangeable, they are nevertheless distinct from one another in several crucial aspects. In our reading of North Korean literature, the two paradigms have a communicative, reciprocal relationship. They are meant to speak to and mirror each other. The political literacy of today's North Korea requires that this relationship between the two paradigms be recognized as a relationship of love.

In her essay on the rhetorical power of love as manifested in North Korean literature, Ryang argues that an ideal love relationship in North Korea is a triangular relationship. Focusing on how the relationship between a worker in a steel mill and his lover, the man's friend's sister, is represented in a piece of fiction from the 1980s, Ryang observes that the couple's mutual sexual attraction is not enough to make a meaningful relationship and that the completion of their relationship requires that each comes to grips with his or her separate yet common affective ties with the leader. The steelworker discovers his true love for his friend's sister only after he has discerned the reciprocal relationship of absolute love and absolute faith between himself and the leader. Thus, Ryang concludes that in North Korea's totalitarian society, the realization of love between individuals is dependent on the affective unity realized between the individual citizen and the sovereign leader. This "love triangle" may appear shocking but is nevertheless hardly unfamiliar; an identical motif was a prominent feature in the public culture of Stalin's Russia. The heroic productive achievement of Soviet shock workers in the 1930s was meant not only as proof of superhuman capacity to transcend the forces of nature but also, equally crucially, as a labor of love attributed to Comrade Stalin made in return for his boundless paternal love for all Soviet peoples. According to Jeffrey Brooks, the personal moral ties to Stalin "replaced bonds to family, friends, colleagues, the community, and ultimately to society itself. The workers' dependence on Stalin and the state was particularly evident in the case of Stakhanovites. . . . Thus proletarian and peasant notables acted out rituals of the gift and celebrated their miraculous rebirth as new people with a special relationship to their benefactor."[45] Brooks calls this a moral play enacted according to a ritualized economy of the gift.[46] We will come back to the moral economic dimensions of socialist politics in the North Korean context (see chapter 6); for now, it suffices to mention that today's North Korean love polemics are distinct from the Stalinist "moral play" in at least one crucial aspect. The political love rhetoric advanced in the era of military-first politics is related to the particular historical condition that gave birth to this political form—most notably, the fate of hereditary charisma in the time of a radical domestic economic crisis and generalized international political crisis relating to the fall of the Soviet empire. In this context, the political "love" of today carefully circumvents any economic implications of the reciprocal relations between the leader and the people (i.e., the exchange of heroic labor for gestures of recognition by Stalin in the form of symbolic and material entitlements, a characteristic of Stalin's Russia). Instead, it singularly focuses on the sovereignty question and on the military implications of the power of love.

The Great General of Sŏn'gun and the World of Love (2005) asserts that the most powerful weapon of all is "the love and trust between the Leader and the army, between the Leader and the people." It postulates that the power of this love is unlimited and immeasurable and is therefore "the object of intense envy for all the revolutionary peoples the world over and the object of intense fear for the enemies."[47] This book starts out with the premise that military-first politics is the highest expression of the North Korean leader's love for his people and develops a series of arguments that aim to explain how a politics that privileges the military is conceptually equivalent to a "politics of love." It introduces a number of episodes in which the military-first politics of love is allegedly expressed in concrete, empirical terms. These episodes consist mostly of Kim Jong Il's on-the-spot-guidance field visits to various military locations and major construction sites allocated to the army.[48] During these visits, the leader pays caring attention to the minute details of living conditions within the army, whose constituents in turn experience the grace of the leader's unconditional paternal care and love—"the affection that is as strong as the entirety of love shown by 10 million parents to their children."[49] On the other hand, the episodes also feature the leader's encounters with the model families of the military-first political era—families that have contributed an exceptional number of children and grandchildren to the armed forces. Called "*ch'ongdae* families," these are Stakhanovite families of the military-first political era. Individuals can also be *ch'ongdae* heroes. The book lists a number of them and, like other North Korean literature about military-first politics, presents a man named Lee Su Bok as one of the most eminent barrel-of-a-gun heroes. Lee Su Bok is a martyr of the Korean War known to have carried out a suicide mission against the Americans (see chapter 4). Most other listed *ch'ongdae* heroes are also fallen soldiers of the Korean War, including An Young Ae, a martyred army nurse who sacrificed her life while trying to evacuate wounded soldiers from a field hospital under American bombardment.

Based on these literary renderings of "the world of love" in the realm of the military-first political leadership, as well as other visual, musical, and theatrical expositions on related subjects, it seems apparent that the barrel of a gun is a master symbol of Kim Jong Il's rule that replaces in significance the classical symbols of the proletarian revolution and workers' state, the sickle and the hammer (in North Korea, these symbols include a brush, representing intellectuals). The barrel-of-a-gun symbol also unifies the traditional class-based symbols, thereby becoming a single source of power and meaning for agricultural, industrial, and intellectual laborers. The last is demonstrated by numerous contemporary events reported in the North Korean media, in which the People's Army has taken a lead in state construction projects (including the construction of memorials for the late founding leader). The army also actively participates in seasonal agricultural work, especially during rice-seeding and harvest times. The substitution of the barrel of a gun for the sickle and hammer means also, conceptually, that the economy and the society are modeled after the army and that, in practical spheres, all resources of the state should first concentrate on strengthening the army prior to sustaining the society. In short, we may call this general theoretical development a turn from the labor theory of value to a theory of human and material values according to the paradigm of partisan politics.

In the end, therefore, *ch'ongdae* refers to all resources, animate or inanimate, necessary to sustain the partisan state. Its broad, encompassing referential terrain includes North Korea's entire armed forces, all military hardware and personnel, and all the country's patriotic individuals and communities, as well as their moral dispositions and practical commitments. Kim Jong Il is reported to have said more than once that a gun is the most loyal comrade for a *sŏn'gun* revolutionary and that, as such, it never betrays the revolution.[50] Indeed, the barrel of a gun is not merely a thing but rather an embodiment of the purest loyalty and fidelity, the obligatory spiritual quality of the citizen of the military-first-era partisan state. According to a key slogan of military-first politics, in today's North Korea 10 million gun barrels are poised to defend the revolutionary center to the death. In this context, the barrel of a gun is both a being and an object; it is a person of loyalty to the North Korean revolution's exemplary center and a means of sustaining political rule for the revolution's hereditary-charismatic center.

The literature on the *ch'ongdae* philosophy acknowledges the difficulties in being a human barrel of a gun, which requires having a powerful longing for the Great Leader (see chapter 1) and absolute loyalty to the leader's legacy, as well as to the keeper of this legacy, the loving general of military-first politics. It also requires maintaining as intense and strong a comradely love for and fidelity to the keepers of the legacy as that held by the Manchurian heroes for their partisan leader. Very recently, however, North Korean literature has begun to acknowledge that being a barrel of a gun might involve overcoming the pain of hunger, like the Manchurian heroes did, as well as vanquishing the sorrow of losing loved ones to hunger.[51] At the same time, the *ch'ongdae* philosophy claims that these self-disciplinary and human-existential difficulties can be conquered if one has an adequate faculty and correct force of love. The literature about this philosophy introduces the life histories of many *ch'ongdae* heroes as proof that these obstacles can be overcome. In the next chapter, we turn to the most eminent heroic barrel-of-a-gun persona in North Korea's military-first-era public history and art, Kim Jong Suk. We will see how, in her life, the obscure love rhetoric and love-triangle phenomenon in North Korea's body politic actually becomes intelligible and how paternalistic-familial love can coexist with such preeminently disciplinary, regimental solidarity as exists in the North Korean army. Kim Jong Suk is the most brightly shining barrel-of-a-gun persona in North Korean history and, at the same time, the most exemplary caring mother figure. In her iconic persona, the love and violence of military-first politics becomes intelligibly integrated.

On a final note, let us briefly return to the stories of the three small guns said to have been passed down through the Kim Il Sung–Kim Jong Il family line. Obviously these are not ordinary guns. The Arirang Festival introduces the image

Figure 3.4. Kim Jong Suk defending Kim Il Sung. *Source: Sŏn'gun, sŭngliŭi kich'i* (Pyongyang: Chosun Art Book Press, 2003), 44.

of two handguns—those handed over to Kim Il Sung by his father in 1926—at the spectacle's critical juncture between the story of the heroic Manchurian legacy and that of the country's visionary future in the military-first era. The two pistols represent "the dearest hope to realize national liberation by armed revolution across generations," according to *The Great General of Sŏn'gun and the World of Love*, and they make up the origin of the "barrel-of-a-gun bloodline" (*ch'ongdae hyŏlt'ong*).[52] These arms, together with the single gun given to Kim Jong Il by Kim Il Sung in 1952, are meant to explain not only the historical roots and genealogical depth of military-first politics but also its purpose and nature. In our understanding of this reasoning, Kim Jong Il's military-first politics is meant to inherit the long family tradition of leading armed struggle and, at the same time, to represent the creative invention of this great tradition in accordance with novel historical conditions. The idea of *ch'ongdae*, in this context, refers to the deeply rooted family tradition from which the new revolutionary paradigm of military-first politics originates.

Therefore, *ch'ongdae* is the tradition of *sŏn'gun*, and *sŏn'gun* is the renovation of the *ch'ongdae* tradition. This apparently simple conceptual relationship between military-first politics and the barrel-of-a-gun philosophy, however, does more than provide historical background to legitimize the political paradigm. Within the conceptual scheme, the revolutionary career of Kim Il Sung becomes, in a crucial way, a hereditary phenomenon; likewise, the founding leader's charismatic authority appears to be more a hereditary authority than a strictly personal charisma. His eminent career as the partisan leader and as the leader of a partisan state was, according to the scheme, in part a genealogical matter and prescribed destiny rather than merely a self-acquired, personal achievement. By extension, the career of the leader's successors repeats the same scenario; they are at once an inheritor of a tradition and its defender. The so-called *ch'ongdae* philosophy thus plays a crucial role in the challenging task of replacing irreplaceable personal charisma with hereditary charisma by transforming the personified charisma into a form of hereditary authority. More importantly, it is also intended to advance the existing hereditary charisma to the next generation of leadership, as we will see in the conclusion to this volume.

Notes

1. Han S. Park, *North Korea: The Politics of Unconventional Wisdom* (Boulder, CO: Lynne Rienner Publishers, 2002), 85–88.

2. See Ilya Zbarsky and Samuel Hutchinson, *Lenin's Embalmers* (London: Harvill Press, 1998).

3. Sung-Ho Cho, *Kim Jong Il changgun ilhwachip* [A collection of anecdotes of General Kim Jong Il] (Pyongyang: Pyongyang Press, 2003), 45–48.

4. Emile Durkheim, *The Elementary Forms of Religious Life*, trans. K. E. Fields (New York: The Free Press, 1995).

5. Jeffrey Brooks, *Thank You, Comrade Stalin!: Soviet Public Culture from Revolution to Cold War* (Princeton, NJ: Princeton University Press, 2000), 3–18.

6. "Segyeminjokhaebangt'ujaengsae gili bitnal pulmyŏlŭi ŏbjŏk [Immortal achievement in the world liberation war]," *Rodong Sinmun*, August 17, 2006.

7. San-Pil Chun, *Sŏn'gun jŏngchie daehan lihae* [Understanding the *sŏn'gun* politics] (Pyongyang: Pyongyang Press, 2004), 1.

8. Chun, *Sŏn'gun jŏngchie daehan lihae* [Understanding the *sŏn'gun* politics], 6.

9. Chun, *Sŏn'gun jŏngchie daehan lihae* [Understanding the *sŏn'gun* politics], 3.

10. Chun, *Sŏn'gun jŏngchie daehan lihae* [Understanding the *sŏn'gun* politics], 15.

11. "Sŏn'gunryŏngdonŭn sahoijuŭichosunŭi sŭngriŭi kŭnbonyoin [The military-first political leadership is the foundation for the victory of socialist Korea]," *Rodong Sinmun*, August 24, 2010.

12. Chun, *Sŏn'gun jŏngchie daehan lihae* [Understanding the *sŏn'gun* politics], 7.

13. Chun, *Sŏn'gun jŏngchie daehan lihae* [Understanding the *sŏn'gun* politics], 8, 9.

14. Chun, *Sŏn'gun jŏngchie daehan lihae* [Understanding the *sŏn'gun* politics], 11.

15. Melvyn P. Leffler, *For the Soul of Mankind: The United States, the Soviet Union, and the Cold War* (New York: Hill and Wang, 2007), 403–14.

16. Chun, *Sŏn'gun jŏngchie daehan lihae* [Understanding the *sŏn'gun* politics], 44.

17. Chun, *Sŏn'gun jŏngchie daehan lihae* [Understanding the *sŏn'gun* politics], 45.

18. Chun, *Sŏn'gun jŏngchie daehan lihae* [Understanding the *sŏn'gun* politics], 8 (original emphasis).

19. Song-Kil Kang, *Sŏn'gunsidaeŭi jokukŭl kada* [A tour of our fatherland in the military-first era] (Pyongyang: Pyongyang Press, 2002); In-Ok Kim, *Kim Jong Il changgun sŏn'gun jŏngch'i iron* [The military-first political theory of General Kim Jong Il] (Pyongyang: Pyongyang Press, 2003); Bong-Ho Kim, *Sŏn'gunŭro uiryŏk ttŏlch'inŭn gangkuk* [Our mighty country of military-first politics] (Pyongyang: Pyongyang Press, 2005).

20. Park, *North Korea*, 41.

21. Don Oberdorfer, *The Two Koreas: A Contemporary History* (London: Warner Books, 1999), 20.

22. Tatiana Gabroussenko, *Soldiers on the Cultural Front: Developments in the Early History of North Korean Literature and Literary Policy* (Honolulu: University of Hawaii Press, 2010), 43.

23. Hiroshi Furuta, "Pyongyang: Kitachōsenniokeru 'shutai' hōji no ishi to hyōshokūkan [Pyongyang: The will to protect *juch'e* and symbolic space in North Korea]," *Ajiashinseki* [Asian new century], no. 1 (2002): 181–94; Sang-Jung Kang, "Sugisaranai ajia no shinjyochiri o koete: Nihon no chosenkan o chushin ni

[Overcoming unchanging mental geography of Asia: Focusing on Japan's view on Korea]," *Ajiashinseki* [Asian new century], no. 1 (2002): 77–107.

24. Song-Bak Cho, *Segyerŭl maehoksikinŭn Kim Jong Ilŭi sŏn'gun jŏngch'i* [Kim Jong Il's military-first politics fascinates the world] (Pyongyang: Pyongyang Press, 1999).

25. Charles K. Armstrong, *The North Korean Revolution, 1945–1950* (Ithaca, NY: Cornell University Press, 2004), 71–74.

26. Kim Jong Il, "Juch'eŭi dangkŏnsŏlironŭn rodonggyegŭpŭi dangkŏnsŏlesŏ t'ŭlŏjuigonaagaya hal jidojŏk jich'imida [The *juch'e* theory of party construction is the guiding principle for the construction of the party of the working class]" (speech delivered at the Plenum of the Central Committee of the Workers' Party, Pyongyang, October 10, 1990).

27. Oberdorfer, *The Two Koreas*, 20.

28. Park, *North Korea*, 31–40.

29. Oberdorfer, *The Two Koreas*, 20.

30. Chun, *Sŏn'gun jŏngchie daehan lihae* [Understanding the *sŏn'gun* politics], 22–23.

31. Chun, *Sŏn'gun jŏngchie daehan lihae* [Understanding the *sŏn'gun* politics], 27.

32. These two quotes are from the North Korean online journal *Uriminjok ggiri* [Between us], March 29, 2010.

33. Very recently, the stories of eminent guns told in North Korea came to include another heritage gun that Kim Jong Il is supposed to have received from his mother, Kim Jong Suk, in his childhood. Pyongyang ch'ulpansa [Pyongyang press], *Sŏn'gunt'aeyang Kim Jong Il Janggun* [The sun of military-first (politics), General Kim Jong Il], Vol. 1 (Pyongyang: Pyongyang Press, 2006), 128–34; Pyongyang chulpansa [Pyongyang press], *Sŏn'gunŭi ŏbŏi Kim Il Sung Janggun* [The father of military-first (politics), General Kim Il Sung], Vols. 1–2 (Pyongyang: Pyongyang Press, 2007); Pyongyang ch'ulpansa [Pyongyang press], *Sŏn'gunŭi ŏmŏni Kim Jong Suk nyŏjanggun* [The mother of military-first (politics), Female-General Kim Jong Suk] (Pyongyang: Pyongyang Press, 2007).

34. Also Pyongyang ch'ulpansa [Pyongyang press], *Sŏn'gunt'aeyang Kim Jong Il Janggun* [The sun of military-first (politics), General Kim Jong Il], 1:72–76.

35. Pyongyang ch'ulpansa [Pyongyang press], *Sŏn'gunŭi ŏbŏi Kim Il Sung Janggun* [The father of military-first (politics), General Kim Il Sung], Vol. 1. See also Chin-Hyuk Chung, *Chŏlseŭi wiin'gamum* [The matchless great man's family line] (Pyongyang: Pyongyang Press, 2002), 36.

36. Maurice Halbwachs, *On Collective Memory* (Chicago: University of Chicago Press, 1992).

37. Kwahak baekgwa sajon ch'ulpansa (Science encyclopedia press), *Chongjarone kwanhan ch'ŭlhakronmunjip* [Philosophical anthology of seed theory] (Pyongyang: Science Encyclopedia Press, 2002).

38. Sonia Ryang, "Biopolitics, or the Logic of Sovereign Love: Love's Whereabouts in North Korea," in *North Korea: Toward a Better Understanding*, ed. Sonia Ryang (Lanham, MD: Lexington Books, 2009), 59.

39. Haruki Wada, *Bukjosŏn: Yugyŏkdaegugkaesŏ jŏnggyukungugkaro* [North Korea: From partisan state to a military state] (Seoul: Dolbegae, 2002), 310. See also Atsuhito Isozaki, "Kimujoniru 'sengunseiji'no honsitsu [The essence of Kim Jong Il's military-first politics]," in *Giki no chosenhanto* [Korean peninsula in crisis], ed. Masao Okonogi (Tokyo: Keio University Press, 2006), 283–304.

40. Wada, *Bukjosŏn* [North Korea], 317.

41. Carl Schmitt, *Theory of the Partisan: Intermediate Commentary on the Concept of the Political*, trans. G. L. Ulmen (New York: Telos Press, 2007), 40–48.

42. Schmitt, *Theory of the Partisan*, 44.

43. Schmitt, *Theory of the Partisan*, 60.

44. Hannah Arendt, *On Violence* (New York: Harcourt Brace, 1969), 11.

45. Brooks, *Thank You, Comrade Stalin!*, 89.

46. Brooks, *Thank You, Comrade Stalin!*, 105.

47. Hyun-Chol Oh, *Sŏn'gunryŏngjanggwa sarangŭi segye* [The great general of military-first politics and the world of love] (Pyongyang: Pyongyang Press, 2005), 112–13; Du-Il Kim, *Sŏn'gunsidae wiinŭi jongch'iwa norae* [The politics and songs of the hero of the military-first era] (Pyongyang: Literature and Arts Press, 2002), 254.

48. Oh, *Sŏn'gunryŏngjanggwa sarangŭi segye* [The great general of military-first politics and the world of love], 91–103. See also Ki-Hwan Choi, *Yŏngwŏnhan t'aeyang Kim Il Sungjusŏk* [Eternal sun, Chairman Kim Il Sung] (Pyongyang: Pyongyang Press, 2002), 207–9.

49. Oh, *Sŏn'gunryŏngjanggwa sarangŭi segye* (The great general of military-first politics and the world of love), 102.

50. "Paekdusan nunbora [Snowstorm in Paekdu mountain]," *Rodong Sinmun*, March 21, 2000.

51. It is observed that "in the second half of the 1990s, North Korean literature rarely mentioned the actual effects of Arduous March on the lives of North Koreans. In the 2000s, however, it is remarkable that realistic reflections on the era of Arduous March began to appear. The pain of hunger [depicted in these reflections] was cruel." Chang-Un Oh, "Sŏn'gunsidae bukhan nongch'on yŏsŏngŭi hyŏngsanghwa yŏn'gu [Representation of rural women in the military-first era]," *Hyŏndaebukhanyŏn'gu* [North Korean studies review] 13, no. 2 (2010): 86.

52. Oh, *Sŏn'gunryŏngjanggwa sarangŭi segye* (The great general of military-first politics and the world of love), 46.

4

The Graves of Revolutionary Martyrs

North Korea's current narrative about the military-first political premise claims that the decision of who Kim Il Sung's successor would be was made as early as the time of the Korean War. It also claims that the decision was taken in a private meeting between the father and son in 1952, long before it became public around the time of the former leader's sixtieth birthday in 1972 or before it was formally completed in 1997 after the three-year mourning period for Kim Il Sung ended. The alleged succession decision made in 1952 was mainly symbolic; it was sealed through the gift of a handgun to the then ten-year-old future leader of North Korea. The giver of this gift was the boy's beloved father and later the country's single political father; he was also, at the time of the event, the supreme commander of the North Korean People's Army. This momentous meeting took place in the fog of the Korean War, on one of the war's fiercest battlefields in the rugged mountain area of Kangwŏn Province in the central-eastern region of the Korean peninsula.

These hill fights were a rare military event during the three-year Korean conflict in which Kim Il Sung personally took part as a field commander. Located close to North Korea's postwar border with South Korea, the environs of the hill were highly contested during the later phase of the war in which Chinese and North Korean forces battled furiously with United Nations and South Korean forces for small territorial gains along what became the armistice line in 1953. The brutal combat in this mountainous area resembled the futile, senseless trench warfare on the western front during World War I and resulted in a high death toll on both sides. Postwar North Korean military history, however, records these hill battles as strategic victories over the technologically superior American forces that broke the enemy's will to fight. The glory of these hill fights is associated primarily with Kim Il Sung's actual physical presence on the battlefield and his military genius in leading the troops to victory. However, it also involves some of North Korea's most cherished martyrs of the Victorious Fatherland Liberation War. These include Lee Su Bok, who, as briefly mentioned in the previous chapter, is remembered today as an emblematic "barrel-of-a-gun" hero in the military-first-era North Korean revolution. The hill fights involved also a tremendous sacrifice by Chinese forces and are remembered in China through the heroic sacrifice of the Chinese volunteer soldier Huang Ji Guang, a prominent martyr of the Korean War, who carried out a suicide mission against the enemy during a fierce hill fight in October 1952. He is known to have blocked American artillery and machine-gun fire with his body. Huang's memory is honored in the Memorial of the War to Resist US Aggression and Aid Korea in Dandong, China's important border town with North Korea.[1] North Korea has made a feature film about his heroism, *Red Hill* (*bulgŭn sanmaru*), and also named a school after him. The memory of the North Korean hero Lee Su Bok is related to a similar act of courage in confronting the enemy's stronger firepower with his bare body. Lee received a national hero title in 1952. Other than Lee and 1211 Hill, with which his heroism is associated, North Korea's struggles in the broad hill areas in the central-eastern region of Korea feature other prominent heroes, including those of the 351 Hill fight, infantryman Kang Ho Young, machine gunner Cho Kun Sil, and the heroic nurse An Young Ae mentioned earlier. Their merits all relate to their immense spiritual commitment in the face of a powerful, technologically superior enemy.[2] Apart from that of nurse An, all the hero stories also speak of the virtue of self-sacrifice and readiness to confront the powerful machinery of violence with a bare body if necessary—that is, to turn into a heroic, human barrel of a gun.

It is no coincidence that the place where Kim Il Sung is said to have given his son a gift of such tremendous value (which, according to contemporary North Korean accounts, holds in it "the destiny of the nation and the revolution") was the important, victorious battlefield of North Korea's sacred war against American imperialism. Not only was the gift of the revolver a token of ultimate authority in succession, but today it is also the most preeminent gun of all existing arms and armaments in North Korea in the era of military-first politics. Remember also that this is not the only gun passed down through Kim Jong Il's family line. We saw in the last chapter that the father-son meeting of 1952 had a precedent, in 1926, when the fourteen-year-old Kim Il Sung was handed two revolvers that had belonged to his father as a token of Kim's destiny to lead the honorable quest for armed revolution against colonial power and injustice. Recalling this childhood event, Kim Il Sung later wrote in his memoir that the gift he had received from his father in 1926 was not a thing but a living and animate object.[3] He said that the two humble pistols grew in strength and number to hundreds of guns (during the Manchurian era) and then to many thousands of guns (at the time of the Korean War). If today's North Korean military-first politics is rooted, as is claimed, in these earlier historical events, and if its barrel-of-a-gun philosophy is essentially a heritage ideology grounded in the genealogical history of the Kim family, it is obvious, from the perspective of the present, that the episode in 1952 is as pivotal as that in 1926 to the moral historical authority of military-first politics. By extension, we can say that the history of the Korean War, which forms the background of the second gift episode within the Kim family, is as vital as the history of the Manchurian struggle to the constitution of the contemporary military-first ideology. We know that the Manchurian legacy was central to Kim Il Sung's charismatic authority throughout his long political career. We have seen also how this legacy was forcefully revived in the 1970s to become a singularly important saga in the national history and how this process was intertwined with the unfolding of the drama of the political succession from Kim Il Sung to Kim Jong Il. The questions that follow, then, are: How did the memory of North Korea's Korean War experience figure in the drama of succession? And was the appropriation of Korean War memories as important to the drama as the Manchurian legacy?

North Korea's National Cemetery

North Korean public art makes it abundantly clear that a towering moral hierarchy exists in the country's historical memory of the Manchurian heroism and the Korean War experience. A most spectacular example is North Korea's national cemetery, the Graves of Revolutionary Martyrs, standing on the hill of Daesŏngsan on the outskirts of Pyongyang. First built immediately after the Korean War ended in July 1953, the cemetery underwent relocation and renovation in the mid-1970s and another renovation in the mid-1980s. The timing of the cemetery's original construction may give the impression that the place is a burial ground for North Korea's fallen soldiers of the Korean War. That is far from the case, however.

Figure 4.1. Mansudae War Memorial, Pyongyang. *Source:* Photo by Byung-Ho Chung (2007).

North Korea has no state-instituted, recognized public cemeteries for the Korean War dead, although it has a number of epitaphs, memorials, and museums dedicated to their memory. In fact, North Korea's national cemetery in Daesŏngsan bears no trace of the country's collective Korean War experience or of its countrymen's tremendous mass sacrifice in that brutal, protracted civil and international war. Instead, the cemetery is reserved exclusively for a particular cohort of national heroes from a prewar history that took place many years before North Korea existed—the so-called first generation of the Korean revolution, which refers to the members of Kim Il Sung's Manchurian partisan group of the 1930s.

The above situation confused many foreign visitors to the Daesŏngsan cemetery, which is popularly known among South Koreans as the North Korean equivalent to South Korea's Hyŏnch'ungwŏn, the beautifully landscaped national war cemetery located at the heart of crowded Seoul. Although the national war cemetery in Seoul maintains the graves of prominent patriotic figures from colonial times as well as those of former heads of state, it is primarily considered by the South Korean public as a place of rest for the fallen soldiers of the Korea conflict. It also has a prominent Tomb of the Unknown Soldier, which, together with the chamber of the names of missing soldiers and student volunteers, is regarded as keeping "the soul of the nation," according to the inscription on a memorial stone at the site. Being familiar with this material memorial culture, which is hardly unique to South Korea, many South Koreans expect, on visiting North Korea's national cemetery, to see a Korean War–related cemetery of fallen soldiers (visiting this place is often an obligation for foreign visitors). Understandably, the experience frequently provokes confusion and surprise at the absence of the war dead in the national cemetery of a country that visitors know fought a highly destructive, mass-mobilized war, just as South Korea did.

We were also confused upon visiting. What surprised us was not necessarily the occupation of the premises by old heroes of the anticolonial resistance; as mentioned, the South Korean national war cemetery also keeps a number of graves and memorial stones for its patriotic heroes from the colonial-era national independence movement. The patriotic heroes kept in South Korea's national cemetery are primarily historical figures from the independence movement's nonsocialist, noncommunist factions and trajectories. Similarly, the national heroes placed in North Korea's national cemetery are exclusively from a communist faction of the movement. This division of national memories of anticolonial resistance along politically left and right lines is regrettable, yet hardly surprising if we consider Korea's turbulent modern history. By the time visits to North Korea were made possible for South Korean citizens in the late 1990s, and especially after the historic summit meeting in 2000 between the two Korean heads of state, heated debates broke out in the South Korean public media about extending titles of honor to the nation's patriotic ancestral figures of socialist and communist orientations.

The most notable outcome of this development was the awarding of a national hero entitlement in 2005 to Yŏ Un-Hyŏng, a prominent figure in the independence movement and later a leader in the failed self-government mass movement during the brief period of Korea's postcolonial autonomy after the nation's liberation from Japanese rule in 1945 and before Korea was divided into the US- and Soviet-occupied zones. Also notable was the rehabilitation of Kim San, an anarchist Korean revolutionary in the Chinese communist movement whose commitment to the ideals of internationalism and national liberation were made famous in his biography, *Song of Arirang*, compiled by Helen Forster Snow, an American journalist and the wife of Edgar Snow.[4] The political bipolarization and division of postcolonial Korea involved a bifurcation in historical knowledge, particularly with regard to the independence movements of the 1920s and 1930s, between the particular revolutionary heritage enshrined in the North and the heritage of the independence movement claimed by the South. Against this background, the division of colonial-era resistance history into the North's "revolutionary" history and the South's "patriotic" national memories was a familiar phenomenon; we were not surprised, therefore, to see the embodiment of the revolutionary national memory in the Daesŏngsan cemetery. What puzzled us instead was the absence of any trace of Korean War sacrifices in a place that claims to keep the national memory. The absence was not confined to the Daesŏngsan cemetery. The long list of national memorials provided by the North Korean authority for outside visitors made no mention of a war cemetery. As a matter of fact, the voluminous North Korean literature that we surveyed gave no indication that a war cemetery existed in the country. So we asked ourselves: If not in this place, then where are they? What happened to the bodies of North Korea's fallen Korean War soldiers?

We asked a number of people and diverse groups of informants about the composition of the Daesŏngsan cemetery. These people included Western diplomats and aid workers who had long-term experience in North Korea, as well as scholars specializing in North Korean history. We also spoke to a number of South Korean policy experts in North Korean affairs. Our interlocutors also included a number of recent refugees from North Korea now settled in South Korea or elsewhere. The responses of these various informants were diverse and revealing.

Most Western and South Korean specialists in North Korean affairs shared our bewilderment as to the absence of war cemeteries in North Korea, and they offered various interesting observations. One longtime North American observer of North Korea (we shall keep his identity anonymous) proposed that the absence should be understood in the context of North Korea's broad revolutionary culture. North Korea is a land where people do not very often see the material traces of human death, according to him; it is a society that focuses its attention on the well-being of the living, consciously departing from the prerevolutionary, feudal tradition that put great moral weight on the well-being of dead ancestors. Another commentator, a scholar of Korean and Chinese history, raised a broadly similar point. This historian drew attention to the similarity that he believes exists in the material culture of war commemoration in North Korea and China. Public war commemoration in revolutionary China, according to him, focuses on the collective spirit of fallen soldiers rather than their individual identities and bodies (this is, in fact, not entirely true, as there are some graves for individual martyrs of the Korean War in Chinese provinces); this contrasts with the art of war commemoration developed in Western bourgeois societies, which, although intended to engender a sense of collective purpose and spirit, nevertheless must acknowledge the individuality of fallen soldiers. This explains, according to the historian, why China does not have a modern war cemetery in the form that is familiar to Westerners. It also explains the shape of the material culture of commemoration in North Korea, considering the fact that a main force of the North Korean People's Army, at the time of the Korean War, consisted of Korean revolutionaries who returned home after a long fighting career on the frontier of the Chinese revolution and civil war.[5] Another acute observer of North Korea and a former Western diplomat to Pyongyang expressed a different view, however. He related the absence of public war cemeteries in North Korea to the ambiguous status of the Korean War experience in the country's official historical narrative. Although North Korea continues to advocate the idea that the war ended with a victory for North Korea, according to this observer, it was actually a failed war. North Korea's official history also presents the country's participation in the war as an act of self-defense against the aggression of a foreign power; this rendering, according to him, makes it hard for the North Korean regime to allow the relics of the failed liberation war, especially traces of the war's destruction, to be displayed too visibly in the public space. Another commentator, an academic specialist in East Asian history, emphasized the specific temporality of the Korean War. The Korean War is an unending war for both Koreas, especially for North Korea, according to the scholar, because it ended in an armistice agreement rather than a peace treaty. The 1950–1953 war will remain unfinished for North Korea, according to this commentator, until it liberates the entire peninsula from the grip of American power. The fact that the country still considers itself at war probably explains why it has not laid its war dead in a war cemetery. A national war cemetery is built not merely for the practical purpose of concentrating the corpses in one place but also to generate a sense of closure; it emphasizes that the history of mass destruction has become a thing of the past and that the society must look to the future. In this light, another commentator noted tellingly that "North Korean sources maintain a deafening silence on Korean War cemeteries. The DPRK does not like to commemorate its war losses, military or civilian. Doing so would remind the population how costly the Korean War was and make them more reluctant to fight another war. The regime encourages anger at the enemy but not tears for the departed."[6]

Despite the diversity of views, most people with whom we spoke about North Korea's commemoration of Korean War martyrs generally agreed that the country's war commemorative culture is an exception to the modern cult of fallen soldiers. The latter, invented in interwar Europe, has since become a nearly universal phenomenon in the modern world and a vital element in the moral order of modern nation-states. In the face of mechanical mass death in the trenches of World War I, western European states invested huge efforts in memorial projects for fallen common soldiers and appropriated the universal experience of bereavement to strengthen national unity.[7] Focusing on German public culture during the interwar period, George Mosse describes how the sustenance of Germany's political order at the time was intimately tied to what he calls the cult of fallen soldiers.[8] According to Mosse, this cult is an invention of modern nationalism, and the art of commemoration it empowers is, despite its adoption of elements of traditional religious values and rituals, distinctly modern and inseparable from the principles of fraternity and equality central to modern political life. The cult has many facets, among which Mosse highlights the idea of glorious and joyous sacrifice—that fallen soldiers sacrificed their lives voluntarily, without coercion, and "joyously" for the family and the nation. This notion draws on diverse means of expression, including literature, art, and ritual. As to the literature, Mosse highlights the works of Friedrich Schiller, who glorified death in the battlefield as a sublime form of death that transcends the anxieties of life. For Schiller, the virtue of patriotic sacrifice lies not merely in its contribution to communal security and integrity but in the fact that this death is free from the fear of death, the ontological condition of mortality, as Schiller says with his famous dictum "Only the [dead] soldier is free." In the sphere of material culture, Mosse mentions the cemeteries of fallen soldiers as the most prominent cult object. Here, the glorification of mass death is materialized in various monumental, inscriptive forms, such as neo-Gothic memorial towers. The structure of modern war cemeteries demonstrates the principles of equality and fraternity vividly. These places keep the bodies of fallen soldiers in simple and identical graves irrespective of their differences in class, religion, and sometimes race. Their unity and equality in death embody the ideal of political fraternity and egalitarianism among individual citizens of a modern nation-state who bear equal rights and duties.

Since Mosse's seminal work *Fallen Soldiers*, other cultural historians of modern Europe have delved into the centrality of war commemoration in the making of modern nationalism and the nation-state.[9] A number of historians and anthropologists have written about the diffusion of what Mosse calls "the cult of fallen soldiers" to many newly independent, non-European nations during the turbulent process of decolonization in the mid-twentieth century. In writing about the experience of Zimbabwe, for instance, anthropologist Richard Werbner states that war cemeteries provided a crucial theatrical arena "for proving the individual's subjection to the state, for asserting the state's encompassment of the personal identities of citizens, and for testing their identification with the nation."[10]

Similar observations have been made regarding the Vietnamese experience of civil and revolutionary war (1961–1975). The postwar Vietnamese state hierarchy put great emphasis on controlling commemorative practices and propagated a genealogy of heroic resistance wars, linking the death of a soldier in the Vietnam War (called the "American War" in Vietnam) to a line stretching back from the French War to the legendary heroes of ancient victories. Every local administrative unit in Vietnam has a war martyrs' cemetery built in the middle of the community's public space, and the reminder "Our ancestral land remembers your merit" is inscribed on the gothic memorial placed at its center. This construction of national memory, according to Patricia Pelley, shifted the focus of commemoration from the traditional social units of family and village toward the state.[11] As Shaun Malarney notes, however, the process was just as much about bringing the state into the living space of the family and the community, ensuring that people felt and experienced a common national memory and revolutionary sentiment, even within the most intimate domains of life.[12] Thus, the memorabilia of war heroes and revolutionary leaders replaced ancestral tablets in the domestic space, and the communal temples gave way to the people's assembly halls. In the latter, ordinary citizens and their administrators discussed community affairs and production quotas surrounded by the vestiges of the American War, in a structurally similar way to the prerevolutionary time, when villagers and notables talked about rents for tenancy and the ritual calendar in the village's communal house, surrounded by the relics of their founding ancestors.

The Vietnam and Korean wars share many common elements. Both nations were liberated from colonial rule at the end of World War II and subsequently experienced radical political bipolarization of society and national partition as part of the postcolonial process and the concurrent advancement of global Cold War conflicts. These wars commonly took the form of a civil war, waged nevertheless as an international and global conflict. Considering this historical fact and also the centrality of war commemoration in the progression of modern national politics noted earlier, it is surprising to observe a remarkable disparity between postwar Vietnam and postwar North Korea in the material culture of commemoration.

In Vietnam, the commemoration of the heroic dead from the era of the Vietnam War constitutes the central component of civic duty and morality. This was the case throughout the postwar years and continues to be so even today in the era of *doi moi*, the Vietnamese term for market economic reform. On national or local anniversaries of the "glorious victory in the liberation war," local residents and schoolchildren crowd the cemeteries of revolutionary war martyrs to clean the premises and lay flowers on their graves. The country's Communist Party committees, from Hanoi to the provinces and villages, hold mass rallies on these occasions, and all other important public organizations, such as local youth, labor, and women's associations, bring colorful wreaths to the cemeteries of war martyrs. Vietnamese art and music abound with songs, poems, paintings, and sculptures dedicated to the meritorious sacrifice of the soldiers and partisan fighters of the American War; learning these songs and poems is an important part of schoolchildren's education. All these vital, national and local, moral cultural activities focus on the cemeteries of war martyrs, which exist in all urban districts and rural communities of Vietnam, and they are made possible, in fact, by the physical presence of the material remains of the war dead in the intimate spheres of communal lives. North Korea also has a large body of songs and other cultural artifacts dedicated to the memory of its heroic soldiers from the time of the Korean War. Unlike in other societies that fought a revolutionary civil war, however, including Vietnam, these artifacts of memory exist in North Korea without what is, in other social contexts, the most important material cultural basis of public memory: cemeteries of war martyrs.

We asked a number of other informants about the absence of war cemeteries in postwar North Korea. We had one particularly interesting conversation with a prominent South Korean North Korea watcher. This expert works now in an academic establishment but used to be a close advisor to the South Korean administration on inter-Korean relations—what the South Korean administration calls national unification policies. The scholar contested the idea of absence, arguing that North Korea had a national cemetery just as South Korea did, and he pointed to the Daesŏngsan Graves of Revolutionary Martyrs and another relevant site, the Graves of Patriotic Martyrs in Hyŏngjesan (see below). He also cited a series of recent events relating to these important sites, including the visit of South Korean trade union leaders to Daesŏngsan in 2006 and the controversy this provoked in the South Korean public media. Some conservative South Korean newspaper editors accused the union leaders of violating the country's national security law, interpreting the visit as close to an act of aiding the enemy. Their accusation was grounded in the alleged fact that people buried in the Daesŏngsan cemetery should be considered communist revolutionary elements rather than anticolonial patriots. The union leaders countered this accusation by arguing that their decision to visit North Korea's national cemetery was in accordance with the broad national policy of inter-Korean reconciliation and rapprochement. The visitors also pointed out an earlier event in which delegates from North Korea came to South Korea's national cemetery in Seoul to make a gesture of tribute to the memory of "virtuous patriotic ancestors" buried there, referring to the activists of the colonial-era national independence movement. In detailing these events, the expert intended to say that national cemeteries exist in both political communities of Korea and to convey his hope that, in the future, there would be a reciprocal recognition between South Korea and North Korea of their sacred symbols of national memory.

We agreed with the expert's emphasis on the imperative of reciprocal recognition between the two Koreas and sympathized with his effort to highlight similarities rather than differences between the two societies. We also recognize the importance of a sense of a common prewar, colonial-era collective heritage in building up better relations between the two communities. However, the expert's view clearly ignored the fact that a crucial structural difference exists between South Korea's national war cemetery and what he believed to be North Korea's equivalent. The Graves of Revolutionary Martyrs in Daesŏngsan, as noted earlier, is no national cemetery in a conventional sense;

no bodies of common fallen soldiers of a citizen's army are buried in that place. The other place the expert mentioned, the Graves of Patriotic Martyrs, has two individual graves for the soldiers of the People's Army martyred during the Korean War.[13] However, it is extremely difficult to call this place a modern war cemetery.

Our interlocutors of North Korean origin offered a different view of the issue. Most of these recent refugees from North Korea, now settled in South Korea or China, were quite clear about the meaning of the Daesŏngsan cemetery—that the place was exclusively for Kim Il Sung's close comrades from the leader's Manchurian years and that the sacred burial ground had no connection with the Korean War (most of the old Manchurian-era heroes were dead by the time the war broke out). Our conversation clearly pointed to the fact that the cemetery was understood, in North Korean public knowledge, in a particular spatiotemporal scheme and according to a historical-genealogical order manifested in a concentric spatial form. According to this understanding, the sacredness of the cemetery stems from the fact that those buried on the premises were members of the first generation of North Korean revolutionaries, that these people were personally closest to Kim Il Sung, and that they were his most loyal followers during his formative years. Kim thus had great personal affection for people buried in Daesŏngsan. As for the graves of fallen soldiers of the Korean War, our informants told us that they had never seen or heard of a war cemetery existing in North Korea. In fact, many of them expressed surprise at our question, saying that it had never occurred to them while they were living in North Korea. Some informants told us, however, about local mass graves of Korean War dead. In these places, local residents buried en masse, during the war, the bodies of the People's Army soldiers they discovered in the vicinity. Some of these places developed into memorial sites after the war. In the immediate postwar years, these graves attracted steady visits from locals, which later prompted the local people's committees in some communities to erect a wooden marker or tombstone. In the city of Kyesŏng, close to the border with South Korea, a large mass grave exists on a modest hill in the city's historic quarter, which is now a favorite destination for foreign tourists. The tour guides in this place knew that the grave had been built for a certain number of North Korean army officers killed during the war. The grave looked well preserved from a distance; however, the guides were not able to offer any more detail about the place.[14] Apart from these scattered examples, we failed to get a clear sense of North Korea's burial culture regarding the Korean War's fallen soldiers. We found no information about this in the large body of North Korean publications we surveyed; in fact, North Korea's national encyclopedia makes no mention of the number of the country's casualties in its voluminous section about the victorious war, which provides detailed information about the casualties suffered by the enemy and the large amount of the enemy's war machinery captured by the North.[15] Although we interviewed a large number of frequent visitors to North Korea and recent emigrants from the country, no one was able to say much about the whereabouts of North Korea's Korean War dead. The absence in North Korea of material traces of the Korean War becomes even more striking when we consider the abundance of memorials dedicated to the memory of an armed struggle waged by a handful of partisan fighters during a previous era.

Memorials for Revolutionary War Martyrs

The Graves of Revolutionary Martyrs was first built in 1954, following a proposal submitted by Kim Il Sung to the Workers' Party assembly immediately after the end of the Korean War in July 1953. The cemetery brought together in one place about one hundred graves of Manchurian partisans that had been widely scattered around the country and in the northeastern region of China. Kim's intention in bringing the remains of his old comrades into Pyongyang was to show, according to his instruction, which is today inscribed prominently in a memorial stone, that "the honorable revolutionary spirit of the martyrs of anti-Japanese revolution will be forever alive in the heart of our party and our people." However, his initiative unquestionably had objectives other than purely paying respect to the memory of his old comrades. As discussed earlier in relation to the formation of North Korea's partisan state, not only were the postwar years in North Korea a time of forceful mass mobilization for economic recovery from the devastation of war, but they also witnessed vicious power struggles and political purges within the Workers' Party. By the end of the 1950s, the Kim Il Sung–led Manchurian faction had won the power struggle, having purged (and neutralized, exiled, or executed) members of the contending factions: the indigenous Korean communist movement and the groups whose backgrounds and political orientations were closely allied with the Soviet or Chinese communist movements. Charles Armstrong aptly describes this power struggle as "centering the periphery," pointing to the fact that it resulted in a group with relatively marginal revolutionary credentials, represented by Kim Il Sung, triumphing over all other historically more major streams of the Korean communist movement.[16] The postwar decision to build the Graves of Revolutionary Martyrs close to the country's capital and to bury in it exclusively the heroes of Kim Il Sung's Manchurian partisan movement (which was, in fact, a very small part of the Manchurian-based Korean independence movement) was therefore an important initiative to center the periphery and, on the part of Kim Il Sung and his Manchurian-faction comrades, to seize and consolidate power. In his memoir Kim later reminisced about how grateful he felt to his old Manchurian comrades and to the unrelenting trust and fidelity they had shown him. In previous chapters, we saw how the stories of these old revolutionaries have been forcefully brought into North Korea's public culture since the 1970s, becoming a principal part of the sublimation of Kim's authority and the concurrent preparation for the succession of Kim Jong Il. The concentration of the graves of the Manchurian partisans was an important episode in the consolidation of Kim's institutional power base and in the construction of his charismatic authority.

In this respect, it is important to recognize that North Korea's statehood in the postwar era was built up, in a crucial measure, on a culture of commemoration, as was the case in many other modern nation-states in Europe and elsewhere. This culture of commemoration was advanced immediately after a devastating war, one of the most brutal of the twentieth century, claiming innumerable human lives. Strikingly unique about the North Korean case, however, is the fact that the country's postwar culture of commemoration chose engagement with a handful of martyrs from the previous generation rather than the mass destruction of the immediate past.

North Korea's postwar culture of commemoration did not (and probably could not) ignore the mass sacrifice of the Korean War entirely, however. Five years after the Daesŏngsan cemetery for Manchurian partisans was completed in 1954, North Korea built a monument in memory of the Korean War's fallen soldiers on another hill near Pyongyang, now called Hyŏngjesan (hill of brotherhood). This initiative was based on a decision made by the Supreme People's Assembly, rather than the Workers' Party, as had been the case with the decision to erect the cemetery for Manchurian heroes, following a recommendation from Kim Il Sung and his "high political consideration of the revolutionary [war] martyrs."[17] Named the Tower of the People's Army Martyrs, the memorial was first completed in February 1959 and renovated later in 1968. The tower employs a bird motif common to memorial art in other socialist countries and consists of a twenty-four-meter-high neo-Gothic tower with two lower, horizontal wings on each side. The wings depict heroic battle scenes of the People's Army, including a scene from the Wŏlmido fight famous in the North Korean history of the Korean War. Contemporary North Korean memorial art history emphasizes that the cenotaph faces eastward. This probably relates to the fact that in the ensuing era, the authority and grace of Kim Il Sung were increasingly symbolized as the rays emanating from the rising sun. Some of the images depicted in the memorial's two horizontal wings were later replicated in the grandiose bronze sculptures of the Victorious Fatherland Liberation War Memorial erected in Pyongyang in 1993. The city of Pyongyang also has a museum with a similar name, the Victorious Fatherland Liberation War Museum, which first opened in August 1953, shortly after the July 27 armistice that ended the three-year conflict. The museum that visitors see today, however, was built in April 1974. The Victorious Fatherland Liberation War Memorial is formally dedicated to the memory of the Korean War's fallen soldiers and patriotic citizens. The most honored object in this memorial complex, however, is the stone where Kim Il Sung's handwritten dedication is inscribed: "Our People's Army and our people, inheriting the tradition of anti-Japanese struggle, honorably defended our fatherland's freedom and independence against the allied imperialist forces during our great Fatherland Liberation War. Their heroic merit shall shine across ten thousand generations." The Victorious Fatherland Liberation War Museum, in its current form, tells the story of North Korea's Korean War experience in terms of the heritage of the heroic Manchurian anticolonial armed struggle.

Before they reach the displays about the Fatherland Liberation War, visitors to the museum must pass through several other exhibit halls. The most prominent of these are the hall reserved for Kim Il Sung and one dedicated to the heroism of the Manchurian partisans.

The above discussion shows one particularly exceptional element in the public culture of commemoration in North Korea compared to equivalent cultures found in other societies that experienced a mass-mobilized people's war. This element is better observed in memorial installations outside Pyongyang. North Korea's provincial towns also have museums where the locals have access to a displayed account of the nation's revolutionary history. These museums are typically called the Kim Il Sung Museum of Revolutionary Historical Relics and, as such, incorporate the history of the Korean War as part of the Great Leader's long revolutionary career and as a modern-day manifestation of the tradition of the Manchurian partisan war. The incorporation of the history of the Korean War into the Manchurian partisan heritage is also observable in the genesis of the Hyŏngjesan memorial for Korean War martyrs. This monument was opened to the public on February 8, 1959, the anniversary of the founding of North Korea's People's Army in 1948. The anniversary was changed in 1978 to April 25, however, as it was claimed that the real origin of the People's Army should be traced instead to the founding of the Manchurian partisan army on April 25, 1932. The new birthday of the People's Army has taken on added significance in North Korea since 1996, when it became a national holiday together with the birthdays of Kim Il Sung and Kim Jong Il. This development in North Korea's postwar memorial art and commemorative calendar clearly shows that, at the heart of the state's memorial projects for the Korean War and its fallen soldiers, there was actually the imperative to empower the Manchurian partisan legacy. In other words, the Korean War was commemorated primarily to sublimate the Manchurian legacy, functioning as a modern background against which the old legacy was to stand out. Subsequently, from the 1970s, the legacy was made into a full-blown, singularly meaningful, and all-encompassing founding historical episode, in view of which the national historical events in the following eras were given meanings retrospectively.

Crucial to this emerging process to center North Korea's national narrative on Kim Il Sung's biographical history was the establishment of the Daesŏngsan cemetery for Manchurian partisans in 1954. The cemetery was an important political instrument in Kim's early postwar power struggle; it continued to play a pivotal role during the subsequent era in the consolidation and eventual transfer of his power and authority to Kim Jong Il.

The Political Afterlife of the Manchurian Partisans

The Graves of Revolutionary Martyrs has undergone two major renovations since it was originally built in 1954. The first renovation took place in 1975, three years after the celebration of Kim Il Sung's sixtieth birthday, and the second in 1985, three years after the leader's seventieth birthday. Both of these major renovations are known to have been conducted under the guidance of North Korea's designated future leader, Kim Jong Il. The work of renovation was indeed an important part of the process of political succession; it was meant to be the appointed new leader's act of tribute to the memory of the country's founding revolutionary martyrs and, therefore, to the glory of their partisan leader. Thus, North Korean literature portrays the renovation of the cemetery as a testament to Kim Jong Il's profound filial piety toward Kim Il Sung in his honoring of the people for whom the leader had deep affection. In fact, Kim Il Sung was reportedly fond of telling foreign visitors how much he appreciated Kim Jong Il's affectionate care for the memory of his old comrades and how impressed he was by the young leader's deep respect for the founding generation of the North Korean revolution. This was a very suggestive remark, considering that Kim Jong Il's nomination as North Korea's future leader reportedly received strong support from the surviving members of Kim Il Sung's Manchurian partisan group. Also notable was the fact that many descendants of the Manchurian partisans held positions of influence, having enjoyed advantages in educational and career opportunities thanks to their distinguished family backgrounds. Contemporary experts in North Korean affairs broadly agree that these families of Kim Il Sung's Manchurian-era comrades were among Kim Jong Il's strongest supporters (he had close personal ties with many of them) and today comprise a most privileged group in North Korean society. It is not difficult to imagine, therefore, what the future leader's initiative to beautify the Graves of Revolutionary Martyrs—essentially a family graveyard for the descendants of these martyrs—would have meant to these powerful families.

The 1985 renovation introduced another important element to the Graves of Revolutionary Martyrs. Today, at the summit of the hillside cemetery, are found the tomb and bronze statue of Kim Jong Suk, Kim Il Sung's first wife and the birth mother of Kim Jong Il. The structure of the cemetery is such that visitors cannot escape the impression that Kim Jong Suk's tomb enjoys the most honored, innermost status within the sacred space of the dead. Her grave is backed by a magnificent stone sculpture of flying red flags. The bronze statue depicts Kim Jong Suk as the commander of the northeastern Anti-Japanese army, an honorific for Kim Il Sung's Manchurian partisan group. Next to her statue, on both sides, stand statues of Kim Hyung Gwon and Kim Chol Ju, Kim Il Sung's paternal uncle and younger brother. Kim Jong Suk's tomb and statue look out over rows of graves and statues of other first-generation North Korean revolutionary martyrs, whose proximity to her grave determines their rank and significance in North Korea's national memory. In 2007, it was reported that the cemetery held about 150 graves, the majority of which belonged to Kim Il Sung's Manchurian partisan group members. This spatial organization of the cemetery clearly delivers the message that Kim Jong Suk should be remembered as the most esteemed leader of the Manchurian partisan army. This regard stems not from the fact that she held a commanding role in

Figure 4.2. The Graves of Revolutionary Martyrs with Kim Jong Suk statue at top center (close-up image, top right). *Source: Chosunŭi ŏmŏni Kim Jung Sukdongji* (Pyongyang: Chosun Art Book Press, 1997), 148.

the army, which she did not, but from the same principle of degree of proximity to the partisan leader as reflected by the concentric spatial organization of the graves of other Manchurian heroes in relation to the grave of Kim Jong Suk.[18]

As mentioned earlier, Kim Jong Suk's towering presence in the pantheon of national heroes, in contemporary North Korea, is mainly associated with her public historical reputation as the most loyal defender of the partisan leader (rather than her ties of marriage and blood to the leader and his successor). In public speech, Kim Jong Suk is referred to as "the unbending, unbreakable communist revolutionary who showed endless patriotic loyalty to the Great Leader of our revolution, Comrade Kim Il Sung."[19] She is also the "Mother of Sŏn'gun" in today's North Korean public language, although the word "mother" in this context does not covey the sense of an inventor or creator as is often the case in the English language. As we saw in the previous chapter, the honorable status of creator of *sŏn'gun* was given exclusively to Kim Jong Il in the early years of his rule. Although this has undergone notable changes in recent years, and the origin of this political form has been forcefully extended to the era of Kim Il Sung and even to his earliest revolutionary experiences, the genesis of the *sŏn'gun* idea remains strictly within a patrilineal political order of descent and allows no space for the Mother of Sŏn'gun.

Kim Jong Suk's place in military-first politics is not in the genealogy of the *sŏn'gun* idea but rather in the idea itself, as it were, as the most exemplary partisan fighter. She was the most faithful follower of the partisan leader and the most dedicated defender of the leader's life and authority; thus, today she represents the most shining, virtuous persona of the *sŏn'gun* era, whom the followers of this political guideline must revere and try to emulate. In this sense, we can conclude that Kim Jong Suk is the Mother of Sŏn'gun because her biography exemplifies how to be a proper and righteous barrel-of-a-gun (*ch'ongdae*) citizen in the era of military-first politics. The ideal of military-first politics is, then, that all North Korean citizens will defend the country's revolutionary heritage with dedication and fidelity as strong as that once shown by Comrade Kim Jong Suk to Kim Il Sung. The barrel-of-a-gun idea postulates that the virtuous citizen of North Korea does more than hold tight to a gun in defense of the country's revolutionary heritage. According to this idea, the ideal citizen is like a gun, never wavering in the face of the enemy's threat and remaining absolutely faithful to those who operate the means of violence. Kim Jong Suk is the Mother of Sŏn'gun because she is the most shining ancestral partisan-warrior exemplar for all virtuous *ch'ongdae* citizens of military-first-era North Korea, whose vital purpose in life and primary duty as citizens are just what they were for the mother: to defend the Great Leader, his legacy, and his hereditary authority. The North Korean song *Kim Jong Suk, Our Mother* says,

> The heavenly face we miss always,
> Looking up, it comes to embrace us.
> Your single-minded patriotic fidelity to the Supreme Leader
> Has blossomed all over our land as flowers under the sun.
> Our Mother Kim Jong Suk,
> We look up to you and we follow your steps.

"Mother of Our Country," the tribute to Kim Jong Suk made in 2005 on her birthday, makes the following interesting observation about her legacy:

> What did we think about while listening to the celebratory music of Arirang? We thought about the loss of national sovereignty in 1905 and our mighty country of the *sŏn'gun* era in 2005. We thought about the transformation of the Arirang of sorrows into the Arirang of prosperity. We thought about our Parent-Supreme Leader and our Supreme Commander General Kim Jong Il, who made the world-making transformation possible. However, why is it that each time we recall the Supreme Leader's face, the founding ancestor of *Sŏn'gun* Chosun, we see also the bright smiles of our Mother? Why is it that each time we look up to the honorable face of our General who shines over the world, we also feel in our heart this deep affection of gratitude to our Mother? General Kim Jong Suk, Mother of Baekdu-san: Her entire life was a burning dedication to the Supreme Leader, the country and the people. We sing in our hearts the songs of praise for her revolutionary life that shines along the past, present and future of *Sŏn'gun* Chosun. . . . Mother of our country! This honorable appellation refers to the great teacher of our nation who taught us the true way to love our motherland [*joguk*, literally "ancestral land"]. Mothers are the first teachers we encounter in our lives. We learn our language and how to survive from them. What we learn from them becomes our spiritual nour-

ishment throughout our lives. Comrade Kim Jong Il said: "I consider my mother not as the mother of me as an individual but as the most faithful revolutionary for the Supreme Leader, as the Mother of Chosun who dedicated her life to the cause of liberation on behalf of the country and people."[20]

The 1985 renovation of the Graves of Revolutionary Martyrs entailed two principal elements. On the one hand, it continued the objective of the earlier renovation in 1975, which was to strengthen the status of the first-generation revolutionary martyrs and therefore, according to what we discussed earlier, the authority of the partisan state.[21] On the other hand, the renovation in 1985 sought to bring the memory of Kim Jong Suk to the vital center of the first-generation revolutionary heritage.[22] This was also evident in the memorial projects that took place outside Pyongyang, particularly in Hoiryŏng and other places in the far northeastern region of Korea associated with her revolutionary relics. One highly revealing episode in the sublimation of Kim Jong Suk took place in her natal home, Hoiryŏng. While the Graves of Revolutionary Martyrs was under renovation from 1984 to 1985, the People's Committee of Hoiryŏng mobilized a special labor task force of the town's students and youth groups to renovate the town's proudest monument, its statue of Kim Jong Suk. Before the renovation,

Figure 4.3. Kim Jong Suk statue in Hoiryŏng. *Source: Juch'e yesulŭi widaehan yŏllun* (Pyongyang: Art and Education Press, 2002), 203.

the Mother of Chosun on the pedestal wore a traditional Korean dress and held a bouquet of wildflowers. When the renovation was completed, the townspeople of Hoiryŏng saw that their familiar local hero had disappeared, giving way to a shining bronze statue wearing a military uniform. This change was, according to Suk-Young Kim, part of a broader change in North Korean women's public dress patterns (and the state's changing policy on the issue) from the predominant traditional dress (*hanbok*) in the postwar years to the combination of *hanbok* with military uniforms.[23] Kim observes that Kim Jong Suk became an iconic figure changing from an exemplary, virtuous, traditional Korean woman (dressed in *hanbok* and dedicated to her husband and children) into a new type of role model, representing both a virtuous woman and a dedicated defender of revolution and the revolutionary leader.

Heroic maternal icons have played an important role in other revolutionary traditions. Best known is probably the Soviet *mat'geroinya*, the Mother Hero Order given to mothers who bore and raised ten or more children. The *mat'geroinya* was awarded in the Soviet Union from 1944 to 1991. In Vietnamese revolutionary history, the honor of Mother of Vietnam (*Ba Me Vietnam*) has a different meaning. This title is awarded to mothers who lost all or many of their children (including those who lost their only child) to the revolutionary war against America. The postwar Vietnamese memorial landscape is dotted with monuments dedicated to the heroic maternal struggle during the war. Some of these monuments depict mothers trying to shield their children from the enemy's violence; others depict grieving and defiant mothers who overcome the loss of their children to the enemy to stand defiantly against the machinery of violence. Vietnamese mother icons are also powerful symbols of adoption and adoptive filial piety. The Vietnamese revolutionary war harnessed the image of motherhood as an important instrument of mass mobilization, particularly in southern Vietnam. Each southern and central Vietnamese village was supposed to be a "mother" in the ideology of the Vietnamese resistance war; it was expected to adopt, care for, and protect the volunteer soldiers sent from the north as if they were the village's own children. In urban areas, the powerful covert revolutionary networks encouraged women to forge intimate ties with young peasant soldiers conscripted by the southern regime, create a relationship of substitutive motherhood with the displaced youth, and work to dissuade them from following the wrong path (against the revolution). After the war was over, the Vietnamese revolutionary state continued to appropriate forceful symbolism of maternal sacrifice. Thus, mothers who lost many of their children to the revolutionary war were given the title of Heroic Mother of Vietnam, which came with modest state welfare benefits. The scheme operated within a broad affirmative system of revolutionary merit and welfare, which privileged the families of revolutionary martyrs in material and social terms, involving easier access to education and employment in public administration. Earlier we mentioned the centrality of the heroic war memory in postwar Vietnamese political lives and the materialization of this phenomenon in the war cemeteries built at the center of the postwar community. Heroic motherhood is integral to this sacred space. In Vietnamese war martyr cemeteries, mothers with a Mother of Vietnam title are buried along with the fallen soldiers (who are all categorically these mothers' children), and their graves occupy prominent locations within the cemetery. On important national days, students and representatives of public organizations visit these tombs, clean the sites, and make offerings of incense and flowers. The idea is that these mothers sacrificed their children to the honorable national cause, thereby losing the social basis on which they could be remembered and cared for as family ancestors; therefore, society has a moral obligation to care for their memory in place of their lost children, thanks to whom the society achieved independence and peace. The tombs of the Mothers of Vietnam, therefore, embody the morality of substitutive filial piety, performed by the society on behalf of the heroic mothers and in place of their own heroic children.

The Mothers of Vietnam occupy the most honored spots in the Vietnamese cemeteries of war martyrs; the Mother of Chosun is buried at the vital center of North Korea's sacred cemetery of revolutionary martyrs. The symbolism of these maternal heroes commonly encompasses the domestic and public spheres, expressing the collective historical experience and public morality in terms of familial idioms and norms. A radical difference exists, however, between these two forms of heroic motherhood. The title Mother of Vietnam is bound up with the history of a violent war and mass human death and suffering. The icon is most prominently manifested in the cemeteries of war martyrs, where the former in fact represents a mother to all the fallen soldiers buried on the premises. It is also a channel through which the caring maternal feelings of the Mother of Vietnam (the structure of emotion demonstrated by the burial of hero-titled mothers in the war cemetery where their "children" are buried) are reciprocated by the collective actions of filial piety (visits and offerings made by the living members of the community where the cemetery is located). The Mother of Vietnam is therefore an important medium for the commemoration of war, whose relevance is anchored in the historical reality of the Vietnamese revolutionary war as well as Vietnam's traditional norms of kinship relations, which highlight the Confucian ethics of filial piety. By contrast, the Mother of Chosun has no meaningful relationship with Korea's history of war or the history of mass human sacrifice it involved. The location of this icon is exclusively in colonial history and postcolonial memory. She is an important figure in North Korea's revolutionary politics of adoption, appearing as the principal caregiver for the orphaned children of the displaced population in Manchuria, as mentioned earlier, who are spiritually adopted by the nation's supreme paternal figure, Kim Il Sung.

The last provides some insight into the renovation of the Graves of Revolutionary Martyrs and the related efforts to empower the memory of Kim Jong Suk in the mid-1980s. Before the renovation, Kim Jong Suk's public image was largely that of a caring and benevolent mother, associated particularly with the displaced orphans of the Manchurian Korean communities and standing as the

mediator between these revolutionary orphans and the nation's supreme anticolonial hero and paternal figure, Kim Il Sung. After the renovation, however, her
political motherhood came to incorporate the status of militant. She became a
partisan leader herself, and her revolutionary merit derived then not merely from
her role as a substitute mother for children adopted by Kim Il Sung but primarily
from her status as the most loyal partisan follower of Kim Il Sung, that is, the hero
closest to the Supreme Leader in terms of interpersonal ties and therefore intensity
of loyalty. This is amply demonstrated in the many recent North Korean literary
and theatrical productions depicting Kim Jong Suk as the mother of military-first
politics. They typically describe the mother as the most loyal and dedicated defender, outstanding among her comrades from the Manchurian partisan group, of
the supreme revolutionary leader.

In this light, it then becomes clear why the Graves of Revolutionary Martyrs
is such an important site in the political order and process of North Korea. The
place embodies the main principles of the partisan state: the state's legitimacy in
anticolonial armed resistance and the empowerment of the members of the Kim
Il Sung–led resistance group as the founding heroes of the state. It also solidifies
the morality of the family state. Kim Jong Suk, whose grave is at the cemetery's
sacred center, represents all the virtues of patriotic family solidarity: she set the
preeminent example of familial loyalty to the partisan leader in the latter's clos-

Figure 4.4. Kim Jong Suk and Kim Il Sung with children. *Source: Pulmyŏllŭi yŏngsang*
(Pyongyang: Literature and Art Press, 1992), 154.

est circle of relations; she took on the task of defending the center (the partisan leader) as her manifest destiny and singular purpose in life, thereby leaving a vital legacy for the era of military-first politics, wherein the citizen's supreme patriotic duty is once again to defend and protect the sovereign center. That Madame Kim has become the commander of the revolutionary army in recent years is due precisely to the vital role of the Manchurian partisan army's legacy in military-first politics. Just as Kim Jong Suk, the Mother of Chosun, devoted her life to the defense and protection of Kim Il Sung, so should her "children," the people of North Korea, dedicate their lives to the task of guarding and standing by the nation's new sacred center, Kim's successors. According to this logic, promulgated unabashedly in the literature about "the spirituality of military-first politics," the core spirit of this politics is to follow the mother's footsteps faithfully and to turn her heroic revolutionary life into a drama relived in the present and enacted collectively by the soldiers of military-first politics.

The Completion of Hereditary Charisma

The Graves of Revolutionary Martyrs was an important material object in building Kim Il Sung's charismatic authority and preparing for the routinization of his charisma. For the Great Leader, the cemetery represented fulfillment of his debt to his loyal comrades from the Manchurian era. The leader's personal satisfaction was also a collective wish fulfillment. For the citizens of North Korea, the cemetery provides a home for the memory of the country's founding heroes and, more importantly, that of the most loyal, dedicated defenders of the Great Leader. As such, the place can be seen to embody the national memory and the soul of the political community, just as the cemeteries of fallen soldiers do in other modern nation-states, including South Korea, despite their considerable divergence in form from the North Korean site. For Kim Jong Il, moreover, the Graves of Revolutionary Martyrs assisted remarkably well in the succession process and the related transformation of the leader's personal charisma into a form of hereditary charisma. Through his successor's efforts and dedication, the Great Leader's wish to repay the debt was fulfilled, and the political community was subsequently provided with a commendable site of national memory and civic morality. By this logic, Kim Jong Il performed a most exemplary patriotic, filial duty to Kim Il Sung through the renovation of the graves: filial duty in that the place fulfills the dearest wishes of the country's political father and patriotic duty in that it honors the memories of the country's founding revolutionary heroes.

At the center of this important site of national memory, furthermore, lies the legacy of Kim Jong Suk, the most exemplary partisan and the birth mother of Kim Jong Il. The empowerment of her legacy helped facilitate the succession process by offering the successor genealogical legitimacy from the maternal as well as the paternal side. However, it also helped solve the structural problem inherent in the succession drama of charismatic authority, which is, according to Max Weber, the fundamental irreplaceability of the charismatic persona. By empowering the maternal icon, which is at the same time the iconic partisan, the child-successor came to be the exemplary filial-patriotic defender of the paterfamilias and his legacy rather than a substitute leader in a bureaucratic-organizational sense or a new prince in a traditional, dynastic sense. By renovating the Graves of Revolutionary Martyrs, North Korea's new leader succeeded in presenting himself not merely as a descendant of the country's founding leader but also as one of the country's most eminent partisan fighters and defenders of the leader. In other words, he created his entitlement to leadership by putting himself both within and without the position of the irreplaceable leader—as the only child who received the gift of a handgun from the Great Leader and as the child of the mother who was the most preeminent barrel of a gun for the Great Leader in the history of the North Korean revolution. Thus, the new leader came to personify the core spirit of military-first politics, which is the defense of the national revolutionary heritage in an era of international crisis, as well as of the barrel-of-a-gun philosophy, which advocates that the citizens of this era make up 10 million gun barrels in the sacred defense. Through this artful transformation of the meaning of succession, in which the successor comes to occupy both the unoccupied position of power and the position of defender of this power, North Korea achieved a remarkable success in countering and resolving the formidable paradox involved in the succession of charismatic authority.

The resolution was made on several fronts. We saw earlier how the post-1994 political process hammered into North Korean society the moral unity of *ch'ung* and *hyo*, that is, political loyalty in the spirit of the absolute ethic of filial piety. In parallel with the reinvention of these traditional concepts, the succession of power also involved a crucial adjustment in what Weber would call rational-bureaucratic authority. Most notable in this matter was the establishment of the position of perpetual, transcendental head of state for the late Kim Il Sung in 1998. This meant, as described in chapter 3, that Kim Jong Il's succession of Kim Il Sung was not quite a succession of office and therefore contributed to resolving the structural contradiction in the reproduction of charismatic authority. The empowerment of Kim Jong Suk proved crucial in the all-out, multifrontier unfolding of the drama of succession. Kim Jong Suk's iconicity provided a vital link between the old partisan legend and the new partisan state paradigm of military-first politics.[24] It created the bridge between the old familial morality of partisan unity and the new moral doctrine of the unity of loyalty and filial piety. Central to the efficacy of her iconicity has been the duplicity and ambiguity of her public persona in relation to her consanguine identity. She is the mother of military-first politics and, at the same time, the mother of the leader in the military-first political era. She is the mother of all citizens of Kim Jong Il's North Korea and, at once, the mother of the singular leader of this polity. She loves flowers, in particular the wildflowers in Korea's prairie,[25] whereas she is also the most determined, unbreakable, and exemplary barrel of a gun. She is closest to the love of the Great Leader and to the rays of grace emanating from the benevolent sun; yet, she is not merely a passive recipient of the sovereign love but also a powerful commander of the partisan army whose existential purpose is to defend the power and authority of the sun. A December 2000 *Rodong Sinmun* editorial titled "The Woman Who Leads Immortal Life in Our Hearts" salutes the memory of Kim Jong Suk with reference to a Peruvian broadcast by Radio Santa Rosa, which ran a program of the same title: "People of Chosun have high esteem for her. She defended with her life the Supreme Leader, Kim Il Sung, the founder of socialist Chosun. Her other esteemed contribution was to *embrace and lift* the guiding leader Kim Jong Il."[26]

Notes

1. About the display of the Korean War in this museum and how it subtly yet importantly differs from the display of the war in Pyongyang, see Tessa Morris-Suzuki, "Remembering the Unfinished Conflict: Museums and the Contested Memory of the Korean War," *Asia-Pacific Journal*, July 27, 2009, http://www.japanfocus.org/-Tessa-Morris_Suzuki/3193 (accessed September 13, 2009).

2. In addition to the battles on 1211 Hill, 351 Hill, and Wŏlmi Island, North Korea's most cherished heroic battle histories of the Korean War include the naval battle in Jumunjin and the fight along Daejon in the early days of the war.

3. Kim Il Sung, *Segiwa dŏbulŏ* [Together with the century] (Pyongyang: Workers' Party Press, 1992), 128–30.

4. Nym Wales and Kim San, *Song of Arirang: A Korean Communist in the Chinese Revolution*, rev. ed. (San Francisco: Ramparts Press, 1972).

5. It is reported that about thirty-five thousand ethnic Korean troops who had fought the Chinese civil war alongside their Chinese Communist comrades returned to Korea shortly before the Korean War broke out. The Chinese troops that later joined the Korean conflict amounted to 1.3 million combatants with casualties surpassing 300,000. See Kenei Shu (Zhu Jianrong in Chinese), *Motakutō no chōsen sensō* [Mao's Korean War] (Tokyo: Iwanami shoten, 2004), 10–36. Cumings estimated the number of Korean Chinese combatants who joined the Korean War to be between seventy and one hundred thousand. See Bruce Cumings, *Korea's Place in the Sun: A Modern History* (New York: W. W. Norton, 1997), 241. Hideki Takizawa interviewed some of these veterans and reported the results in *Chōsenminzoku no kindaikokka keiseishi jyosetsu* [An introduction to the formation of the modern Korean nation-state] (Tokyo: Ochanomizu shōbo, 2008), 101–40.

6. Personal communication with Chris Springer, author of *Pyongyang: The Hidden History of the North Korean Capital* (Gold River, CA: Saranda Books, 2003), on June 29, 2006.

7. Jay Winter, *Sites of Memory, Sites of Mourning: The Great War in European Cultural History* (Cambridge: Cambridge University Press, 1995).

8. George Mosse, *Fallen Soldiers: Reshaping the Memory of World Wars* (Oxford: Oxford University Press, 1991).

9. For example, John R. Gillis, ed., *Commemorations: The Politics of National Identity* (Princeton, NJ: Princeton University Press, 1994); Winter, *Sites of Memory*.

10. Richard Werbner, "Smoke from the Barrel of a Gun: Postwars of the Dead, Memory, and Reinscription in Zimbabwe," in *Memory and Postcoloniality*, ed. Richard Werbner (London: Zed, 1998), 2.

11. Patricia M. Pelley, *Postcolonial Vietnam: New Histories of the National Past* (Durham, NC: Duke University Press, 2002).

12. Shaun K. Malarney, *Culture, Ritual, and Revolution in Vietnam* (New York: RoutledgeCurzon, 2002).

13. See "*Aegukryŏlsarŭng* [The graves of patriotic martyrs]," *Rodong Sinmun*, December 28, 2004. See also Chosŏn daebaekkwa sajŏn [Chosun encyclopedia], "Lee Soo Bok," in *Chosŏndaebaekkwasajŏn* [Chosun encyclopedia], Vol. 8 (Pyongyang: Baekkwasajŏnch'ulpansa [Encyclopedia press], 1999), 211–12.

14. We thank Jim Hoare for bringing this information to our attention.

15. See Chosŏn daebaekkwa sajŏn [Chosun encyclopedia], "Chokuk haebang chŏnjaeng [Fatherland Liberation War]," in *Chosŏndaebaekkwasajŏn* [Chosun encyclopedia], Vol. 17 (Pyongyang: Baekkwasajŏnch'ulpansa [Encyclopedia press], 2000), 501–5.

16. Charles K. Armstrong, "Centering the Periphery: Manchurian Exile(s) and the North Korean State," *Korean Studies* 19 (1995): 1–16.

17. Cited from Dae-Hyung Oh and Kyung-Ho Ha, *Dangŭi ryŏngdomit'ae ch'angjakkŏllipdoin daeginyŏmbidŭlŭi sasang yesulsŏng* [The ideological-artistic quality of the commemorative monuments established under the party's leadership] (Pyongyang: Literature and Art Press, 1989), 219.

18. Before the final renovation in 1985, Kim Jong Suk's grave was among, not above, those of twelve other highly esteemed old partisan heroes of North Korea. See Oh and Ha, *Dangŭi ryŏngdomit'ae ch'angjakkŏllipdoin daeginyŏmbidŭlŭi sasang yesulsŏng* [The ideological-artistic quality of the commemorative monuments established under the party's leadership], 237.

19. This reference to Kim Jong Suk is inscribed in the memorial stone on Osandŏk, in Hoiryŏng, erected in November 1978. Osandŏk is a small hill located at the center of the town, where in childhood, Madame Kim used to collect wild vegetables. According to North Korea's official biographical accounts of Kim Jong Suk, it was also on this hill that the young Kim nurtured her hatred of the Japanese and love for her country, after witnessing the pitiful scenes of dispossessed Koreans crossing the Tumen river in search of a better life in Manchuria. See Hee-Bok Choi, *Paekdusan nyŏjanggunŭi insaenggwan* [The life philosophy of the woman-general of Paekdu mountains] (Pyongyang: Labor Group Press, 2009); Pyongyang ch'ulpansa [Pyongyang press], *Sŏn'gunŭi ŏmŏni Kim Jong Suk nyŏjanggun* [The mother of military-first (politics), Female-General Kim Jong Suk] (Pyongyang: Pyongyang Press, 2007).

20. "Uri jokukŭi ŏmŏni [Mother of our country]," *Rodong Sinmun*, December 23, 2005.

21. Oh and Ha, *Dangŭi ryŏngdomit'ae ch'angjakkŏllipdoin daeginyŏmbidŭ lŭi sasang yesulsŏng* [The ideological-artistic quality of the commemorative monuments established under the party's leadership], 225.

22. Woo-Kyung Kim, Ki-Chun Dong, and Jong-Suk Kim, *Kŭmsusan'gin yŏmgungjŏn chŏnsŏlchip* [Legends of Kŭmsusan memorial palace], Vol. 1 (Pyongyang: Literature and Art Press, 1999), 96–102.

23. Suk-Young Kim, "For the Eyes of the Dear Leader: Fashion and Body Politics in North Korean Visual Arts" (lecture given at the U.S. Library of Congress, Washington, DC, March 17, 2009).

24. Chin-Hyok Chung, *Jŏlseŭi wiin'gamum* [The matchless great man's family line] (Pyongyang: Pyongyang Press, 2002), 22–32.

25. Especially the red azaleas, which symbolize the female partisan followers of Kim Il Sung in contemporary North Korean literature and art. See Kim Jong Suk's fictional biography, Jong-Ryol Lee, *Jindalae* [The azalea] (Pyongyang: Literature and Art Press, 2007), 401–2. The Kim Jong Suk statue in Hoiryŏng (figure 4.2 in this chapter) depicts a cluster of rhododendrons next to the heroine.

26. "Inminŭi maŭmsoge yŏngsaenghasinŭn nyŏsa [The woman who leads immortal life in our hearts]," *Rodong Sinmun*, December 22, 2000. The phrase "embrace and lift" is our translation of *ana olisida*. See the image figured on the front cover of this volume.

5

Gifts to the Leader

The 1970s were a formative decade for North Korea's political culture. Many of the striking features that we witness in today's North Korean political process and development took root during that period. It was a time of many contradictions. Domestically, the North Korean economy, after enjoying a successful recovery over the previous decade from the devastation of the Korean War, began to show signs of stagnation, in sharp contrast to a rapid industrial growth in its neighboring competitor and antagonist, South Korea. The decline in economic performance was soon manifested in the disturbing instability, beginning in the early 1980s, of North Korea's most important mechanism of social and political integration: the national distribution system for food and other subsistence items. According to Lee Woo-Young, who conducted an interesting study of North Korea's political and economic changes based on the country's changing revolutionary slogans, the first indications of the food-shortage problems appeared in 1977, in slogans such as "All forward to the conquering of the hill of 8 million tons of grain production!" "Save, save, and again save [the food]!" and "Rice is socialism."[1]

However, in the political arena, in contrast to the loss of economic vitality, the theatrics and pomposity of the North Korean state's power and authority were systematically magnified during the 1970s. During this time, the full-throttled sublimation of Kim Il Sung's personality cult took place, involving a radical empowerment of his glorious Manchurian partisan legend. The process was referred to in North Korea at that time as the consolidation of the unitary ideological system—the idea that the entire society must unite in and for the thinking of Kim Il Sung, the only meaningful theory of social revolution—and it created powerful new slogans such as "Production, study, and everyday life: All according to the anti-Japan partisan method!" As described in earlier chapters, the making of the unitary thought system was advanced not only for the sake of the Supreme Leader's own majesty but also as part of the long process of transferring his authority and power to Kim Jong Il. The succession process involved a multitude of cultural productions and memorial projects, as well as a systematic effort to build a universally politically literate society along a singular historical narrative centered on Kim Il Sung's life. In this sense, we can locate in this era the actual birth of North Korea as a theater state, despite the fact that in the literature discussed earlier, the idea of the theater state is more closely associated with the political development of North Korea after the death of Kim Il Sung in 1994 (see chapter 2). In this respect, the theater state idea refers not merely to the role of rituals and spectacles in the political process in general terms but rather, more specifically, to a contradiction in the practice of state power—that is, to how the state may become more active and effective in asserting its power by demonstrative means and in fantastic ways as it becomes more inefficient and weaker in the sphere of material power and economic capacity. In other words, the theater state idea that we employ in this book includes, first, how the theatrics of state power develop in relation to the routinization and succession of charismatic authority and, second, the notion that the theatrical politics of a state may intensify in an inverse relationship to the actual material power of the state.

We have seen how the stories of the old partisan struggles in Manchuria in the 1930s were brought back in powerful dramatic forms in the 1970s. We also saw, in chapter 4, how the postcolonial historical reconstruction was manifested in the material culture of commemoration, focusing on the structure of the Graves of Revolutionary Martyrs. Chapter 6 pursues the same question in relation to the great famine of the mid-1990s, the most destructive human and social crisis North Korea has faced since the time of the Korean War, and how the country's leadership has reacted to the catastrophe. In order to grasp the magnitude of this catastrophic event and its consequences for the moral fabric of North Korean society, which are still unfolding in painful ways, it is necessary to look at some additional sociological parameters and institutional reifications of North Korea's partisan family state, which we discussed previously with reference to the invented concept of traditional patriotic filial piety and the symbolism of the barrel of a gun. Notable in this matter is the idea of the gift, which permeates, in many explicit and implicit forms, political and economic life in North Korea. This idea is instructive for understanding the moral relationship between the people and the sovereign leader, and it also helps to explain the conceptual relationship between the symbols of the partisan state and the family state paradigm. We saw earlier how state sovereignty and the entire familial political order have been rendered in North Korea as a gift from the preeminent leader of the country and his Manchurian comrades. The idea of the gift is therefore constitutive of how the North Korean polity's exemplary center asserts its moral authority over the realm it governs. Furthermore, the idea is central to how North Korea locates itself in relation to the outside world and, in fact, how it perceives the meaning of its historical genesis in modern global history. We focus on this last aspect in this chapter and argue that the organizing principle of North Korea's modern political sovereignty is based on an idea of the gift in relation to the international community.

Global North Korea

The life cycle ceremonial calendar has been an important element in North Korea's political process. The country's two most important seasonal markers are the birthday celebrations for the founding leader and his successor. We saw earlier how the claimed "revolutionary leap" in the early 1970s in North Korea's public art coincided with the country's momentous ceremonial occasion, Kim Il Sung's sixtieth birthday. The sixtieth birthday celebration is traditionally an important part of Korean family life and ritual culture, and the custom remains strong in North Korea. The same applies to the spectacle of Arirang, one of the most preeminent displays of state art in today's North Korea. The Arirang spectacle was first opened to the public in 2002, which marked the ninetieth anniversary of the birth of the late leader and provided an occasion to commemorate his exemplary life history and, at the same time, celebrate his immortal political life. Arirang is clearly an important tool of the state, intended to consolidate the domestic realm as well as to send vital diplomatic messages to the outside world. North Korea claims, "Arirang displays the one hundred years of our nation's history in a performance that lasts an hour and a half. It implants into the people the pride and dignity of a nation having a great supreme leader and great guiding leader. It says loudly what sort of country the *sŏn'gun* Chosun is and what kind of people we are."[2] However, the mass spectacle, performed by tens of thousands of immaculately trained women and children, also has powerful moral meanings. Arirang is meant to be a gift from the people of North Korea to their Great Leader; it is also a gift from the new leader to his predecessor: "Arirang is not a mere work of art. It contains our greatest respect to the Supreme Leader. It is our warmest song of gratitude dedicated to him. It is a gift with deep meaning prepared by our Dear Leader, General Kim Jong Il, for the Great Leader, in the name of the entire nation."[3]

The gift aspect of the actual performance of Arirang is shown most explicitly when the narrative it tells parts with the historical trajectory of the revolutionary state and moves into North Korea's contemporary story in the era of military-first politics. At that moment, the stadium's twenty thousand schoolchildren, mobilized for what some call the "video wall" created by changing multicolor handheld pickets, display the founding leader's portrait surrounded by thousands of flowers. Simultaneously, the hundreds of women dressed in traditional costumes of different colors are gathered in the stadium's field to perform the beautiful collective dance "Flowers to the Supreme Leader." The video wall then delivers the messages "Honor to the nation's father, our Great Leader" and "Honor to the iron-willed general who won over two imperialisms in one generation." Later, close to the finale, the flower-giving women (who actually are flowers themselves, according to the famous North Korean song "Women Are Flowers") come back to the stage to perform their dance, "The Sun of the Twenty-First Century [Kim Jong Il] Shines All over the World." This dance, followed by a grand gymnastic fanfare performed by schoolchildren, takes place around a large model of the globe carried into the stadium by a group of youth athletes. While this is underway, on the spectacle's human video wall, the twenty thousand schoolchildren's multicolor pickets display tributes to Kim Il Sung ("Honor to the nation's father"), then to Kim Jong Il ("Glory to the Dear Leader"), then, followed by images of flowers and flying doves, writes the slogan, "Independence, peace, and friendship."

The Arirang performance provides a succinct, exemplary narrative of North Korea's past and future that the state wishes to convey to its people and to the outside world at a given historical moment. The narrative opens with the miseries and humiliations of the colonial occupation and the exodus of dispossessed people (and future revolutionaries) to Manchuria. If we look at the spectacle's concluding performance involving the image of the globe in relation to the opening scene about the sorrowful diasporas, the message is clear. The introduction of the globe to the spectacle speaks of the dignity of the North Korean people and their leader, who together overcame the destitution of colonial displacement and built a proud political home, the authority of which is recognized and respected by the world. According to a North Korean columnist, the message of Arirang is, "Our country, Kim Il Sung Chosun, was built by our father–supreme leader and has walked on the glorious path toward victory and prosperity under his leadership. Once it lost its place in the world atlas; now its esteem and authority shine the world over. This is entirely thanks to the wise leadership of our great Supreme Leader."[4] The concluding scene is also a statement of collective determination to keep the Great

Figure 5.1. "The sun of the 21st century [Kim Jong Il] shines over the world!" Arirang Festival, 2005. *Source:* Photo by Jae Soo Liu (2005; permission granted).

Leader's gift of a political home intact. To do so is the moral obligation of all who have benefited from the leader's gracious gift—"the entire people of Chosun and the entire progressive humanity," as Kim Jong Il said in his important commemorative speech in February 1996.[5] Furthermore, it is necessary to mention also that North Korea's dignity, displayed in the closing scene of Arirang, is not merely about having a place in the world as a sovereign and independent entity. The symbol of the globe is meant to convey the message that North Korea is a state with global esteem and that the country's founding leader is a global leader. South Korean anthropologist Lee Moon-Woong observes, "It is argued that the sphere of Kim Il Sung's influence is not limited to North Korea. Instead, he is a twentieth-century hero born in Korea and a man respected by all the world's revolutionary peoples."[6] Kim Jong Il said in 1996, "The great comrade Kim Il Sung is not only our nation's father and the first genuine hero whom our nation ever had in its thousands of years of history. He is humanity's sunshine recognized by the entire world." While this statement may sound excessively self-centered, the ethos it delivers is nevertheless a vital aspect of contemporary North Korea's self-awareness and its perception of its rightful place in the world community. Moreover, the idea of a global North Korea becomes less strange if considered from a historical perspective. Important to this consideration is another preeminent North Korean national monument built in the 1970s, one not yet discussed in this book—the International Friendship Exhibition Hall.[7]

The International Friendship Exhibition Hall

The ten years between Kim Il Sung's sixtieth birthday in 1972 and his seventieth birthday in 1982 provided the foundation for North Korea's contemporary musical and theatrical productions. The era was also the heyday of the country's monumental art. Most foreign, as well as domestic, visitors to Pyongyang are normally expected to visit and pay respect to at least three of the most important memorials existing within and around the city: the gigantic bronze statue of Kim Il Sung on Longevity Hill (Mansudae), Kim's birthplace (Mankyŏngdae), and the granite Juch'e Tower along the Daedong river. The statue opened in 1972 to mark the late leader's sixtieth birthday, prior to the 1975 renovation of the Graves of Revolutionary Martyrs. The leader's seventieth birthday in 1982 saw, among other things, the completion of the Juch'e Tower and the Victory Gate, the North Korean version of the Arc de Triomphe, which celebrates Kim Il Sung's triumphant anticolonial revolutionary activity from 1925 to 1945. Both of these pieces are meant to be more than national monuments—they also assert global prestige. In terms of material structure, therefore, the Juch'e Tower is claimed to be the tallest stone monument ever built by a human civilization, and the Victory Gate was constructed to be taller and more imposing than its Napoleonic counterpart in Paris.[8] These world-leading material forms were meant to represent the global fame of the country's founding revolutionary leader, which was the focus of the era's North Korean memorial art.

The rendering of Kim Il Sung's global fame is realized most sumptuously in the International Friendship Exhibition Hall (Gukje ch'insŏn ginyŏmkwan). Completed in 1978 and located in one of North Korea's most cherished natural beauties, the Myohyang mountains, the hall functions as the storage site and museum for the tens of thousands of gifts that state leaders, communist parties, "progressive peoples," and individual admirers from around the world have dedicated to Kim Il Sung. It also has a room that depicts, rather than the gifts from the outside world to the leader, the leader's outward interaction with the world, listing the transnational locations that have earned the prestige of receiving the leader for a visit as well as the mileage of his overseas on-the-spot-guidance trips.[9] Since Kim Il Sung's death in 1994, the hall has also included rooms reserved for gifts given in honor of the late leader's living memory (Hall of Eternal Life), particularly for his postmortem birthday celebrations held each April. In 1989, a separate building for the gifts received by Kim Jong Il was added to the memorial complex. International Friendship Exhibition Hall stores about two hundred thousand gifts to Kim Il Sung available for public viewing in 150 exhibition rooms. The number of gifts to Kim Jong Il is relatively modest, amounting to about fifty thousand objects received from 165 different countries. There are also sections devoted to the modest number of gifts received posthumously by Kim Jong Suk.[10] The North Korean guides working at the hall usually like to remind visitors that it would take a year and a half to look through all the gifts to the leaders, allowing one minute to examine each item. The displayed gifts include medals, certificates of honor, and letters of admiration, as well as a dazzling variety of precious objects, cultural artifacts, and industrial goods. These were sent from all corners of the world—by revolutionary leaders in Latin America, tribal leaders in Africa, progressive political groups in Europe and North America, and state leaders in Asia and former Soviet bloc countries. The place is open to foreign visitors (it is often an obligatory stop for them), and for citizens of North Korea, it is an important national pilgrimage site. The front of the hall consists of a pleasant, well-proportioned building in the traditional Korean style. On entering the massive bronze gates (which are allegedly resistant even to the explosion of an atomic bomb, as the museum guides like to emphasize), however, visitors are dazzled by the sumptuous interior, which employs pompous elements of European palatial architecture, and discover that the entire twenty-thousand-square-meter museum (the Kim Il Sung Hall) is actually a gigantic fortress dug into a rocky mountain. The impression created is that the materials stored and displayed in this fortress are regarded as truly precious treasures by those who would go to such great lengths to ensure their safety. Indeed, the hall is often referred to as the "treasure house of Chosun." Comparing it to the Hermitage in Saint Petersburg, the Louvre in Paris, and the Palace Museum in Beijing, North Korean writer Kwak Sŏng Ho says of his visit that, on entering the hall, he felt as if he were entering a treasure house in an ancient fable. He adds, "Then, I understood why people said that here, one would be able to see, rather than Chosun in the world, the world in Chosun."[11]

Figure 5.2. International Friendship Exhibition Hall. *Source:* Photo by Byung-Ho Chung (2006).

After this evocative statement, Kwak continues to recall the feelings and thoughts the tour of the hall provoked in him. He reflects on the sorry story of old Korea, particularly on how numerous national treasures were lost or stolen in the past during the age of imperialism and colonialism. Then he writes,

> At that time, our people were unable to protect even household copper ware, not to mention the country's treasures. But remember the moment when all this changed, when we were allowed to keep our own historical relics and, moreover, when we began to witness the extraordinary phenomenon that treasures of the world began to arrive in our country with deep emotions of respect. That was the moment that we began to look up to Comrade Kim Il Sung as the father of our nation and as the founding ancestor of the socialist Chosun. . . . These are the gifts sent by peoples of all nations and states, including eminent state leaders, transcending their differences in political opinion, religion, nationality, social system, language, and skin color.[12]

As Kwak mentions, the collection at the International Friendship Exhibition Hall is indeed global in geographic terms, transcending national, cultural, and racial differences and boundaries. It is also global in qualitative terms, treating fabulous gifts from eminent state leaders structurally as equal to those sent by the leader of a humble tribal group or by individual foreign friends of North Korea.

The gifts to Kim Il Sung include a bulletproof automobile from Joseph Stalin; a large handicraft depicting a roaring tiger from Mao Zedong, sent in November 1953 in celebration of Kim Il Sung's victory in the Korean War (these items are "tributes" to Kim Il Sung made by Comrades Mao and Stalin, according to the labels next to the gifts); and a gigantic porcelain vase offered in 1978 by the Central Committee of the Chinese Communist Party specially for the opening of the Hall of Gifts. Most of the gifts are displayed according to their geographical region of origin. Gifts from Latin America include a silver machete and a machine gun from Nicaragua, decorative plates from Ecuador and a Peruvian university, an oil painting of an Andean market from Guiana, and a briefcase made of crocodile skin from Fidel Castro. A stuffed, standing crocodile holding a plate of wine glasses, a gift from the Sandinista leadership, is a favorite for many visitors to this section. The African rooms display a variety of gifts, including traditional cultural objects such as ivory candlesticks from Ethiopia; ivory walking sticks from Julius Nyerere, former Tanzanian leader; a stuffed turtle from Guinea; a collection of Senegalese traditional handicrafts; Ghanaian textiles; a large set of traditional spears from Rwanda; and an Algerian camel saddle. Particularly notable in this collection is the seat of chiefly power dedicated in 1994 by Nigeria's Umozi tribe (a subtribe of the Ibu in the country's resource-rich southeastern region). In 1995, according to a report in North Korea's Workers' Party newspaper, the tribe elected the late Kim Il Sung as its honorary sun chief, the first ever such election in Nigerian history.[13]

Many gifts in the Asian collection are from China, and these include some of the most sophisticated artifacts, such as the meticulously sculpted jade "Galloping Horses," given in celebration of the launch of North Korea's version of the Great Leap Forward, Chollima (thousand-mile horse). The Asian collection also contains a large number of artifacts from North Korea's other traditional allies, particularly from members of the Non-Aligned Movement. Most prominent among these are the personal gifts from Indonesia's Sukarno, which include a silver tea set, leather office furniture, and traditional Indonesian ceremonial gongs. Another prominent gift from Indonesia is the orchid flower offered to Kim by Sukarno during Kim's state visit to Indonesia in 1965. The flower was later introduced to North Korea, in 1977, as the "eternal flower" and "flower of revolution." Since then, the Indonesian orchid has been recognized as the Kim Il Sung flower, and since 1998, a large number of workplaces and army units have been allocated the job of cultivating it for Kim's annual birthday celebration in April, when Pyongyang opens a flower festival in memory of the late leader.[14] The Asian collection also contains an ivory figurine given by Ho Chi Minh in 1964, flower vases from the Democratic Republic of Vietnam from 1962, a silver basket from the Laotian Patriotic Front given in 1972, a model junk boat from the Cambodian leader Norodom Sihanouk, a jade teacup set from Myanmar, a miniature temple from Nepal, and a variety of traditional artifacts from India, Pakistan, and Bangladesh. The Asian section also includes rows of gifts from the Middle East and Central Asia, including handicrafts and silverware from Egypt, Iran, Syria, Palestine, Lebanon, and Yemen. The regional collections expand into Europe, North America, and Oceania. The North American section includes a dove sculpture from Billy Graham and a bearskin donated by an unidentified Canadian citizen. The European collection consists of gifts from former Eastern bloc countries and their party leaders (such as Erich Honecker's hunting rifle) as well as from communist parties and *juch'e* philosophy study groups in western European societies (i.e., an entire collection of Spanish translations of Kim Il Sung's voluminous philosophical writings and speeches). There are also large collections of gifts from overseas Koreans, although we were not able to see them.

The structure of the Kim Jong Il museum of gifts closely follows that of the Kim Il Sung museum, although the collection it holds clearly demonstrates the changes that have taken place over time. The former also keeps a large and dazzling collection of gifts from diverse regions and peoples; yet, its most frequently visited rooms are the China, United States, Japan, and South Korea rooms. The most eye-catching gift from the United States is the basketball with Michael Jordan's signature on it, brought by former secretary of state Madeleine Albright, although the room also contains gifts from other important American visitors to North Korea, such as Jimmy Carter and Bill Clinton. The South Korea room consists of gifts from the country's former heads of state, from Park Chung-Hee to Roh Mu-Hyun, as well as those brought by prominent industrialists, party leaders, media groups, and civil society representatives. The Kim Jong Il collections in the International Friendship Exhibition Hall are therefore a museum in the making, continuing to take shape, following North Korea's changing relationship with the world. By contrast, the collections in the Kim Il Sung Hall are supposed to be permanent, although we were told that they might undergo some minor changes over time; new items might be brought out of storage, and some items in the existing collections might be put away. It is also possible that the construction of the Kim Jong Il Hall in 1989, the year that the Berlin Wall fell, affected the organization of the display in the Kim Il Sung collection. Despite these minor modifications, however, it is safe to say that the collection of gifts for Kim Il Sung has remained generally intact since the hall's original public opening in 1978. Our survey of old North Korean literature on the International Friendship Exhibition Hall also confirms this continuity. Bearing this in mind and recalling what we have seen in recent years, we believe that the International Friendship Exhibition Hall displays ideas about the global North Korea imagined in the formative era of the 1970s, or in Kwak Sŏng Ho's words, "Chosun in the world" and "the world in Chosun."

Leader of the Postcolonial World

North Korea's musical and theatrical revolution in the early 1970s is claimed to have given new life to the partisan art tradition originating in the 1930s. We considered this claim previously with reference to some famous North Korean musicals such as *The Flower-Selling Girl*, which draws upon the Kim Il Sung–led partisan group's revolutionary cultural activity in Japan-controlled Manchuria in the 1930s. We also saw how the origin of this musical is even deeper and more international than North Korea would like to admit, relating to an early Soviet revolutionary drama. We may look at the display of gifts to Kim Il Sung in a similar light. The literature about the display, published at the time of its opening, claims that the International Friendship Exhibition Hall was a gift to the Great Leader personally designed by Kim Jong Il and, like other memorials built at the time, prepared by him on behalf of the people of North Korea. However, it seems fairly evident that the idea was not entirely Kim Jong Il's and that its origin should be traced to one among the most prominent forms of Soviet public art in the Stalinist era.

The development in the art of rule in North Korea between 1972 and 1982, the years of Kim Il Sung's sixtieth and seventieth birthdays, respectively, has a close affinity with what happened in the Soviet Union between Stalin's sixtieth and seventieth birthday celebrations in 1939 and 1949. The so-called personality cult of Stalin reached an apex during this period, and regarding the specific theme discussed in this chapter, it is worth noting that the advancement of Stalin's political charisma relied heavily on a logic of gift exchange and theatrics such as birthday celebrations. Jeffrey Brooks explores Soviet public culture in this era, focusing on what he calls the "morality play" of gift exchange between the Soviet leader and the Soviet peoples.[15] He describes how the workers were driven to understand all the amenities of modern life that they were enjoying—be it new housing, schools, or modern transportation—as gifts from Stalin; in turn, they were encouraged to conceptualize it as their duty, as the citizens of the Soviet state and as the workers in the workers' state, to appreciate these gifts from Stalin and to reciprocate. In this light, Brooks focuses on the dramas of the *udarniki*, the Stakhanovite Soviet labor heroes whose superhuman agricultural or industrial labor performances were then widely described by the Soviet press as a form of repayment for the gift of love from Stalin.[16] He writes, "The press made such people's obligation strikingly apparent, as in *Pravda*'s front page on January 1, 1935, which featured a drawing of Stalin at a podium, with diminutive shock workers proffering bouquets of flowers. Thus in the press, personal moral ties to Stalin replaced bonds to family, friends, colleagues, the community, and ultimately to society itself. . . . [Proletarian] and peasant notables acted out rituals of the gift and celebrated their miraculous rebirth as new people with a special relationship to their benefactor."[17]

The "morality play" of gift exchange between the Soviet leader and the Soviet peoples culminated in the famous Stalin Birthday Gifts Exhibition held in Moscow in 1939, and again between 1949 and 1953, at the Pushkin Museum of Fine Arts. The exhibitions drew a great number of gifts from ordinary Soviet people as well as party notables in different Soviet republics. The gifts included portraits of Stalin, a huge bust of Stalin made of chocolate, model industrial plants, samovars, and weapons. Those brought by non-Russian Soviet peoples included carpets, national costumes, and ornamental objects. For the birthday celebration in December 1949, cargoes of foreign gifts were also brought in from the Soviet Union's allies as well as from some of its Cold War enemies. The politburo of the Hungarian Communist Party met five times to discuss preparations for Stalin's seventieth birthday before sending a trainload of gifts to Moscow. It orchestrated the mass production of Stalin's bust for display in factories and public offices and used the occasion to spread the cult of Stalin among the masses as a way to bring Hungary into a leading role in the construction of socialism in the Eastern bloc.[18] From China, Mao Zedong personally led a delegation with a carload of gifts in an armored railcar captured during the civil war from Chiang Kai-shek.[19] Particularly inventive foreign gifts included a smoking pipe with a sculpture of Stalin engaged in a game of chess with Theodore Roosevelt, an avant-garde telephone set featuring a hammer and a sickle, and a lamp made from a dead armadillo (the gift of an unidentified Brazilian).[20] Some gifts carried moving stories: a woman in France who had lost her daughter to the Nazis sent the girl's hat—the only thing that was left of her child. Many gifts came also from indigenous peoples in the far corners of Siberia; a group of Native American tribes in the United States sent a fully feathered headdress, through the Soviet representative in New York, to commemorate Stalin's election as the honorary chief of all Indian tribes.[21]

Anthropologist Nikolai Ssorin-Chaikov examines these birthday gifts to Stalin and, like Brooks, concludes that these objects show how the Soviet politics at the time was based on an imaginative public gift economy.[22] He finds that this demonstrative public, international gift economy was intended to be a powerful political statement—to show the power of the gift-based global solidarity of progressive states and peoples, for whom Stalin stood as the leader, and to set this power of socialist modernity against the commodity-worshipping world of the Soviet Union's Cold War enemies. There was a politics of time as well as the politics of space and geopolitical competition over spheres of influence, according to Ssorin-Chaikov. Gift economies are usually associated with premodern societies or traditional social relations in the development of Western social thought, in distinction to modern social forms identified with the rise of monetary and commodity exchange. The gifts to Stalin turned this central premise of modern Western social thought on its head by using the spectacle of gifts to advance a vision of a progressive global modernity rather than a view of the premodern past; according to Ssorin-Chaikov, it was a "temporal negation of the commodity form."[23]

Another important aspect of the gifts to Stalin needs to be mentioned, however. In conventional social and economic theory, gifts are distinguished from commodities as objects whose values and meanings are inseparable from (and embedded in) the particular social relations within which the objects circulate. They are not a thing, strictly speaking, but a quasi-animate entity, being an extension of the donor's moral selfhood. They are a token of value, but the values they represent, unlike with commodities, are qualitative rather than quantitative, being inalienable from the moral quality of the relationship between the donor and the receiver.

Brooks emphasizes these moral aspects of the Soviet public gift economy, concentrating on the domestic side of Stalin's politics of gifts. He cites eminent British anthropologist E. E. Evans-Pritchard's introductory note on Marcel Mauss's classic *The Gift*, in which Evans-Pritchard contrasts the traditional gift exchange system to modern economic systems in terms of moral versus mechanical transactions. Based on this notion that gift exchange is a moral economic system, Brooks writes, "Stalin and his compatriots developed a society in which public allocations of resources were officially presented as moral transactions, and performers who publicly thanked Stalin validated personal ties to the leader. . . . The official enfolding of economic transactions into the moral economy of the gift implicitly undermined both public and private commitment to more straightforward economic transactions and markets. It also provided a rationale for attributing personal success and achievement to Stalin and the state. Stalin himself validated the moral economy, personally picking recipients of important state prizes."[24]

Both Ssorin-Chaikov's geopolitical and Brooks's moral-economic perspective on the Soviet public gift economy in Stalin's era are instructive for understanding the spectacle of gifts to Kim Il Sung, although the latter shows several elements that are distinct from Stalin's birthday festivities. First, North Korea's International Friendship Exhibition Hall, as its name suggests, is exclusively for the gifts to the leader given by the leader's overseas allies and admirers or by foreign visitors to the leader's realm. Unlike the Stalin Birthday Gifts Exhibition, which incorporated both the gifts from the Soviet peoples and those from the friends of the Soviet Union, the gifts to Kim Il Sung stored and displayed in the Myohyangsan complex cover all the continents of the globe and nearly all national communities of the world except the leader's own. Second, in addition to this formal difference between the gifts to Stalin and those to Kim, we need to consider the fact that the two displays arose under quite different historical circumstances.

A North Korean source from the early 1980s writes of the gifts to Kim Il Sung, "In each of these precious gifts, we find the respect and affection of the world's revolutionary peoples toward our great Supreme Leader. They also contain these people's unchanging support for and solid solidarity with our people's justified work of revolution."[25] Despite these general references to the world's progressive peoples and North Korea's international friends, the idea of international revolutionary solidarity held specific meanings for North Korea at the time, which were manifested quite explicitly in the organization of the exhibition at the International Friendship Exhibition Hall. The picture albums of the hall's inaugural display of gifts to Kim Il Sung, meant for the leader's seventieth birthday in 1982, show clearly that the concept of international friendship at that time focused on the postcolonial world rather than necessarily the socialist bloc under Soviet leadership or Chinese influence. This relates to what Charles Armstrong aptly calls North Korea's anti-imperialist "Third-Worldism" in the 1960s and 1970s, during which North Korea made a huge, conscious effort in the global arena to acquire international recognition and fame as "a model of postcolonial nation-building."[26]

North Korea's pursuit of international fame as an exemplary postcolonial polity has a complex historical background. Armstrong highlights North Korea's self-confidence in the economic sphere—stemming from rapid recovery from the destruction of war and impressive industrial growth until the mid-1960s—and its political pride as a Third World country (before Vietnam) unique in having successfully resisted the military power of the United States.[27] This led Kim Il Sung to highlight, in his important address at the eighth plenum of the party's Central Committee in 1964, the need to strengthen "international revolutionary potential" by forging strong solidarity with revolutionary forces and peoples in the global South—in Asia, Africa, and Latin America.[28] He declared, "We must try to isolate American imperialism to the maximum extent possible and drive it to a corner everywhere in the world. This would encourage anti-American national liberation movements in the South and facilitate the reunification of Korea."[29] Notably, by the time of Kim's seventieth birthday in 1982, North Korea's pledges and polemics about Third World–based global revolutionary solidarity, which by then had begun to adopt a more militant language than in the previous decade, came to be closely associated with the claimed political theoretical efforts of Kim Jong Il, not merely with the teachings of Kim Il Sung.[30] Other, less positive factors existed, however. The North Korean economy began to face problems, both in the industrial and agricultural sectors, in the late 1960s and, in the 1970s, began to fall visibly behind South Korea in economic growth. The country's leadership felt threatened by the US invasion of Vietnam, which resulted in a rapid rise in defense spending despite the stagnation in economic growth. In the political sphere, moreover, North Korea's main blood allies during the Korean War and its principal political-spiritual allies, China and the Soviet Union, were embroiled in escalating, cutthroat ideological and diplomatic battles with each other. As a result, the international socialist movement had "two suns in the heavens," as Sergey Radchenko aptly puts it, between which the movement's humble actors were forced to choose.[31] In the beginning of the 1970s, the Sino-Soviet bifurcation in the socialist world was further complicated by the Soviet Union's and China's separate détente initiatives with the United States, which some historians today call the transformation of the early Cold War's bipolar international order into a tripolar system. The situation was particularly challenging for North Korea, which shares not only geographical borders but also a foundational constitutional and political history with both the socialist big brothers. During this momentous shift in global power relations (the consequences of which, in fact, continue to shape the regional and global environment of North Korea today), North Korea set out to become itself a "sun in the heavens" rather than to remain under the influence of one or the other existing sun of international socialism.

Important events in this development include Kim Il Sung's visit to Indonesia for the tenth anniversary of the Bandung Conference on Afro-Asian Solidarity in April 1965, during which he delivered a speech about three principles of his postcolonial revolutionary philosophy known collectively as *juch'e* (spirit of self-reli-

ance, according to the official North Korean translation): independence in politics
(*jaju*); self-reliance in the economy (*jarip*), which he argued was not incompatible
with receiving foreign economic aid; and self-defense in the military (*jawi*).[32]
During this visit, the then Indonesian president and leader of the Non-Aligned
Movement (NAM) presented Kim with the gift of a flower, which later became
the Kim Il Sung flower. In September 1977, Pyongyang held the first international
seminar devoted to deliberating on the *juch'e* ideology.[33] Shortly before this event,
Marshal Tito, president of Yugoslavia and another key figure in the NAM, came to
Pyongyang, where he received a triumphant welcome as well as the Order of Hero
of the DPRK (North Korea) from Kim Il Sung. The two leaders agreed that the
NAM had a most important role to play in world politics and that all progressive
parties must remain independent (from the Soviet Union and China) and march
along their own roads to socialism. Between these two events, North Korea made
a great effort, independently of China and the Soviet Union, to raise its status
in the NAM and to establish and strengthen ties of friendship with developing
countries in the Third World. It also invested considerable economic and military
resources into assisting revolutionary forces in Africa (Algeria, Angola, Congo,
Mozambique, Somalia, Sudan, Tanzania, Uganda, and Zambia), in Asia (Cambodia, Laos, and Yemen), and in Latin America (Argentina, Brazil, Columbia, Do-
minican Republic, Guatemala, Nicaragua, Uruguay, and Venezuela). At this time
North Korea clearly had ambitions of becoming a world-class revolutionary leader
in the postcolonial world, different from, yet as powerful as, China and the Soviet
Union. The traces of this ambition still reverberate in the contemporary world.
Libraries in places as diverse as Malta, Zimbabwe, and Iran still keep large quanti-
ties of books about Kim Il Sung and his *juch'e* philosophy. Streets and boulevards
named after Kim Il Sung still exist in many places across Asia and Africa.[34] Many
Sudanese still remember how North Korean advisors tried to teach them how to
perform a mass game—North Korea's proud public art form that depicts revolutionary slogans using thousands of handheld, multicolored pickets raised in a series
of absolutely synchronous movements, such as we see today in the Arirang Festival. A militant Ugandan cult, during that country's civil war, promoted the spirit of
Chung Po, representing the supplier of arms from North Korea, to a key position
in its hierarchy of spirit helpers.[35] Most recently, in April 2010, a large Ndebele-
speaking crowd gathered in western Zimbabwe to protest against the government's
plan to invite the North Korean national football team to set up a training camp in
the country in preparation for the 2010 World Cup in South Africa. The demonstra-
tors' grievance originates in the massacre of twenty thousand Ndebele rebels and
civilians in the early 1980s by Robert Mugabe's notorious Fifth Brigade troops,
who were trained, it is believed, by military instructors sent from North Korea.

These stories are known only locally in Sudan, Uganda, and Zimbabwe; they
are not mentioned in the existing literature of Cold War international history and
rarely appear in the ethnographic literature of sub-Saharan and southern Africa.
Above all, the negative and violent aspects of these transnational Cold War histor-

ical episodes are traceless in the many gifts with tags of Sudanese or Zimbabwean origin preserved and proudly displayed in the Myohyangsan International Friendship Exhibition Hall. The stories that these gifts tell are instead carefully crafted to fit into the single narrative that the hall aims to relate about North Korea's international friendships—about the guiding "sun" of the postcolonial world. One story is about a gift from Sudan called "Long Live Walking Stick." According to this story, widely disseminated in North Korea through school and workplace study meetings, a Sudanese teacher named Mohammed wished to present a gift to Kim Il Sung for his sixtieth birthday. He thought of a walking stick, following the Sudanese cultural custom of presenting walking sticks to respected tribal elders. The choice was also made based on Mohammed's reading of Kim's revolutionary biographical history. Through this reading, he learned that the Great Leader walked many miles every year while doing his endless on-the-spot-guidance trips to numerous places. So he decided that a walking stick would make a perfect gift for the eminent leader, whose health and longevity were of supreme importance "not only for Korean revolution but also the struggle for independence throughout the world."[36] But the gift had to be a special walking stick, for it was for a special occasion and a very special person. After failing to find the right type of material that he believed would suit the special gift, Mohammed heard about an aromatic sandalwood that existed only in India. He sent a telegram to his friend there,

Figure 5.3. Kim Il Sung welcoming Third World delegates. *Source: Pulmyŏlŭi yŏngsang* (Pyongyang: Literature and Art Press, 1992), 472.

asking for help finding the wood and explaining how important it would be for him and for people in the Third World to prepare the right kind of gift. His friend was eager to help but was unable to find the special sandalwood his Sudanese friend was looking for. One day, he met a timber merchant in Mumbai and asked him whether he knew about the wood. The merchant asked why he was looking for it and, hearing the story about the wishes of the man's Sudanese friend, was delighted to discover that it would be used to make a gift for the great leader of the Third World. The merchant took the trouble to fly to a distant, remote place in India to find the special sandalwood. The wood was then shipped to Sudan and, after long, hard work by the best Sudanese craftsmen, made into the "Long Live Walking Stick" that Mohammed had dreamt of.

These stories about gifts to Kim Il Sung make it abundantly clear that North Korea sought to attain international authority and fame by becoming a spiritual leader in the postcolonial world equal in status in that realm to the Soviet Union and China in the socialist world. This global diplomatic aspiration was intended to deflect the power and authority of the two superpower socialist states; yet, the manifestation of this ambition drew heavily on the artistic and diplomatic traditions developed by these same powerful neighbors. The display of gifts for Kim Il Sung was clearly an adaptation of the earlier spectacles surrounding birthday gifts to Stalin. The gifts of arms and military training offered by North Korea to various postcolonial revolutionary groups in Sudan, Zimbabwe, and elsewhere also derived from Soviet and Chinese internationalism. North Korea also borrowed from China many important symbolic instruments—for instance, the powerful tool to bring the charismatic leader close to citizens' hearts, the famous Mao badges. The cult of Mao Zedong peaked during the Cultural Revolution, during which Mao transformed himself "from essentially a military figure [into] a cosmocratic one . . . [into] a Chinese Socrates in full possession of logic and word."[37] The mass-produced Mao badges appeared in 1966 at the height of the Cultural Revolution and were universally worn by the Chinese as well as widely exchanged among the Red Guards.[38] North Korea's Kim Il Sung badges were first introduced in 1970 and mass-produced starting in 1972, the year of Kim Il Sung's sixtieth birthday.[39] In that year, contemporary North Korean art history claims, the country's revolutionary art production made a great leap forward in all fronts and genres, thanks to the genius and dedication of the Great Leader's future successor, Kim Jong Il. The Kim Il Sung badges were initially distributed to party cadres, who regarded wearing them as a token of their privilege, but they had been made available to the entire population by 1974. After that, the party cadres invented new, more sophisticated badges so that they could maintain their distinctiveness from ordinary people. Staring in 1982, the year of the Great Leader's seventieth birthday, the mass-produced tokens of intimacy between the leader and the people came to include badges bearing a portrait of Kim Jong Il. Many people subsequently wore two badges, one for the Great Leader and the other for the future leader, whereas others took to a more convenient model with the images of the two leaders etched on the same badge side by side. Not everyone could wear this convenient twin model, however. The outside world saw the badge-wearing custom of North Korea as a material symbol of the country's totalitarian culture and cult of personality. We have heard many painful stories about how North Korean travelers were looked down upon and ridiculed overseas because of the badges on their shirts. Inside North Korea, however, the badges are much more than a symbol of total social unity; they are an important indicator of the wearer's social and political status. As Andrei Lankov observes, "In many cases the badges can be seen as an insignia of a sort which can demonstrate the social status of the bearer."[40] Around the same time as the introduction of the Kim Jong Il badges, the portrait of the new leader was added to the walls of domestic homes, whereas before 1982 people hung only that of the Great Leader. Schoolchildren bow before and speak greetings to these portraits every morning before they greet their parents and grandparents; their parents, usually their mothers, clean the portraits' glass surfaces every morning before going to their workplaces. They do so using a white cloth stored in a special wooden box, which every household keeps underneath the leaders' portraits. After Kim Il Sung's death in 1994, when they prepared for their traditional death-day ancestral rites, North Korean families offered ceremonial greetings and food to the Great Leader's portrait before doing so for any deceased member of their own family. On these occasions, the food offerings pointed not only to the late leader but also to his successor and political partner, who also hung on the domestic wall, despite the fact that the latter was alive and therefore totally unfit to receive ceremonial food offerings to the dead. The successor's death in December 2011 may finally free North Korean households from this contradiction in their domestic ritual life.

The North Korean Exception

The North Korean public arts that developed in the 1970s were not works of great originality, borrowing, as they did, many of their constitutive elements from Stalin's Soviet Union and some from Mao's China. Despite lacking creativity in form, however, in terms of content, these works were exceptionally original. This substantive originality in North Korean public art since the 1970s is closely tied up with the single most exceptional quality of the North Korean polity compared to other revolutionary socialist polities: a transition of power based on hereditary charisma.

Some readers may have noticed by now that in describing the public expression of the North Korean leader's personal and historical charismatic authority either in the domestic or international sphere, we have refrained from using the well-known, obviously relevant expression "personality cult," and they may ask why. The avoidance was a conscious choice, and some explanation is due. The term "personality cult" is most closely associated, although not exclusively, with Stalinist Russia and, historically, with Nikita Khrushchev's secret speech in February 1956, three years after Stalin's death in March 1953, titled "The Personality Cult and Its Consequences." In it, Khrushchev confronted Stalin's *kul't lichnosti* (cult of personality), arguing that "the classics of Marxism-Leninism denounced every manifestation of the cult of the individual." The modern semantics of the cult of personality is therefore associated with the historical process in which such a phenomenon arises under extraordinary circumstances but disintegrates with the end of the cultic persona's physical life; accordingly, it is also associated with a historically retrospective, morally critical perspective on the phenomenon. The "cult of personality" in North Korea is neither a historically redundant nor an ideologically debunked phenomenon. As a matter of fact, it developed, radicalized, and prevailed in the North Korean context precisely because there were such revisionist attempts to discredit the authority of founding and formative revolutionary personae, first in the Soviet Union in the late 1950s and then in China in the mid-1970s, by which the North Korean leadership clearly felt threatened. The North Korean literature that narrates the virtuous character of Kim Jong Il often contrasts Kim with Khrushchev, depicting the latter as an emblematic figure in the history of socialism capable of some of the most undesirable human behaviors in the morality of socialist revolution: betrayal (of senior revolutionary figures) and treachery (toward the foundational revolutionary tradition).[41] Balázs Szalontai observes in his informative study based on Hungarian and former Soviet archives that Kim Il Sung's successful defiance of Soviet de-Stalinization played a major role in the evolution of North Korean politics.[42] The Stalinesque personality cult therefore advanced in North Korea not merely on its own but rather in reaction to the forceful dynamics of de-Stalinization happening in its immediate international environment and among its key allies.[43] That is to say, the cultification of Kim Il Sung from the mid-1960s and its radicalization from the 1970s were a form of crisis management. Following Max Weber, we may understand the development as an effort to routinize personal charisma in the face of structural challenges to the charismatic authority. The cult of Kim Il Sung that developed in this international crisis of revolutionary charisma, therefore, was not a "cult of personality" in the conventional sense. Rather, it was a particular political form representing a local resistance to the general, global process of bureaucratic rationalization of political rule in the socialist international world.

Kim Il Sung said, "We have many revolutionary comrades and friends internationally. The international solidarity of our revolution continues to grow strong." In light of the above discussion, this statement should be understood as actually meaning that North Korea can have as many international revolutionary friends as China or the Soviet Union, despite its movement along a different revolutionary pathway from them. The "international solidarity of our revolution" looked increasingly toward the postcolonial world rather than the existing socialist international order, and in this process, the identity of "our revolution" also took on an increasingly postcolonial character. North Korea indeed played an active role in the postcolonial world within the milieu that some historians call the second Cold War—the eruption of violent bi- and tripolar political conflicts in Africa and the Middle East with prolific interventions by the United States, the Soviet

Union, and China—and we do not doubt that it took its global role and status very seriously. Nevertheless, it is also beyond doubt that the North Korean leadership's truly vital, primarily self-interested and self-serving ambition lay behind its outward ambition to become a global actor separate from the Soviet Union and China. North Korea's true ambition was to be unlike China and the Soviet Union in terms of the fate of charismatic revolutionary authority—that is, it wanted to resist the inevitable demise of personal charisma in the progression of history.

This commitment to transcend the political life cycle of personal charisma, the eventual fall of which is, in Weberian theory, part of a natural historical process, explains why North Korea invented and has propagated the *juch'e* idea since 1965. Other than the principles of political self-determination and economic self-reliance, the idea claims, at a metaphysical level, that human will and agency are ultimately the only meaningful qualities in historical progress and thereby rejects the principles of Marxist historical materialism. In lay language, the *juch'e* idea posits that nothing is determined in the historical process and that human beings can achieve extraordinary historical progress if their individual and collective wills are properly focused and guided. Many observers focus on the last aspect, arguing that the *juch'e* theory is intended to justify the centralization of power in the hands of Kim Il Sung, the only source of proper guidance for the collective will. The super-androcentric theory had a further, implicit, yet far-reaching message, however. This message was that a human society, properly guided and directed, would be able to overcome the constraints of history against the durability of personal charisma.

Figure 5.4. Kim Il Sung birthday anniversary (*T'aeyangjŏl*, "Day of Sun") march by international delegates on April 15, 2002. *Source: Chosun* 542 (June 2002): 10.

The ethos of this politicized androcentrism is referred to, in popular North Korean language, as the "We can do it" (*hamyŏn doinda*) revolutionary spirit or as "We will do it, once the party decides it."[44] In the country's most vital political project to realize the routinization of charisma, only North Korea's recently deceased leader, Kim Jong Il, could have played the most pivotal role since the early 1970s. He directed the most important, inventive state projects concerning the Great Leader's public eminence and aura: the powerful revolutionary performative art that restored and magnified the Manchurian story to legendary proportions. He orchestrated the equally powerful monumental art projects of national and global relevance, including the Graves of Revolutionary Martyrs and the International Friendship Exhibition Hall. It was he who understood that the routinization of revolutionary charisma required nothing less than the power of a theater state in order to confront the force of history that works against the life of charismatic authority—the force that engulfed even the twentieth century's most powerful revolutionary polities. According to the popular North Korean publication titled *Collection of Legends about the Kŭmsusan (Kim Il Sung) Memorial Palace*, "Human beings are the master of their own destiny. All other entities of the world must serve human welfare and happiness. The great ideology teaches that humans are the supreme rulers of the world and able to conquer and tame the heavens. This great philosophical thought was created by the father of humanity and the great man of global fame, Comrade Kim Il Sung. These are the iron principles of *juch'e* and the theory of human self-reliance that Comrade Kim Jong Il inherited and brought forward."[45]

The result was indeed close to a triumph over history. The *juch'e* theory worked: there was no outcry about "the cult of personality and its consequences" after the death of Kim Il Sung in 1994, and the Great Leader's authority continued to shine and thrive in North Korea's political landscape. It is not surprising that the theory worked, however, for it was, from its very inception, meant to be principally a manual written for local purposes and for the routinization and perpetuation of local charismatic authority, despite its apparent claim to universal validity in the postcolonial world.

The North Korean writer Kwak Sŏng Ho said of the gifts for the Great Leader and those for his successor that he saw at the Myohyangsan International Friendship Exhibition Hall "the world in Chosun" as well as "Chosun in the world." He saw, on the one hand, an evident connection between "the world in Chosun" displayed in this place and, on the other, the "Chosun in the world" the display intends to show—North Korea's dignity and majesty in the world community. In order to see this connection as clearly as the writer, we need to leave the hall's many rooms and endless rows of gifts to join the long queue to enter the single most important room of the entire hall. In the far interior of the dark room stands a life-sized wax figure of the late Great Leader wearing a suit and hat, behind him a bright scene of Three Lakes (an important historic site in the legend of the Manchurian partisans). The visitors to this chamber must stand in well-ordered lines to bow toward the wax figure (which is a gift from China; see also the conclusion to this volume), while listening to the song "Song of General Kim Il Sung."

The gifts displayed in the International Friendship Exhibition Hall are demonstratively global in scale; yet, the meaning of this international gift economy is interwoven with the webs of gift relations in the domestic sphere, between the leader and the people. An employee at the hall, a graduate of Kim Il Sung University in literature who was working as a guide for visitors, explained that the hall was actually a great ethnological museum, bringing together in one place all the material cultures of the world. Thanks to the hall, she said, the people of North Korea, unlike peoples in other countries, did not have to travel far to experience and learn about other cultures. Then the guide said that the hall was a very special kind of ethnological museum, for it was a gift to the people of North Korea from the Great Leader. She said conclusively, "In our republic, the Supreme Leader dedicates everything to the people, and the people dedicate all loyalty to the Supreme Leader. All these gifts are what the Great Leader has dedicated to the people." In the next chapter, we turn to North Korea's domestic political gift economy and how this politico-economic order underwent a radical structural and moral crisis after the death of Kim Il Sung.

Notes

1. Woo-Young Lee, *Bukhansahoiŭi sangjingchegye yŏn'gu: Hyŏkmyŏngguhoŭi byŏnhwarŭl jungsimŭro* [A study of symbolic system of North Korean society: Changes in revolutionary slogans] (Seoul: Institute of Unification Studies, 2002), 53.

2. "Sae segiŭi daegŏljak [The masterpiece of the new century]," *Rodong Sinmun*, July19, 2002.

3. "Sae segiŭi daegŏljak [The masterpiece of the new century]."

4. "A, nae choguk! [Ah, my country!]," *Rodong Sinmun*, September 6, 2009.

5. Kim Jong Il's speech delivered at the Central Committee of the Workers' Party, Pyongyang, February 11, 1996.

6. Moon-Woong Lee, *Bukhan jŏngch'imunhwaŭi hyŏngsŏnggwa gŭ t'ŭkjing* [The formation and characteristics of North Korean political culture] (Seoul: Institute of National Unification, 1976), 38.

7. *The International Friendship Exhibition* (Pyongyang: 1990) (pamphlet in English).

8. See B. R. Myers, *The Cleanest Race: How North Koreans See Themselves and Why It Matters* (Brooklyn, NY: Melville House Publishing, 2010), 76–77.

9. His overseas, on-the-spot guidance trips on the train amount to 368,000 kilometers, according to the information displayed on the wall of the exhibition hall.

10. Ki-Hwan Choi, *Yŏngwŏnhan t'aeyang Kim Il Sungjusŏk* [Eternal sun, Chairman Kim Il Sung] (Pyongyang: Pyongyang Press, 2002), 127–28. See also

"Kim Il Sungjusŏknimŭn onŭldo sŏnmulŭl batŭsimnida [Chairman Kim Il Sung continues to receive gifts today]," *Rodong Sinmun* August 8, 2004.

11. Song-Ho Kwak, "Bomulgo [The treasure house]," *Chŏngnyŏnmunhak* [Youth literature], no. 7 (2010): 16–17.

12. Kwak, "Bomulgo [The treasure house]."

13. "Kim Il Sungminjokŭi chonŏmgwa yŏnggwang [Dignity and honor of the people of Kim Il Sung]," *Rodong Sinmun*, July 5, 2009.

14. "Kangkye jŏngsinŭro ŏksege ssawŏnagaja [Let's struggle along force-fully in the spirit of Kangkye]," *Rodong Sinmun*, April 22, 2000.

15. Jeffrey Brooks, *Thank You, Comrade Stalin!: Soviet Public Culture from Revolution to Cold War* (Princeton, NJ: Princeton University Press, 2000), 105.

16. Brooks, *Thank You, Comrade Stalin!*, 74, 83–105.

17. Brooks, *Thank You, Comrade Stalin!*, 89.

18. Reuben Fowkes, "The Role of Monumental Sculpture in the Construction of Socialist Space in Stalinist Hungary," in *Socialist Spaces: Sites of Everyday Life in the Eastern Bloc*, ed. David Crowley and Susan E. Reid (Oxford: Berg, 2002), 77.

19. Sergei Goncharov, John Lewis, and Litai Xue, *Uncertain Partners: Stalin, Mao, and the Korean War* (Stanford, CA: Stanford University Press, 1993), 84.

20. Helen Womack and Tom Harper, "To Russia with Love," *Daily Telegraph*, October 29, 2006.

21. Cited in Nikolai Ssorin-Chaikov, "On Heterochrony: Birthday Gifts to Stalin, 1949," *Journal of the Royal Anthropological Institute* 12, no. 2 (2006): 368.

22. Ssorin-Chaikov, "On Heterochrony," 357.

23. Ssorin-Chaikov, "On Heterochrony," 358.

24. Brooks, *Thank You, Comrade Stalin!*, 83–84.

25. *Exposición de la amistad internacional, ediciones en lenguas extranjeras* (Pyongyang, RPD de Corea, 1982) (pamphlet in Spanish), 4. See also *The International Friendship Exhibition* (Pyongyang: 1990).

26. Charles K. Armstrong, "Socialism, Sovereignty, and the North Korean Exception," in *North Korea: Toward a Better Understanding*, ed. Sonia Ryang (Plymouth, MA: Lexington Books, 2009), 45.

27. Armstrong, "Socialism, Sovereignty, and the North Korean Exception," 45.

28. The quoted phrase is cited from Young C. Kim, "North Korea and the Third World," in *North Korea in a Regional and Global Context*, ed. Robert A. Scalapino and Hongkoo Lee (Berkeley: Institute of East Asian Studies, University of California, Berkeley, 1986), 328.

29. Kim, "North Korea and the Third World," 328.

30. Kim, "North Korea and the Third World," 329.

31. Sergey Radchenko, *Two Suns in the Heavens: The Sino-Soviet Struggle for Supremacy, 1962–1967* (Stanford, CA: Stanford University Press, 2009).

32. Bruce Cumings lucidly writes, "Self-reliance is not a matter of mere rhetoric. North Korea offers the best example in the postcolonial developing world of conscious withdrawal from the capitalist world system and a serious attempt to construct an independent, self-contained economy; as a result it is the most autarkic industrial economy in the world. Unlike Albania in the socialist world and Burma in the 'free world,' two countries that 'withdrew' to no apparent purpose as their economies idled along or got worse, North Korea never idled but always raced. This was withdrawal with development, withdrawal for development." Cited from Bruce Cumings, *Korea's Place in the Sun: A Modern History* (New York: W. W. Norton, 1997), 419–20.

33. For a broad overview of North Korea's relations with Southeast Asian nations within its broader engagement with the Third World, see Kook-Chin Kim, "An Overview of North Korean–Southeast Asian Relations," in *The Foreign Relations of North Korea*, ed. Jae Kyu Park, Byung Chul Koh, and Tae-Hwan Kwak (Boulder, CO: Westview Press, 1987), 353–78. Kim argues that the Bandung Conference of 1955 "turned out to be a watershed in the inauguration of Pyongyang's Third World diplomacy" (Kim, "An Overview of North Korean–Southeast Asian Relations," 368). For a concise introduction to *juch'e* principles, see Charles K. Armstrong, "A Socialism of Our Style: North Korean Ideology in a Post-Communist Era," in *North Korean Foreign Relations in the Post–Cold War Era*, ed. Samuel S. Kim (New York: Oxford University Press, 1998), 34–38; also Jacques L. Fuqua, *Nuclear Endgame: The Need for Engagement with North Korea* (Newport, CT: Praeger, 2007), 37.

34. For a brief overview of North Korea's vigorous engagement with Africa in the 1960s and 1970s, see Jae Kyu Park, "North Korea's Foreign Policy toward Africa," in *The Foreign Relations of North Korea*, ed. Jae Kyu Park, Byung Chul Koh, and Tae-Hwan Kwak (Boulder, CO: Westview Press, 1987), 436–61.

35. Janice Boddy, *Wombs and Alien Spirits: Women, Men and the Zār Cult in Northern Sudan* (Madison: University of Wisconsin Press, 1989), 165; Heike Behrend, "Power to Heal, Power to Kill," in *Spirit Possession: Modernity and Power in Africa*, ed. Heike Behrend and Ute Luig (Oxford: James Currey, 1999), 25–26.

36. Song-Chol Cho, "Jŏlseŭi uiinŭl gyŏngmohanŭn maninŭi sun'gyŏlhan maŭm [The pure hearts that worship the great human being of all times]," *Rodong Sinmun*, June 1, 2007.

37. David E. Apter, "Yan'an and the Narrative Reconstruction of Reality," in *China in Transformation*, ed. Tu Wei-Ming (Cambridge, MA: Harvard University Press, 1994), 211.

38. Michael Dutton, *Streetlife China* (Cambridge: Cambridge University Press, 1998), 244–45.

39. Andrei Lankov, *North of the DMZ: Essays on Daily Life in North Korea* (Jefferson, NC: McFarland, 2007), 7.

40. Lankov, *North of the DMZ*, 8.

41. For instance, see the manuscript *The Character of a Just Man: Who Is General Kim Jong Il?*, Chongryon.com, http://www.chongryon.com/k/mc/kim/21-new/2-4.htm (February 17, 2010).

42. Balázs Szalontai, *Kim Il Sung in the Khrushchev Era: Soviet-DPRK Relations and the Roots of North Korean Despotism, 1953–1964* (Washington, DC: Woodrow Wilson Center Press, 2005), 241.

43. On Kim Il Sung's reaction to Khrushchev's secret speech, see Szalontai, *Kim Il Sung in the Khrushchev Era*, 85–112.

44. The slogan "We can do it" (*hamyŏn doenda*) is hardly unique to North Korea. Similar ideas were prevalent in the state-driven economic and social mobilization in South Korea under the rule of Park Chung-Hee as well as in Japan's Meiji-era mass politics.

45. Woo-Kyung Kim, Ki-Chun Dong, and Jong-Suk Kim, *Kŭmsusan'ginyŏmgungjŏn chŏnsŏlchip* [Legends of Kŭmsusan memorial palace], Vol. 1 (Pyongyang: Literature and Art Press, 2004), 75–76.

6

The Moral Economy

Ideas about gifts provide insights into North Korea's formal domestic politico-economic order as well as its asserted stateliness in international relations. As in Joseph Stalin's Russia and Mao Zedong's China, both of which explained the structure of their mass politics and mass-mobilized economy partly in terms of reciprocal gift giving between the charismatic leader and the people, these ideas were vital to the political process and development in North Korea, especially since the 1970s.

Socialism is often referred to as substantive economic democracy based on the principle of egalitarian access to and distribution of social goods, in contrast to the formal democracy of liberal states founded on ideas of universal suffrage and personal liberty to pursue better access to social goods.[1] In its early years, North Korea had great success in building a state and economic system along the model of substantive democracy, rapidly transforming the impoverished, highly stratified, and primarily agrarian society left by long colonial domination into an energetic, industrial society enjoying distributive justice and universal literacy. The country achieved this in a relatively short period and with relatively little social turbulence and political violence, compared to other revolutionary social-ist states. The last was, in large measure, an ironically positive consequence of the Korean War, which, although it literally reduced North Korea to ashes and caused unimaginable suffering among its population, nevertheless contributed to eliminating existing class conflicts and social inequalities. The war resulted in poverty and deprivation for everyone; it also uprooted potential class and politi-cal enemies, many of whom moved to South Korea during the war. On the other hand, the Korean War also led to the rise of an elaborate mechanism of mass mobilization in North Korea, which, after the war, was effectively used in eco-nomic recovery and, subsequently, in building a state-controlled, collectivized economy. The result was impressive. By 1956, merely three years after the end of the devastating war, North Korea had recovered its prewar level of agricultural production and, in industrial output, doubled its prewar capacity, achieving a stun-ning annual industrial growth rate of 45 percent in 1957.[2] The collectivization of agriculture was completed by the end of the 1950s. During the same period, the country achieved a series of other major social reforms, including, among others, free education for primary and secondary schools, state-sanctioned equal rights for women in workplaces, state-subsidized medical service, and a welfare system for war invalids and the families of the fallen. Against this background of successful mass mobilization, famous British Keynesian economist Joan Robinson, after her visit to Pyongyang in October 1964, wrote a report called "Korean Miracle," praising "the intense concentration of the Koreans on national pride" in North Korea's social economic development, led by the country's leader, Kim Il Sung, who was "a messiah rather than a dictator."[3]

A great number of people in postwar North Korea undoubtedly held a firm commitment to bettering their economic and social conditions, and they indeed showed genuine, intense concentration of will, as Robinson noted, in making their collective community a proud place. It is also beyond doubt that the country's "messiah," Kim Il Sung, played a pivotal role in raising and directing the popular commitment and will toward a focused, mobilized social force for the collective good. North Korea adopted, from its very early days, the Stakhanovite drive for labor heroism, propagating passionate and miraculous labor as the principal civic virtue. Later, its labor heroism changed character, taking on a more militaristic

Figure 6.1. Chollima (thousand-mile horse) movement memorial. *Source: Chosun* 541 (May 2000): 140.

form and adopting slogans and images relating to the heroic Manchurian partisans and the heroic martyrs of the Korean War. However, it also created some unique ways to arouse passion and enthusiasm for labor among the masses. Notable in this matter was Kim Il Sung's on-the-spot-guidance art of rule, a very modern form of pageantry involving intimate contacts between the charismatic ruler and the ordinary worker-citizens. A foreign observer of North Korea who travelled widely in the country told us how very impressed he had been by the extent to which the late leader had practiced his on-the-spot guidance during his lifetime, as testified to by the large number of local sites of memory existing in all corners of North Korea dedicated to the leader's visits. He observed that anyone who could engage in this intimate contact with people so prolifically would make a powerful charismatic leader.[4] Helen-Louise Hunter writes about the power of Kim's signature art of modern pageantry, "He conveyed a deep personal interest in the lives of the people, worked tirelessly for the national good (as he saw it), and maintained the image of a man of the people. Moreover, his particular style of leadership, featuring endless tours of the country, kept him in close touch with the population where his personality was used to the fullest."[5] Hunter quotes Prince Norodom Sihanouk of Cambodia, who spent some time in North Korea: "Kim has a rela-

Figure 6.2. Kim Il Sung during his on-the-spot-guidance trip to Hwang-hae steel mill. *Source: Kim Il Sungdongjiŭi widaehan juch'esasangŭi kich'iddara* (Pyongyang: Foreign Literature Press, 1972), 2.

tionship with his people that every other leader in the world would envy."[6] Due to the combination of these two great arts of socialist economy, the virtue of miraculous labor and the efficacy of modern pageantry in generating this civic virtue, one borrowed from the Soviet Union and the other largely original, the public gift economy in North Korea took on a different form from that in the Soviet Union. Unlike Soviet shock workers, who received entitlements or gifts from Stalin, the labor heroes of North Korea did not necessarily have to be rewarded with material benefits from the state. For the North Korean heroes, the most meaningful gift from the state was supposed to be the leader's visit to their workplace, which constituted the ultimate public acknowledgment of their dedicated labor. This became particularly the case in the late 1960s when, according to some observers, "North Korean society became centered on the Supreme Leader to such an extent and intensity that we cannot even easily apply the general idea of the cult of personality to the phenomenon."[7]

The above process was further radicalized in the 1970s amid a declining domestic economy and mounting political crisis in the international socialist solidarity, as described in the previous chapter, and it gave birth to a new logic of the gift. As Kim Il Sung's charismatic authority evolved from a sublime form to an

Figure 6.3. "We are all our general's family" (calligraphy hung on the wall of many households). *Source:* Photo by Byung-Ho Chung (2003).

extreme degree, it aspired not only to encompass the entire foundation of North Korea's political sovereignty but also to incorporate the entire working order of its national economy and the entire spectrum of civic life from the public to the domestic sphere. The Great Leader became the beating heart of the revolutionary polity as a historical entity, the genesis of which, in turn, became equivalent to the leader's biographical history. This made the life of every citizen conceptually part of the leader's personified sovereign body and the citizen's economic life part of the superorganic household economy headed by the leader—hence, the slogan "We are the general's family (*janggunnim siksol*), which is widely displayed in the domestic space of North Korean households. Moreover, it made the very material fact of being a North Korean, and having a political home and enjoying a meaningful political life in the home, fundamentally a gift from the leader's exemplary historical life—the élan vital of the revolutionary partisan statehood and of the collective organic life of the family state. Lee Moon-Woong observes in his work on North Korea as a family state, "Children at nursery school are taught that the food they receive at school is a gift from the Supreme Leader. They also learn how to express gratitude to the leader for the gift."[8] The ethos of the state as a superorganic family is well expressed by the song "We Celebrate Our Supreme Leader's Longevity and Health," released in the wake of Kim Il Sung's sixtieth birthday in 1972:

To the single purpose of bringing us happiness,
Our Supreme Leader dedicates his entire life.
From his parental love and embrace,
Has blossomed our happiness today.
We shall follow you to the end of the heaven and earth,
We shall serve you until the day that the sun and the moon disappear.
Keeping our indebtedness to you for generations and generations,
We shall be loyal to you in one single heart.
Looking up to our great parent,
Your people celebrate your longevity and health.

The related ideas of the political community as a household writ large and of the political home as a gift from the exemplary leader are also prominent in other songs released in the same anniversary context. The song "Nothing to Envy in the World" is explicit about the ethos of North Korea's family state:

The sky is blue; my heart is in joy,
And I hear the sound of an organ.
I love my country
Where people live in harmony.
Our father is the Supreme Commander Kim Il Sung,
Our house is the [Workers'] Party's embrace,
And all of us are real blood brothers and sisters.
I have nothing to envy in the world.

Another song titled "In One Single Heart" is clear about the moral obligations of the dwellers in the happy political household. This song is not only important in the repertoire of North Korea's political literacy but also widely used as a love song among the youth:

> The happiness we enjoy today,
> Who gave it to us?
> It is the Workers' Party,
> It is our leader.
> Along the way led by the Supreme Commander Kim Il Sung,
> We shall follow it to our death,
> In one single heart.

As poignantly mentioned by Marcel Mauss, however, gifts may contain poison (in the old Germanic language, "poison" and "gift" have the same epistemological root), creating a relationship of dependence and subordination between the donor and the recipient. With reference to "the law of the gift" observed among the Brahmans, Mauss mentions the old saying that "To receive from the king is honey at first and ends as poison."[9] Part of his insight applies to the gift of political life that concerns us here. Citizenship in North Korea includes not only the right to enjoy the gift of true political life given by the founding leader but also the obligation to recognize deeply one's personal indebtedness to this gift of life and to show this recognition in concrete actions through deeds of loyalty to the donor and to his house of dominion. As we saw earlier with regard to the idea of the partisan state, this reciprocal relationship between the head of state and the citizens is explained in North Korea's political literacy as having originated in the era of the patriotic Manchurian anticolonial armed resistance. Considering the flip side of the partisan state idea, the family state, we may also say that the reciprocal relationship between the leader and the people takes on ethical principles as well as political imperatives. The state takes the form of a household writ large according to this scheme, which means, by extension, that members of the political household (i.e., citizens) are all entitled to benevolent care and material provision from the head of the household (i.e., the leader of the political organic community). It also means, as manifested in the idiom of "unity of loyalty and filial piety" discussed in chapter 2, that the beneficiaries of the material and spiritual care must reciprocate with deep filial loyalty to the head of the political household and, after the household head passes away, by cherishing his legacy as if it were a family ancestral memory. North Korea's politico-economic order since the 1970s is, therefore, based on a particular, politicized form of human reciprocal relations: a paternalistic, patriarchal formation modeled on domestic relations, particularly the relationship between parents and children.

Anthropological literature refers to the above form of relations as generalized reciprocity, as opposed to restricted reciprocity. The latter points to what we would normally mean by exchange relations, including barter, commerce, and commod-

Figure 6.4. Children receiving bundles of gifts from the leader.
Source: T'aeyanggwa ch'ŏngch'un (Pyongyang: Gǔmsǔng Youth
Press, 1999), 122.

ity or monetary exchanges. In this exchange system, the actors are rational and calculating agents, playing within and respecting the rule of the game, which is to part with one's valuable object for the purpose of obtaining another valuable, more needed object from someone else. People may practice this exchange to fulfill concrete mutual economic needs (such as fishermen exchanging fish with farmers for cereals) or for cultural and ceremonial reasons (such as two groups of hunters exchanging game meat with each other). Although a varying degree of practical rationality exists in restricted reciprocity (e.g., sharing meat has relatively weaker practical rationality than exchanging fish for grain), this form of reciprocity must have some degree of rationality, as defined in the premise of the *Homo economicus*. In contrast to restricted reciprocity, in which some kind of economic reasoning is embedded, generalized reciprocity is characterized by the absence of this reasoning. Actors in this circuit part with a valuable object not for the purpose of acquiring a different valuable object or in expectation of an equivalent or higher return but for moral reasons. Sharing food and care within a family or other similarly close circle of people is a prominent example of generalized reciprocity. This form of reciprocity does not necessarily have to involve altruistic attitudes; yet, it must be based on some form of moral principle of sharing, although the details may vary across societies.

According to a former high-ranking North Korean official who defected to South Korea in the mid-1990s, "In a situation where all means of production actually belong to the Great Leader, the economy itself naturally serves the interests of the Great Leader before all else. The national economy is nothing more than the household economy of the Great Leader."[10] If it is indeed the case that managing the national economy is equivalent to running a household economy in North Korea, we may ask, in light of the contrast between generalized and restricted reciprocity mentioned above, what moral principles constitute the order of the political household economy. When the household economy runs into difficulties, moreover, who will take the blame for the hardship suffered by its members? In other words, within the scheme of the partisan family state, is there a structural contradiction between, on the one hand, the historical authority and the personal and hereditary charisma derived from the revolutionary partisan legend and, on the other, the moral authority of the charismatic leaders deriving from their role in good household management and securing the subsistence of the members of the house? We briefly touched upon this question in chapter 1 with reference to the supremacy of politics over economy in post–Kim Il Sung North Korea.[11] The death of Kim Il Sung coincided with a grave economic and subsistence crisis unprecedented in the country's history. We agree with other observers that an understanding of today's North Korean society is not possible without an understanding of its experience of the Arduous March, the extreme food crisis that started in the mid-1990s. In this final chapter, we return to the critical question with which we started our discussion of North Korea's stateliness in the physical absence of the country's founding charismatic leader, and we will consider how North Korea's paternalistic political order has coped with the most radical moral failure for a family state: allowing the collective household suffering from hunger and famine.

North Korea after 1994 is not same country as North Korea before that year. This is in part because the country lost its paramount center of moral and spiritual unity, Kim Il Sung, in July 1994, which has since provoked forceful commemorative politics (see chapter 1). However, 1994 was also the beginning of an unprecedented human crisis in modern North Korean history and one of the most devastating humanitarian catastrophes in modern Korean history as a whole: the great North Korean famine, or the Arduous March, as the disaster is called in contemporary North Korea.

Kim Jong Il's rule of North Korea began with these two powerful death events: the death of the country's irreplaceable founding father and the mass starvation and death of countless numbers of the leader's political children. Although these tragedies happened coincidentally and bore no apparent relationship to each other, they nevertheless became closely intertwined in the experience and memory of the North Korean people. The two events are intertwined also in the sense that an understanding of how the state and society coped with one was closely related to how they reacted to the other. The two death events overlapped in their unfolding as well. The mourning for Kim Il Sung nominally lasted for three years, from 1994 to 1997; the most critical period of the North Korean famine was from 1995 to 1998. Whereas the shock of losing the Great Leader later developed into a commemorative heritage politics that aimed to minimize the impact of Kim's death on society by defining the current-day politics as a revelation of the late leader's historical legacy, the mass suffering and death caused by the famine destroyed any possibility of an unproblematic continuity of North Korea's social order across the threshold of the mid-1990s. The legacy and continuity paradigm that was loudly advocated in the process of political succession, therefore, faced a tragic upheaval and radical rupture in the socioeconomic order, which had fundamentally to do with the collapse of the country's centralized economic and food-distribution system. Earlier we discussed this system in terms of politicized gift-exchange relations between a radically personified paternalistic state, on the one hand, and a society made into a household writ large, on the other. The rest of this chapter discusses how the shortage of food changed the moral ties and practical relations between the state and society. Before we proceed to the origin and meanings of the famine in North Korea, however, it will be instructive to introduce the idea of moral economy, which we believe helps to speak about the unspeakable human tragedy of the Arduous March and what it meant to ordinary North Koreans.

The Idea of Moral Economy

The idea of moral economy is being strongly revived in contemporary social studies, particularly in the scholarship of former socialist societies in Russia and eastern and central Europe. In fact, the idea defines one of the principal research arenas in what is today commonly called postsocialist or postcommunist studies. Eminent anthropologist of the former Soviet Union Caroline Humphrey employs the idea (related to the notion of everyday economy) in describing the transitional dynamics in today's Russian society from a command economy to a different politico-economic form characterized by the privatization of the means of production and the inception of market relations. Humphrey describes how the imported ideas and imposed forces of the liberal market are negotiated, in communities of the former Soviet Union, with the preexisting economic practices and norms that she calls everyday economy. The latter in this context refers to the experience of relative economic security within institutional, bureaucratic socialism and that of the informal economy, which prospered in socialist societies in parallel with the institutional forms. Humphrey emphasizes the informal barter network and practice in the Soviet Union and Mongolia, whose importance, in her observation, continues and is even increasing in the current situation of increasing deregulation of economic life.[12]

Anthropologist and specialist in contemporary eastern Europe Chris Hann similarly tries to redefine socialism in the language of moral economy rather than that of political economy. He writes, "The everyday moral communities of socialism have been undermined but not replaced. Nor does lacing capitalist consumerism with increased doses of national sentiment seem to produce the desired results."[13] The emphasis of these scholars on the moral economy of everyday life is partly a reaction to the dominance of liberal macroeconomic ideas at the institutional level, both among the policy makers of the former Eastern bloc states and among advisors from Western states.[14] It is observed that the former are sometimes stronger believers in the assumptions about *Homo economicus* than the latter, as well as more militant advocates of outright market liberalization. According to some observers, in the radical transition of the Eastern bloc states from previously paternalistic providers of social security to aggressive pursuers of corporate freedom and economic utopianism, society is thrown into a state of limbo, since it has to deal with "the debris left over from communism as well as the chaos of the new order."[15] For sociologist Zygmunt Bauman, postsocialism signifies a liminal condition—suspended in the uncertain state of neither being severed from the socialist past nor being integrated into a wider capitalist reality—and this condition is engendered by the prevailing forces to classify social entities in terms of either this or that social form.[16]

Following these accounts, it transpires that the duality of socialism and capitalism has changed from a spatial notion based on geographically discrete political blocs, passing the threshold of 1989, to a temporal notion, which entails a movement from one to the other form, plus all the repercussions that this transition involves. "Transition" is indeed a keyword in postsocialist studies, being used sometimes almost synonymously with the idea of postsocialism and understood as "a temporary state between two fixed positions, a movement between the point of departure and that of arrival."[17] Opinions vary as to what the prospective point of arrival should be and whether it will entail a full incorporation of a western European–style free market economy and liberal democracy or, rather, a perpetual process of coming close to (yet never reaching) that ideal. About the point of departure, however, researchers of postsocialist social transitions seem to have a broad consensus, identifying it unambiguously with the end of the Cold War.

Hann defines the Cold War as the "struggle between capitalism and socialism" and writes that this struggle has been over since 1989.[18] At the same time, he characterizes the struggle as "a long drawn out contest that decisively framed the political consciousness of most of the world's population while it lasted and continues to exercise pervasive effects a decade after it was apparently won by 'the free world.'"[19] Trying to come to terms with his apparently contradictory statements about the end of the ideological struggle, on the one hand, and about the old struggle's persistent and pervasive effects on the contemporary world, on the other, it transpires that the latter is in fact what Hann intends to address with the idea of postsocialism. Hann divides the bipolar history of Europe into two kinds and places them selectively across the threshold of 1989. One is the Cold War as a geopolitical order, and this is left in the pre-1989 background. The other is called

the postsocialist transition after the Cold War, in which the conflicts between local norms and global forces are highlighted. The idea of moral economy is introduced into the descriptions of these conflicts, allocated to popular conceptions of
economic justice and related resistance against all-out liberalization of economic
relations according to the laissez-faire free market ideology.

A set of intriguing issues arises from Hann's postsocialist research agenda.
One of them concerns the revival of the idea of moral economy, an important conceptual tool among certain social historians and anthropologists in the 1960s and
1970s. British historian E. P. Thompson excavated the term from the pamphlet-
eers of the eighteenth-century English food riots in his monumental social history
of that period.[20] In its original meaning, the idea of moral economy represented
the ethos of popular resistance against the ideology of free trade, particularly concerning subsistence goods. For Thompson, the idea of moral economy permitted
a critical review of the rising philosophy of the free market in the eighteenth
century. He described the food crisis among the English workers during early industrialization, explored it in relation to Adam Smith's proposition that local food
shortages in Europe would be solved only by a general, full liberalization of grain
distribution, and concluded that Smith's philosophical treatise on the free market
in *The Wealth of Nations*, which turned into a bible for policy makers during the
time, in fact contributed to aggravating rather than solving the food crisis. Anthropologist James Scott later studied the peasant rebellions in colonial Southeast
Asia from a related perspective and explored what he called "the moral economy
of peasants" in terms of their subsistence ethic.[21] Scott argued that peasants took
to organized acts of protest when the intensity of economic exploitation reached
an unbearable level, which broke their traditional ethical principles about subsistence and communal survival.

Thompson and Scott wrote about moral economies at the height of the Cold
War conflict, when a growing number of historians and sociologists were interested in social and political movements, stimulated by the multitude of revolutionary upheavals in the decolonizing world and also disturbed by the intensity
of the countermeasures taken by Western industrial powers against revolutionary
movements. The idea of moral economy therefore arose from critical intellectual
engagement with Cold War global politics, despite the fact that the idea was expressed in literature with reference to eighteenth-century England or nineteenth-
century French Indochina. Thompson's intellectual career testifies to the above
point. He was a historian who wrote about the moral economy of English food
rioters, but at the same time, he was a public intellectual who was deeply engaged
with the predicaments of bipolarized Europe. For Thompson, moral economy
spoke essentially of an economic and social history "from below," and he approached the divided political reality of Europe from this perspective, empha-
sizing the mobilization of popular consciousness and initiatives "from below"
against the Iron Curtain. Against this background, it is interesting to note that
the idea of moral economy has been revived today in the academic discourse of

postsocialism, now identified with the negative effects of parting the curtain and everyday resistance to these effects.

The idea of moral economy is also relevant in the North Korean context and for understanding the transition the society is undergoing today. This is so, however, not according to how the idea is discussed in current postsocialist studies, which are mainly based in the former Soviet Union and former eastern and central European socialist societies. The great famine of the mid-1990s has set North Korea on an irrevocable path of social transformation that has some elements in common with what observers refer to as postsocialist or postcommunist social transition, such as the state's changing role in the provision of economic security. Questions of moral economy raised in the North Korean context are, however, not collapsible to the abstract conceptual contrast of socialism versus capitalism or that of state-instituted economic security versus the propensity of the liberal market. Instead, these questions require us to return to the original idea of moral economy and to think seriously about the ethics of subsistence, which, in fact, constitute the idea's core message and original spirit.

The Arduous March

North Korea's great famine in the mid-1990s attracted considerable attention from the international community, resulting in several informative, authoritative reports on the political origin and economic and social consequences of the tragedy.[22] British academic Hazel Smith, who worked in North Korea as a consultant to international humanitarian efforts, explains that the food crisis forced North Korea, for the first time in its history, to open its territory to Western observers, although the opening was limited in scope and enacted very reluctantly on the part of the country's leadership, which was concerned about the implications for national security.[23] These concerns were not unwarranted. The food crisis indeed opened a window onto the reclusive country. A prominent example is Smith's own report of her experience with famine relief work in North Korea, which we believe is one of the first serious ethnographic reports of North Korean economy and society written in English. The crisis also resulted in a massive exodus of North Koreans to China and further afield; their testimonies have been vital to recent growth in empirical knowledge of contemporary North Korean society.[24] Thus, the famine not only strained the moral relationship between state and society within North Korea but also weakened the wall of containment within which the North Korean state had so judiciously sheltered its citizens from the outside world and constricted its society. The opening of this wall was, of course, far from a celebratory event, unlike the fall of the Berlin Wall in November 1989, and the consequence of this opening may turn out to be quite different from the Berlin experience. Nevertheless, the exposure of the Arduous March to the international community was still the first opening of North Korea in recent times, and it occurred in a way that was relatively uncontrolled by the state. Although the implications of this upheaval are still unfolding and uncertain, it is nevertheless fairly certain that the year 1994 was a historic threshold for North Korea and that it will be recorded as such by future historians.

As for the relationship between state and society, evidence suggests that the most critical challenge caused by the crisis was the breakdown of the moral authority of the Workers' Party in relation to the general population. This apparatus had previously been understood by the North Korean population as the provider of subsistence and welfare security; thus, the authority of the party suffered a devastating fall during the food crisis. The last was evidenced by shocking statements like "Life was not so bad as now even under the Japanese rule," which were rumored to circulate in popular communication, as well as by reported language plays such as that which shifted reference to the Workers' Party to the "Communist Party" (the name used by North Korea's enemy forces during the Korean War). Another statement characterized the current North Korean state as "a landlord in a remote mountainous region" whose thought is singularly focused, in a highly anachronistic manner (as in colonial-era rural Korea), on ways to extract extra small wealth from impoverished tenant farmers.[25] However, these subversive language practices, although they expressed deep disappointment and indignation, were careful political statements, always within acceptable limits of political and moral criticism in North Korea. Within the order of a family state, the society's economic prosperity is a tribute to the grace of the country's singular leader; likewise, the responsibility for economic hardship should lie, in principle, in the hands of the leader. The North Korean leadership carefully sought to avert these tremendous challenges to the unchallengeable authority of the leader, most importantly, by associating the leader's role primarily and exclusively with noncivil, noneconomic state affairs. This was, in significant measure, why North Korea came to take on the political path called military-first (or army-first) politics. Apart from other historical reasons for the rise of this political form (discussed in chapter 3), Kim Jong Il's privileging of the army and the military hierarchy was also related to the imperative to escape culpability for the economic failure and consequent human catastrophe. This way out was to reverse the traditional hierarchical order of the party over the army and then to base his rule primarily on the empowered military apparatus institutionally and on the scheme of revolutionary heritage politics ideologically. This maneuver was necessary, for by it alone could the political leadership detach itself from culpability for the economic failure, relegating the latter, in the perception of the population, to the party and other related state administrative apparatuses.

Famine in North Korea was known to the outside world first as a temporary crisis relating to consecutive harvest failures from 1995 to 1997—the mass flooding followed by severe drought that reduced the country's annual grain production by 20 to 30 percent.[26] The North Korean administration took to the natural-cause explanation, understandably, while carefully avoiding any mention of the man-made aspects of the crisis or its responsibility for it. Meredith Woo-

Cumings argues in her 2003 article that the argument for a natural cause was not merely a face-saving gesture but might have some credibility.[27] In this regard, Woo-Cumings mentions changing climatic conditions in the Korean peninsula. It is a widely held view among South Korean climate scientists that the massive flooding suffered by North Korea in the mid-1990s (and again in the early 2000s) partly relates to global warming, which is pushing northward the monsoon line that used to fall on the traditional center of wet rice cultivation in southern Korea. Woo-Cumings's report integrates the global ecological background of North Korea's agricultural crisis (which is a man-made crisis in a broader perspective) with another global origin of the human crisis. Both origins are man-made, certainly, but the second is much more recent in history and primarily political rather than ecological in nature.

As we noted in chapter 1, the North Korean food crisis is an epiphenomenon of the end of the Cold War as a global geopolitical order. The disintegration of the socialist international order from the late 1980s to the early 1990s brought to an end the international economic ties and division of labor maintained among the socialist polities and societies.[28] North Korea relied heavily on this division of labor; despite its incessant assertion of the idea of economic and political self-reliance, it relied heavily on overseas aid and focused on bartering its industrial products for agricultural produce and subsidized energy resources from its brotherly partners in the socialist world. The breakdown of this international barter and trade network in the beginning of the 1990s suddenly exposed North Korea to the hard-currency-based international trade system for procurement of energy and food, which the country was not able to join due to a lack of foreign currency and credit, as well as the sanctions imposed on the country by the United States.[29] The country was, in fact, already in a serious foreign-debt crisis, which analysts argue was brought about, in part, by the heavy importation of expensive industrial machinery from overseas during the 1970s and 1980s (and by the launching of many large-scale state construction projects in Pyongyang and elsewhere, as well as the hosting of costly international events such as the World Festival for Youth and Students in 1989) in order to compete with the fast-growing South Korean economy. By the early 1970s, according to Bruce Cumings, North Korea "clearly had exhausted the extensive development of its industry based on its own or prewar Japanese or new Soviet technologies, and it therefore turned to the West and Japan to purchase turnkey plants. . . . Ultimately these purchases caused North Korea to run into problems in servicing its external debt."[30] In agricultural sectors, North Korea insisted on collective and cooperative farming, unlike other Asian socialist economies that introduced private family-based production in earlier decades. North Korea also took pride in its successful mechanization of agricultural production. As James Hoare and Susan Pares observe, "In conjunction with the industrialization of the country from the 1950s through to the 1970s, progammes were put in hand to mechanize and modernize agriculture. . . . Self-sufficiency in food production was taken as a marker of the country's independence."[31] However, the heavy reliance on fuel-intensive farming technology, including excessive dependence on chemical fertilizers, became an obstacle when the subsidized energy supply was no longer forthcoming from the country's major traditional trade partner, the Soviet Union.

It is unclear why North Korea's economic planners did not address the country's serious structural problems before they exploded dramatically in a sudden collapse of nearly the country's entire production and distribution system in the early 1990s. It appears that Kim Il Sung and his close advisors were aware of some of these problems and that they sought to avert them by planning to follow the China-Taiwan economic exchange model in relation to South Korea.[32] This effort was clearly manifested in Kim's visit to China in October 1991 during which the North Korean leader is reported to have had engaging discussions with his Chinese counterparts Deng Xiaoping and Jiang Zemin about the imperative to coordinate North Korean development along the Chinese economy-first socialist model. This led to the historic signing of the Agreement on Reconciliation, Non-Aggression, and Exchanges and Cooperation between the two Koreas on February 19, 1992. These efforts did not come to fruition, however, partly due to the reluctance and resistance of some conservative political circles in the United States and South Korea, which were then preoccupied with the early inception of the North Korea–related nuclear crisis. Later, in the very beginning of the 2000s, both the South Korean and US administrations managed to change course and sought to improve their economic and diplomatic relations with North Korea. However, this initiative was frustrated, tragically, by the subsequent onset of the ill-advised, belligerent "regime-change" rhetoric pursued by the new US administration under President George W. Bush beginning in 2002. Regarding the last development, Bruce Cumings tellingly wrote in 2004, "[The United States'] last foray into North Korea helped to bring about an armed-to-the-teeth garrison state, and fifty years later it is still with us. If North Korea does finally get the [nuclear] bomb, there's very little we can do about it. So let's just call it Bush's bomb."[33] However, the failure of Kim Il Sung's initiative to follow the Chinese path of social development also stemmed from opposition to the efforts arising from within North Korea. The opposition must have involved the then powerful new leader of the country, Kim Jong Il, who, as described earlier, chose the opposite path of development that he later named military-first socialist revolutionary politics.[34]

The collapse of the Soviet and international socialist order was undoubtedly another major factor, and this must have come as a great shock to North Korea, as it did to the outside world. The gravity of the crisis led the North Korean leadership to acknowledge publicly, for the first time in the country's history, "big losses in our economic construction" and "a most complex and acute internal and external situation" at the Workers' Party assembly in December 1993.[35] However, worrying indicators about the country's economic future long pre-dated the implosion of the Soviet empire. North Korea's industrial output had been declining for quite a few years by the early 1990s; the distribution of food and other basic subsistence materials was already highly precarious in parts of the country by the second half of the 1980s. Although it remains uncertain why the state stood inactive in the face of a whirlwind of disaster gathering force on the horizon,[36] the consequence of its passivity was to become brutally clear.

An adequate allocation of subsistence goods was vital to the integrity of the North Korean state in relation to the society. Most North Korean families were entirely dependent on the state for subsistence, living on monthly state food rations provided through work or residential units. In 1992, the ration system began to flounder for a month or two; in 1994, it shrank again and became available only for three to four months a year (in some places, even only for a month). In 1996 (in some places, already in 1995), food rations were stopped entirely, and people were told by their local party organizations that they should now find ways to fend for themselves.[37]

The situation was particularly dire in the northeastern region of Hamgyŏng Province that borders China. By the time residents of this region were told that the ration system had fallen apart, a chronic food shortage had already set in for many, and famine-related deaths were already widespread. Even in the late 1980s, in this region, the monthly ration was barely enough to survive for twenty days, and residents were obliged to gather whatever they could lay hands on from the hills and fields—a practice that also claimed a number of lives due to food poisoning. The region is comparatively more industrialized and has less access to arable lands than neighboring regions in the south. The fact that people of this region suffered particularly speaks to serious failures in the Pyongyang government, indicating that the central government failed to coordinate different provinces in confronting the crisis. The failure apparently also resulted from a seemingly rational decision by the security-preoccupied North Korean leadership: to sacrifice the remote northern regions, which are relatively less important in terms of national security as they are distant from the militarized frontier with South Korea. In addition, the situation was already so grave and widespread that the provincial governments, preoccupied with protecting their own local food security, were reluctant or unable to help the neighboring provinces.

At more local levels, according to testimony from survivors, people initially confronted the crisis in good collective spirit. According to one survivor, "We received no rations in 1994 [the year of Kim Il Sung's death], but people were not in panic. Strong among us was the resolve to defend 'socialism in our style' even without rations. When food rations were not forthcoming after a year, our determination became even stronger, and we thought that, well, from now on we must find our own ways to survive rather than simply looking up to the higher authority for food handouts."[38] Certain collateral mutual assistance also existed in the early stage of the crisis: between cooperative farms and city districts, between workplaces and residential units, and between neighbors and relatives. A woman from a mining town in northern Hamgyŏng province told us how her workplace's party chairman and chief engineers struggled to barter part of their coal produce for grain with a cooperative farm in another region. Another informant who worked in a tobacco factory in the same province told us in detail how the workers of this factory initially sought to exchange their tobacco produce for maize and flour with a local army unit whose food situation was relatively better. We were also told that people who faced particularly dire situations were initially helped by others within the neighborhood or the workplace. These individuals often had access to small garden plots or had a foreign income source through kinship ties with ethnic Korean families across the Korean-Chinese border. These barter and mutual-assistance networks were based on preexisting, long-term relationships of trust and solidarity among relatives, neighbors, workmates, and members of a common local public organization, such as the elderly women's association. As the situation worsened, the initial barter network developed into localized makeshift marketplaces, where locals could sell and purchase homegrown grains, as well as those brought in from other regions or from China, and processed foods.[39] At the same time, existing mutual-help relations became strained and in many cases broke down, leaving the vulnerable and weak helplessly exposed to great hardship to the extent that in one home, at the height of the crisis, the desperate mother of a child struggling with hunger-caused illness pleaded with and prayed to the portraits of Kim Il Sung and Kim Jong Il, which she had preciously preserved in her home, to help save her child's life.

Figure 6.5. *Kk'otjebi* (wandering children) during the famine. *Source:* Good Friends (permission granted).

Most observers of the North Korean famine agree that throughout this painful time, women—particularly married women with children and elderly women with married children and grandchildren, whom Barbara Demick aptly calls "mothers of invention"—played a most active role both in forming mutual-assistance networks and later in the rise of marketplaces.[40] It was mainly these people who travelled great distances to find food in the countryside, sometimes in other provinces, defying the official rule against unauthorized human mobility. It was also primarily these women who later took the initiative to gather in public spaces to create marketplaces in defiance of the administration's rule against the transaction of goods unauthorized and uncontrolled by the state. Moreover, many of these women later had the courage to make the extremely hazardous border-crossing journey into China.[41] Their objective was not to leave their home for a better life elsewhere (or to seek "freedom," a completely nonsensical notion in this context, as some outside media irresponsibly characterized the border crossing) but chiefly to help keep their families at home alive by taking on the role of breadwinner as temporary migrant laborers.[42]

The situation must have greatly worried the party hierarchy. There is ample testimony that local party leaders at the town or provincial level, unlike their superiors in Pyongyang, were actually supportive of the local residents' survival efforts, including their mobility and marketplace activity. In regions where residents had experienced the food shortage for longer, since the mid-1980s, local party cadres were well aware of the severity of the problem. Some of them were highly frustrated with the lack of government intervention and occasionally expressed their frustrations at lower-level party cell meetings with rank-and-file party members or at meetings with workplace or residential groups. In these regions, the families of party cadres also struggled for survival, although probably not so desperately as ordinary working families. Judging from the testimony of diverse sources, as well as reports made available by several nongovernmental organizations that had access to local realities in North Korea, it seems fair to conclude that local communities confronted the onset of the "age of nondistribution [of food]" (*bibaegŭp sidae*), as the era of famine is commonly called at the grassroots level in North Korea, with great shock, yet also, initially, with great resilience and communal solidarity.[43]

The situation changed, however, when the collapse of the food-ration system, which in 1994 and 1995 had been more or less confined to the northeastern region of the country, spread to other areas (except the country's capital of Pyongyang). The generalization of the food crisis quickly paralyzed the entire economic and social system of North Korea, destroying medical and other social welfare sectors. The severity of the situation was well illustrated by changes in the classroom. In a primary school in northern Hamgyŏng Province, in 1998, only a quarter of the students were able to bring their lunch to school. Another quarter attended the day's classes without a meal, and a roughly equal number of students attended only the important morning classes, which were reserved for the study of Kim Il Sung's and Kim Jong Il's biographical histories. The last quarter were absent from the school entirely, believed by the teachers either to have died of starvation or to be looking for food in the fields or marketplaces.[44] Moreover, the teachers at this school confronted a situation just as challenging as that faced by students and their families. Unlike workers in industrial plants where production was halted, which left them relatively free to devote their time to food-gathering activities, these teachers, like employees in other public sectors such as hospitals, were obliged to come to their workplace, despite the fact that their work was not re-munerated at that time with a salary or food allocation. This caused some teachers to force students and their parents to pay for their school lessons in corn and other grains, whereas other teachers tried to cope with the situation as best they could. Some teachers joined the marketplace activity after work, even though they ini-tially feared encountering students and their parents in the marketplace and thereby losing their dignity as members of the teaching profession. As the crisis deepened and more people came to rely on the marketplace for survival, however, the mar-ketplace shed this negative stigma and became a crucial social space where diverse groups of people gathered to exchange goods and information. The initial stigma of the marketplace gave way to the opposite image of this space as the embodiment of the common, general will of people to survive. Thus arose a shocking, powerful saying at that time: "The marketplace is our party [or new Workers' Party]."

Figure 6.6. *Jangmadang* (open market). *Source:* Good Friends (permission granted).

The state administration's reactions to the mounting food-distribution crisis were extremely haphazard at best and, in the end, deplorably self-destructive, with unimaginably tragic consequences. We have noted briefly how the North Korean state, in the face of the escalating subsistence crisis, opened its borders and territory to foreign aid and international humanitarian assistance for the first time in its history (apart from during the postwar years when the country invited a large number of Russian and eastern European engineers and industrial experts to assist with economic reconstruction). This was an encouraging move, one that no doubt involved serious compromise, for the North Korean state leadership, of its perceived national security imperatives. Later the state also opened its territory to humanitarian aid agencies from South Korea, although in a more restricted way than it had with international nongovernment aid organizations. In the domestic sphere, however, the Pyongyang leadership acted highly ineptly, possibly because it did not grasp the extremity of the situation, which was entirely new to the country.

The first mistake was, of course, failure to confront the food-shortage problem earlier, even though, as mentioned, it had been apparent in some regions as early as the mid-1980s. An equally grave mistake was the state machinery's focus, after Kim Il Sung passed away in 1994, primarily on solidifying the chosen commemorative and hereditary politics. Although the leader's death was a serious, injurious event, and it is therefore understandable that a political system would make efforts to minimize the impact of the rupture, the post-1994 commemorative politics, which focused on further sublimating the late leader's heroic and victorious legacy, contributed to repressing the voices of hunger within the society, thereby aggravating the scale and intensity of the crisis. The commemorative political process also involved the onset of military-first politics, which empowered the army as the principal state institution beyond the authority of the party. This political form had a logical and historical background, as discussed previously with reference to the partisan theater state idea and in relation to the complexity involved in transforming a preeminent personal charisma into a hereditary charismatic authority. However, the privileging of the army (over the party and over the society) had a hugely destructive consequence for the fragile human-security conditions. The empowerment of the army made sense in terms of the chosen hereditary politics, but it became entangled with the prioritization of military personnel and organizations in the allocation of resources over the civilian population during the general food crisis.

The North Korean army acted aggressively to protect itself from the food crisis, sometimes competing with the civilian population. In one telling incident, a local army base sent a convoy of solders to a nearby collective farm during the harvest time. The convoy seized the harvested grain, amid vigorous protests from the farmers. The local party and public-security offices were informed of the incident by the farm management but were not able to intervene. Such incidents were, fundamentally, an outcome of Pyongyang's stated policy privileging the army over the civilian population in the struggle for survival and over the party in the national political arena. North Korea's literature about military-first politics does not mention the army's priority in subsistence as part of its ascribed merits as the vanguard of socialist revolution. However, this message was communicated to the public in subtle ways. One notable communication tool was the choice of sites for the new leader's field visits. During the Arduous March, Kim Jong Il's on-the-spot-guidance visits took him predominantly to army bases and military installations.[45] Art also played an important role. North Korea recently loaned to the Austrian Museum of Applied Art a number of paintings meant to be the most representative pieces of contemporary North Korean fine art. The collection included a 2000 painting by Ri Chul titled *The Supreme Commander of the People's Army Deeply Concerned over the Soldiers*. The painting depicts Kim Jong Il's on-the-spot-guidance visit to an unidentified army base; the leader is observing food preparation for the soldiers and giving instructions for improving the soldiers' dietary conditions. The scene was widely disseminated in newspaper editorials and other publications, which, in North Korea, are typically used as study materials in workplace political-study meetings.

As the crisis deepened, the pain of hunger affected the army as well, particularly rank-and-file soldiers. Hazel Smith reports, "The armed forces were given priority for food distribution, but this did not mean that all members of the armed forces received generous rations. The army was told to find ways to grow its own food and to develop industries so that it could purchase food and other necessities from the markets and from abroad. There were no indications that the ranks of the army were given excessively large rations, but unlike the general population they were more or less assured of a basic food supply all year round."[46] In the sphere of subsistence economy, therefore, military-first politics takes on, in principle if not always in practice, a most literal "military-first" meaning in that the army should be given priority over the people in the allocation of scarce resources. This draconian hierarchy of value imposed on the civilian population may have appeared to be a difficult yet rational and necessary choice for the North Korean leadership. However, it complicated enormously the outside world's humanitarian intervention in North Korea and, in the end, contributed to worsening the humanitarian crisis. The tacit rule that privileged the military (and the population of Pyongyang) in the allocation of resources provoked critical responses from international aid agencies and donors, raising issues of transparency and accountability on the part of the North Korean state hierarchy as to the destination of the humanitarian aid, which was, by definition, in the view of these agencies and donors, intended strictly for the civilian population and primarily for the weak and the vulnerable. It also complicated South Korea's engagement policy with North Korea after the former took on the role of a major donor of food and other humanitarian aid to North Korea in the early 2000s. Doubts about the destination of food aid later created a bitter divide in South Korean public and political circles, one as corrosive as the nuclear-armament and other dangerous, belligerent military maneuvers that

North Korea pursued in parallel with opening relations of economic exchange and economic and humanitarian aid with South Korea.[47]

Within North Korea, the military-first political form had complex implications at the grassroots level. The North Korean army is organizationally a people's army in a genuine sense of the term, consisting of, as North Korea's public media puts it, "sons and daughters of the people." To serve in the army is traditionally recognized as a privilege as well as a duty for North Korean youth and their families. The service experience is vital for young males to obtain a meaningful and functional status as adult males in society; it affects their marriage prospects, profession, educational opportunities, and personal esteem. Youths with dubious family backgrounds (i.e., today, people closely related to those who left for China or South Korea) are not entitled to join the army. In addition, military service in North Korea is long, amounting to ten years, and the country keeps one of the largest armies in the modern world, both proportionally and in absolute size.[48] This means that numerous families are connected to the army institution through intimate family ties. In this context, the privileging of the army, in terms of food allocation, meant for many suffering North Korean families that their beloved children or siblings serving in the armed forces experienced relatively less severe pain due to hunger. Especially for the parents of servicemen, military-first politics, in its manifestation in the subsistence economy, had a consoling aspect in this sense. For the mobilized youth, on the other hand, their relative advantage in subsistence compared to the civilian population meant that their beloved parents and siblings back home were enduring extreme hardships. Food shortages affected the army as well as the society, especially rank-and-file soldiers. Many soldiers suffered from malnutrition, and some were sent home to recover. However, a disparity existed in the intensity of hunger between the army and the society, in relation to the politically engendered hierarchy of value in human survival between these two social spheres. This disparity became a source of profound shock and sorrow for many soldiers of the People's Army when they later returned to their devastated homes.

The hierarchy of survival was manifested not only between the army and society but also within the society.[49] While the party hierarchy lost some of its muscle in relation to the army within the institutional structure of military-first politics, which is in fact sometimes referred to as "army-first, party-second politics" (*sŏngunhuro jŏngchi*), it nevertheless jealously guarded the privilege of its hierarchical order through its own shrewd food-allocation politics. At the height of the subsistence crisis, when the state's food-allocation system totally broke down outside Pyongyang and when the local food-distribution centers virtually closed down, evidence suggests that the party hierarchy maintained an exclusive, internal food-distribution network, within which employees in security sectors, officials on local people's committees, and cadre members of communist youth organizations continued to receive food rations along their separate institutional channels, independently from the national food-distribution system. In some areas, local officials abused their organizational privilege in a variety of ways. In one shrewd exploitative maneuver, a district official purchased a large number of unused food-ration coupons from the local residents, buying them with a fraction of the amount of food that the coupons were worth. Later he exchanged these coupons for food at the district's food depot, using his family network, when an overseas relief food supply arrived. When the supply ran out, he then released the obtained grain to the local marketplaces, thereby making a handsome profit. This was by no means an isolated abuse of power and privilege.

The Ethics of Common Survival

Let us return to the popular saying that arose during the Arduous March in parts of North Korea: "The marketplace is our party." Like all powerful social and historical metaphors and idioms, this saying has multiple meanings. Before we consider them, a note on the term "Arduous March" is necessary. It refers to two distinct periods of hardship in the evolution of the North Korean revolution. One is the extreme hardship of scarcity and famine suffered by nearly the entire population of North Korea since the second half of the 1990s. Although the North Korean administration declared in October 2000, while celebrating the birth anniversary of the Workers' Party, that the period of the Arduous March was over, the dire economic and subsistence crisis nevertheless continues today for a great portion of the population.

The other historical era referred to as the Arduous March goes all the way back to the end of 1938. At that time, the Kim Il Sung–led Manchurian militia, pressed by Japan's revamped counterinsurgency activity, was forced to undertake a long march for survival, fighting against hunger and the harsh winter of northeastern China, as well as the enemy troops on their tail. The march is known to have lasted for about one hundred days throughout the winter, and it is recorded in North Korean history as the time of greatest trial for Kim and his early revolutionary comrades. Kim's militia suffered a high loss of manpower during this time, as well as several betrayals by longtime comrades. However, North Korean history also depicts the one hundred days of the Arduous March, like the Long March in the Chinese revolution, as a glorious time when the country's revolutionary ancestors struggled against impossible odds to succeed in a final victory and thereby lay the ground for the proud home of a revolutionary state. In North Korean arts and literature, the one-hundred-day Arduous March is typically depicted not only as a heroic episode but also as a beautiful time—when the most beautiful of all human virtues flowered amid extreme hardship.[50] These virtues included comradely solidarity and iron-like commitment to the cause of national liberation. Paramount were fidelity and faithfulness to the partisan leader, according to how these values are depicted in countless songs, stories, and works of art about the era. The famous North Korean song "Song of Comradely Love" (1980) depicts these sublime human virtues born in the experience of the Arduous March:

No matter how arduous the way may be,
We shall climb over the hills of hardship.
No matter how strong the wind of fire may be,
We shall stay together in life and death.
You can't purchase even with tons of gold,
The boundless love of comrades.
Let our resolve live forever,
Looking up to the single star.

The partisan who embodied the virtue of comradely love—both collateral love for ordinary comrades and filial loyalty to Kim Il Sung, the "single star" of Korean revolution—in the most distinguished way was, of course, the Mother of Chosun and later the Mother of Sŏn'gun, Kim Jong Suk.

In the mid-1990s, North Korean state arts released a number of new songs and dramas about the virtue of comradely love. Among them was the popular television drama *Sea Routes*, which depicted how a group of people, cast adrift on a ship after a sea storm, came to discover true comradely, altruistic love for one another amid the hardship of hunger and thirst. The drama's theme song, "Comradely Love," says,

We didn't know in the quiet days,
How precious the true comrades are.
The love of a comrade who shares my fate,
I discovered in turbulent days that without you, I am no longer.
In the embrace of our General who taught us what true love is,
Let you and me stay as eternal comrades.

These songs and dramas sought to create an analogy between the crisis of hunger and the old historical episode of the Arduous March from the late 1930s, which had been, as discussed earlier, forcefully empowered in the 1970s and again in the mid-1990s in the face of the new challenges of political isolation and economic hardship. The analogy meant to propagate the power of the human spirit and moral solidarity in overcoming adverse historical conditions—to instill the conviction that there are no insurmountable obstacles in the historical world for people who are armed with proper spiritual and moral strength. This spiritual power is not a dialectal force (shaping and being shaped by historical conditions) but a transcendental force that, properly guided, is free from constrictions imposed by objective historical conditions. Key to this spiritual power is the moral solidarity among fellow travelers on the Arduous March, which the above songs depict as "comradely love." Yet, the transcendental quality of this spiritual solidarity lies not merely in the collateral moral ties among comrades. More crucially, it consists of their unshakable collective faith in the all-embracing, encompassing authority of the leader of the march, and it is only through this faith that the morality of comradely love finds its ultimate purpose and genuine strength.

Figure 6.7. *He Who Leads the Arduous March* (painting depicting the Kim Il Sung–led Arduous March in Manchuria, 1938–1939, partial image). *Source: Pulmyŏlŭi yŏngsang* (Pyongyang: Literature and Art Press, 1992), 184.

The civic morality propagated by today's narrative of the Arduous March is therefore of heritage politics in form and, in substance, in the service of hereditary politics. It brings into full flower the family-partisan state aesthetics developed since the 1970s, adding to them a powerful montage of the past and the present—a continuity between the old episode of crisis in the revolutionary movement and the new reality of crisis in the life of the revolutionary state, as well as between the morality of old Manchurian partisans and the civic ethics required of members of today's North Korean political family. In doing so, however, the political narrative of the Arduous March confronts a critical inner contradiction.

The Manchurian story of the Arduous March tells of a revolutionary movement, involving a handful of vanguard revolutionaries and a relatively simple social organization formed by these battle-hardened actors. In contrast, today's Arduous March involves a complex state society that has an elaborate system of division of labor, including that between the army and economic society. In this regard, the logical contradiction embedded in the historical-analogical scheme of the Arduous March refers to the attempt to extend the rules of military-regimental moral unity born in extraordinary historical circumstances to a complex modern society. Even in the Manchurian context, it is unthinkable that the rules meant exclusively for the professional militia could be extended at face value to civilian lives.

This contradiction goes to the heart of the partisan state idea. The life of partisans is an extraordinary form of life, and it may not continue, by definition, without material and moral support from sympathetic nonpartisan, civilian groups. This is why the violence of modern counterinsurgency warfare often targets communities of civilian populations for destruction as a way to destroy the partisan groups. When this violence occurs, the mobile partisan militia may attempt to escape encirclement by counterinsurgency forces, as did Kim Il Sung's Manchurian partisans in the winter of 1938 and 1939, leaving the civilian communities to fend for themselves. This art of survival in partisan warfare, however, is not an option available to a partisan state. The partisan state is a territorially bound entity, unlike classical partisans, and it has no place to go other than the place it keeps. Moreover, its survival depends on the survival of civil society as much as on that of the army.

The decision based on military-first politics to privilege the state's armed wing against its social and civil wing in the struggle against starvation was clearly made according to the logic of partisan warfare. The draconian decision may have seemed difficult yet necessary to the North Korean leadership, given the circumstances and in view of the glorious Manchurian legacy it was determined to preserve and appropriate. However, the affirmative action for the army resulted in a radical contradiction between the two faces of North Korea's stateliness, characterized, on the one hand, by the paradigm of the partisan state and, on the other, by the paradigm of family state (see chapter 1).

These paradigms are closely intertwined in the art of rule in North Korea. The unity of familial moral solidarity and partisan regimental discipline is also a prominent theme in the narrative of Manchurian heroism. Nevertheless, the family state idea has a distinct moral conceptual dimension that may, in certain situations, resist partnership with the partisan state idea. As discussed earlier, the idea that a polity is a household writ large entails a moral reciprocal relationship between the state and society: the state provides security in basic economic life and human welfare in return for citizens' fidelity to the political system and contribution to the national economy. This is the case whether this relationship takes on a personalized paternalistic character centered on a charismatic leader, as in Kim Il Sung's North Korea, or a more institutionalized form of socialist politics (in the Weberian sense) explained in terms of the relationship between the party and the masses.

Max Weber's insights into the nature of charismatic authority engage with the above issue. Weber defines charisma as "a certain quality of an individual personality by virtue of which he is set apart from ordinary men and treated as endowed with supernatural, superhuman, or at least specifically exceptional qualities."[51] In order for this personal quality to develop into a public and political authority, it is vital that the charismatic individual be recognized as such; as Weber writes, "This recognition is a matter of complete personal devotion arising out of enthusiasm or of despair and hope."[52] Once this recognition begins, the authority of the charismatic personality seeks to influence people from within, in contrast to the powerful institutional agents of modern times, such as rational bureaucracy and capitalism, which instead focus on making people adapt to external material circumstances. For Weber, charisma is therefore, by its nature, *against* the socioeconomic force: it has to dismiss everyday economic concerns and matters because, by its very nature, charismatic authority strives to be extraordinary and enchanting, to go beyond and ultimately transcend ordinary, routine, everyday life. Although Weber believes that charismatic authority is fundamentally antieconomic (and this is in part why he doubted its durability), he also notes the central importance of engaging with mundane economic concerns for its sustenance, including the transformation of this authority into a hereditary form. Following him, the most vital question in the routinization of charisma concerns the charismatic authority's struggle against its own natural tendency, which is, for Weber, the propensity to transcend the imperatives of ordinary, everyday life.

North Korea's pre-1994 stateliness as a family state can be seen in relation to this vital question in the routinization of charismatic authority. The same perspective applies to the late founding leader's renowned art of rule—most prominently in his lifelong practice of on-the-spot-guidance visits, during which the leader displayed his enchanting attentiveness to the minute details of the working masses' mundane, everyday routines. Before 1994, North Korea took the form of a partisan state ruled by a charismatic partisan leader; in content, however, it contained elements of apparently anticharismatic politics in which the ruling charismatic authority was aware of the limits and perils of its power of enchantment.

In comparison, North Korea's hereditary charisma in the era of *sŏn'gun* began its career on the ruins of the everyday economy and as an authority whose power of enchantment knew only the power to influence people from within, whether it liked it or not, and not how to counterbalance this dangerous, ultimately self-destructive power with an authority derived from the management of an economically sustainable political household. The military-first-era North Korea is a proud partisan state but a failed family state. It has failed because the state violated the most elementary normative principle of any viable family organization, political or social: the protection of the subsistence of its dependants. It has also failed according to the principles of moral economy, which celebrate, among all human values, common survival and the ethics of subsistence. It is not certain how, or even if, this gross failure can be rectified. One thing is certain, however: if the North Korean state genuinely hopes to recover from its failure as a family state, it must first reform its partisan state paradigm and change its approach to the glorious Manchurian partisan legacy. It must confront the historical truth that no revolutionary partisan group ever survived the crisis of an Arduous March in the long run without returning to and rebuilding the mass base, which alone can guarantee the political life of partisans. Ideally, the reform will include a principled commitment to moral economy so that an unimaginable human tragedy such as the Arduous March of the 1990s never occurs again. If this can be achieved, moreover, we hope that North Korea's neighbors will also follow suit and commit themselves to the principles of moral economy. Our hope goes especially to South Korea, which, despite its claims of a common nationhood with the North, seems to have forgotten the ethics of common survival when it comes to the suffering of its compatriots across the artificial northern border. Human subsistence is a moral question that transcends politics—it is not reducible to politics or political economy—and this principle must be adhered to not only by North Korea but also by its neighbors.

Notes

1. Susan Buck-Morss, *Dreamworld and Catastrophe: The Passing of Mass Utopian East and West* (Boston: MIT Press, 2002), 3.
2. See Seong-Bo Kim, Kwang-Su Kim, and Sin-Cheol Lee, *Bukhan hyŏndaesa* [Modern history of North Korea] (Seoul: Ungjin, 2006), 121–22; Bruce Cumings, *Korea's Place in the Sun: A Modern History* (New York: W. W. Norton, 1997), 423–24; Joseph Chung, "North Korea's Economic Development and Capabilities," *Asian Perspective* 11, no. 1 (spring–summer 1987): 45–74.
3. Joan Robinson, "Korean Miracle," *Monthly Review* 16, no. 8 (1965): 548. See also Marjorie S. Turner, *Joan Robinson and the Americans* (New York: M. E. Sharpe, 1989), 90. For a concise introduction to North Korea's short-lived post–Korean War industrialization achievement, see Glyn Ford and Soyoung Kim, *North Korea on the Brink: Struggle for Survival* (London: Pluto, 2008), 56–66.
4. Personal communication with Robert Templer in the International Crisis Group, March 16, 2010.
5. Helen-Louise Hunter, *Kim Il-song's North Korea* (Newport, CT: Praeger, 1999), 26.
6. Hunter, *Kim Il-song's North Korea*, 26.
7. Kim, Kim, and Lee, *Bukhan hyŏndaesa* [Modern history of North Korea], 181.
8. Moon-Woong Lee, *Bukhan jŏngch'imunhwaŭi hyŏngsŏnggwa gŭt'ŭkjing* [The formation and characteristics of North Korean political culture] (Seoul: Institute of National Unification, 1976), 36.
9. Marcel Mauss, *The Gift* (London: Routledge, 1990 [1922]), 58. See also Jonathan Parry, "The Gift, the Indian Gift and the 'Indian Gift,'" *Man* 21 (1985): 453–73; Gloria Goodwin Raheja, *The Poison in the Gift: Ritual, Presentation, and the Dominant Caste in a North Indian Village* (Chicago: University of Chicago Press, 1988).
10. Bradley K. Martin, *Under the Loving Care of the Fatherly Leader: North Korea and the Kim Dynasty* (New York: Thomas Dunne Books, 2004), 193.
11. Okonogi Masao, Japanese political scientist and prominent North Korea observer, argues that "the asymmetry of politics and economy" constitutes a principal character of North Korea's social system. Okonogi Masao, "Haji-

meni: Rensahōkai no akumu [Introduction: The nightmare of chain collapse]," in *Kitachōsen handobukku* [North Korea handbook], ed. Okonogi Masao (Tokyo: Kōdansha, 1997), 12.

12. Caroline Humphrey, *The Unmaking of Soviet Life: Everyday Economies in Russia and Mongolia* (Ithaca, NY: Cornell University Press, 2001).

13. C. M. Hann, "Farewell to the Socialist 'Other,'" in *Postsocialism: Ideals, Ideologies, and Practices in Eurasia*, ed. C. M. Hann (New York: Routledge, 2002), 10.

14. Christopher G. A. Bryant and Edmund Mokrzycki, "Theorizing the Changes in East-Central Europe," in *The New Great Transformation?: Change and Continuity in East-Central Europe*, ed. Christopher G. A. Bryant and Edmund Mokrzycki (New York: Routledge, 1993).

15. Frances Pine and Sue Bridger, "Introduction: Transitions to Post-Socialism and Cultures of Survival," in *Surviving Post-Socialism: Local Strategies and Regional Responses in Eastern Europe and the Former Soviet Union*, ed. Sue Bridger and Frances Pine (New York: Routledge, 1997), 1.

16. Zygmunt Bauman, "After the Patronage State: A Model in Search of Class Interests," in *The New Great Transformation?: Change and Continuity in East-Central Europe*, ed. Christopher G. A. Bryant and Edmund Mokrzycki (New York: Routledge, 1993). See also Katherine Verdery, *What Was Socialism and What Comes Next?* (Princeton, NJ: Princeton University Press, 1996).

17. Pine and Bridger, "Introduction," 3.

18. Hann, "Farewell to the Socialist 'Other,'" 10.

19. Hann, "Farewell to the Socialist 'Other,'" 1.

20. E. P. Thompson, *The Making of the English Working Class* (London: Gollancz, 1963).

21. James C. Scott, *The Moral Economy of the Peasants* (New Haven, CT: Yale University Press, 1976).

22. Among the notable works are *Woori minjok sŏrodopki bulkyo undong bonbu* (Korean Buddhist sharing movement), *Bukhansingryangwigi: Bukhansingryangnanŭi silt'ae* [Food crisis of North Korea: Current conditions of North Korean food refugees] (Seoul: Joŭnbŏtdŭl, 1998); Byung-Ho Chung, "Bukhan ŏrini kiawa hankukinryuhakŭi kwaje [North Korean children's famine and the tasks for Korean anthropology]," *Hankukmunhwainryuhak* (Korean cultural anthropology) 32, no. 2 (1999): 155–75; W. Courtland Robinson et al., "Famine, Mortality, and Migration: A Study of North Korean Migrants in China," in *Forced Migration and Mortality*, ed. Holly E. Reed and Charles B. Keely (Washington, DC: National Academy Press, 2001), 69–85; Stephan Haggard and Marcus Noland, *Famine in North Korea: Markets, Aid, and Reform* (New York: Columbia University Press, 2007); Andrei Lankov, "North Korean Refugees in Northeast China," *Asian Survey* 44, no. 6 (2004): 856–73; Andrew S. Natsios, *The Great North Korean Famine: Famine, Politics, and Foreign Policy* (Washington, DC: US Institute of Peace Press, 2001).

23. Hazel Smith, *Hungry for Peace: International Security, Humanitarian Assistance and Social Change in North Korea* (Washington, DC: US Institute of Peace Press, 2005).

24. Testimonies are available at Joŭnbŏtdŭl [Good friends], *Bukhansaramdŭli malhanŭn bukhaniyagi* [Tales of North Korea told by North Koreans] (Seoul: Jŏngto, 2000); Joŭnbŏtdŭl [Good friends], *Bukhansahoi muŏti byŏnhago itnŭnga?* [What changes are taking place in North Korean society?] (Seoul: Jŏngto, 2001). About the growth of markets, see Hyung-Min Joo, "Visualizing the Invisible Hands: The Shadow Economy in North Korea," *Economy and Society* 39, no. 1 (2010): 110–45. About everyday lives during the Arduous March, see Soon-Sung Pak and Min Hong, eds., *Bukhanŭi ilsangsegye: Oaech'imgwa soksagim* [Everyday life in North Korea: Cries and whispers] (Seoul: Hanul, 2010); Woo-Young Lee, ed., *Bukhan dosijuminŭi sajŏkyŏngyŏk yŏn'gu* [Research report on private economy among North Korea's urban residents] (Seoul: Hanul, 2008).

25. Cited from a testimony by a North Korean featured in Kyung-Won Ryu, "Tto dasi kinjanggam hŭrŭnŭn sijang (Tensions grow again in the market)," *Limjingang* [Imjin river], no. 4 (March 2009): 122.

26. Sue Lautze, one of the first outsider specialists permitted to enter North Korea in 1996 to investigate the effects of the floods, reports failures in the public distribution system and changing priorities of the North Korean authority at the time of national emergency. Sue Lautze, *The Famine in North Korea: Humanitarian Responses in Communist Nations* (Cambridge, MA: Feinstein International Famine Center, Tufts University, 1997).

27. Maredith Woo-Cumings, "The Political Ecology of Famine: The North Korean Catastrophe and Its Lessons," Research Paper 31, Asian Development Bank Institute, January 1, 2002, http://www.adbi.org/files/2002.01.rp31.ecology.famine.northkorea.pdf (accessed September 21, 2011).

28. Natsios, *The Great North Korean Famine*, 10–16.

29. See Natsios, *The Great North Korean Famine*, 36–49. See also Byung-Ho Chung, "Living Dangerously in Two Worlds: The Risks and Tactics of North Korean Refugee Children in China," *Korea Journal* 43, no. 3 (2003): 193–96.

30. Cumings, *Korea's Place in the Sun*, 426.

31. James E. Hoare and Susan Pares, *North Korea in the 21st Century: An Interpretative Guide* (Folkestone, UK: Global Oriental, 2005), 43.

32. See the memoir by the former South Korean chief of the Ministry of Unification, Dong-Won Lim, *Pisŭmeikŏ: Nambukgwangyewa bukhaekmunje 20nyŏn* [Peacemaker: Twenty years in inter-Korean relations and in North Korea's nuclear crisis] (Seoul: Jungang, 2008), 279–303, 526–50, 569–75.

33. Bruce Cumings, *North Korea: Another Country* (New York: The New Press, 2004), 102.

34. For more information about this turbulent period, see Selig S. Harrison, *Korea Endgame: A Strategy for Reunification and U.S. Disengagement* (Princeton, NJ: Princeton University Press, 2003), 144–45, 206–7; Cumings, *North*

Korea, 42–102; Don Oberdorfer, *The Two Koreas: A Contemporary History* (London: Warmer Books, 1999), 373–491.

35. Cited from Cumings, *Korea's Place in the Sun*, 426.

36. For careful, persuasive deliberation on this question, see Haggard and Noland, *Famine in North Korea* (New York: Columbia University Press, 2007), 38–41.

37. Natsios, *The Great North Korean Famine*, 89–121.

38. Joŭnbŏtdŭl [Good friends], *Bukhansaramdŭli malhanŭn bukhaniyagi* [Tales of North Korea told by North Koreans], 61.

39. Byung-Ho Chung, "Bukhan kigŭnŭi inryuhakjŏk yŏn'gu [An anthropological study on the North Korean famine], " *T'ongilmunjeyŏn'gu* [Korean journal of unification affairs] 16, no. 1 (2004): 109–40.

40. See Barbara Demick, *Nothing to Envy: Real Lives in North Korea* (London: Granta, 2010), 147–59.

41. See Natsios, *The Great North Korean Famine*, 55–88. See also the moving report of the painful, diverse human experience of the famine in Demick, *Nothing to Envy*, 133–46.

42. See Joŭnbŏtdŭl [Good friends], *Bukhansaramdŭli malhanŭn bukhaniyagi* [Tales of North Korea told by North Koreans]; Joel R. Charny, *Acts of Betrayal: The Challenge of Protecting North Koreans in China* (Washington, DC: Refugees International, 2005); Byung-Ho Chung, "Between Defector and Migrant: Identities and Strategies of North Koreans in South Korea," *Korean Studies* 32 (2008): 1–28.

43. For an informative analysis of the Chinese experience, see Dali L. Yang, *Calamity and Reform in China: State, Rural Society, and Institutional Change since the Great Leap Famine* (Stanford, CA: Stanford University Press, 1996).

44. Chung, "Living Dangerously in Two Worlds," 193.

45. It is claimed that for six years since Kim Il Sung's death in 1994, Kim Jong Il travelled the distance of more than 140,000 kilometers as part of his prolific, on-the-spot guidance trips to military installations across the country. Cited from Ki-Hwan Choi, *Yŏngwŏnhan t'aeyang Kim Il Sungjusŏk* [Eternal Sun, Chairman Kim Il Sung] (Pyongyang: Pyongyang Press, 2002), 209.

46. See Smith, *Hungry for Peace*, 87–88. Also Ralph Hassig and Kongdan Oh, *The Hidden People of North Korea: Everyday Life in the Hermit Kingdom* (Lanham, MD: Rowman & Littlefield, 2009), 108–9.

47. Some of these disputes were based on false reports and ungrounded claims in the international media and South Korean press about the North Korean army appropriating the humanitarian aid. See Byung-Ho Chung, "North Korean Famine and Relief Activities of the South Korean NGOs," in *Food Problems in North Korea: Current Situation and Possible Solutions*, ed. Gill-Chin Lim and Namsoo Chang (Seoul: Oruem Publishing House, 2003), 239–56.

48. Eberstadt and Banister estimate that at least 1.2 million military personnel exist in North Korea, which makes the country in possession of the fourth

largest armed forces in the world. Nicholas Eberstadt and Judith Banister, *The Population of North Korea* (Berkeley: Institute of East Asian Studies, University of California, Berkeley, 1992).

49. Lautze, *The Famine in North Korea*, 7.

50. Kwahak paekkwa sajŏn ch'ulpansa [Science encyclopedia press], *Munhakyesulsajŏn* [Dictionary of literature and art], Vol. 1 (Pyongyang: Scientific Encyclopedia General Press, 1988), 188–89. See also the fictional account of the hardship in Woon-Ki Suk, *Konanŭi haenggun* [Arduous March] (Pyongyang: Literature and Art Press, 1991).

51. Max Weber, *The Theory of Social and Economic Organization*, edited by Talcott Parsons (New York: The Free Press, 1947), 329.

52. Weber, *The Theory of Social and Economic Organization*, 359.

Conclusion

On December 17, 2011, the ailing North Korean leader Kim Jong Il was reportedly on his special personal train, where he suffered a heart attack in the early morning and subsequently failed to recover. The leader's sudden death came as a surprise to the international community; in North Korea, it unleashed collective expressions of painful sorrow across the country followed by a mass-mobilized funerary procession in Pyongyang on December 28, all closely resembling the unfolding of the Great National Bereavement in 1994 following the death of the country's founding father, Kim Il Sung. An obituary in the Workers' Party newspaper stresses that Kim died while traveling to an unspecified location for an on-the-spot-guidance visit: "Our General always traveled by train, in his Train Towards People (*inminhaeng yŏlch'a*), to all corners of our country as well as to the territories of foreign countries. In doing so, he devoted all his life to the well-being of his people and to the victory of the self-determination revolutionary task around the world. Our General died in duty and on his field-trip train, not in a comfortable home or office."[1] On-the-spot-guidance trips have been an important part of the North Korean leaders' charismatic politics. It is asserted that although this important art of mass politics had been invented by the country's founding leader, Kim Il Sung, it was brought to a higher level by his successor Kim Jong Il and provided "the fundamental source for all the miracles of his military-first politics."[2] Kim Jong Il began his high political career as a pioneer of an artistic revolution that brought the power of performative art to sublimating the authority of the country's sovereign center; the dramatic power of the announced circumstances of the leader's death is that it happened while the leader was performing a powerful, miracle-generating art of politics.

The *Rodong Sinmun* article cited above, states that the late leader traveled prolifically to foreign countries as well as within his realm. Indeed, Kim Jong Il made several recent overseas trips to China in August 2010 and May 2011, and, in August 2011, a long-distance tour of Russia, Mongolia, and China. For the trip on August 26, 2010, the leader's train headed toward Jilin, an administrative and commercial center of northeaster China, after crossing the Tumen River along North Korea's border with China.

The following morning, Kim, together with a convoy of senior military and party officials, went to visit Jilin's Yuwen middle school located along the town's

river Songhua. North Korea's founding ancestor, Kim Il Sung, spent a short period here at a tender age in 1926 and 1927, a time depicted in today's North Korean
national narrative as the origin of the Korean revolution. In the afternoon, Kim
Jong Il proceeded to visit the Linjiang Beishan Park, a popular place of recreation
for Jilin's townspeople and a historic monument of the Chinese revolution. The
place is also a site of memory of monumental value in the North Korean revolutionary heritage. Linjiang Beishan Park maintains several memorials dedicated
to the heroes of the Chinese revolution and to the Chinese martyrs of the Korean
War. For North Korea, it is where the fifteen-year-old founder of the North Korean
revolution held secret study meetings with his schoolmates and thereby took his
first step toward the career of a professional revolutionary.

These events were part of Kim Jong Il's five-day informal state visit to China
at a time of important transition for North Korea as well as for China. The destinations of Kim's sightseeing tour in Jilin included not only Linjiang Beishan Park
but also a garment factory. During these visits, the North Korean leader reportedly
met Xi Jinping, a former party secretary of Shanghai, member of the Politburo
standing committee, and son of Xi Zhongxun, a top veteran of the revolutionary
generation. On October 18, 2010, Xi was elected to the powerful position of vice
chairman of the Chinese Communist Party's military commission, which observers hold has sealed his future as the successor to Hu Jintao as China's top leader
in 2012. Shortly before this important decision was made in China, North Korea's
Workers' Party had also elected a new vice chair of its military commission and
a future successor to Kim Jong Il. After his visit to Jilin, the North Korean leader
met Chinese president Hu Jintao on August 27 in Jilin's neighboring town of
Changchun. Then, Kim moved further northward to Harbin, the provincial capital
of Heilongjiang. In Harbin, Kim made further pilgrimage to the town's heritage
sites dedicated to Kim Il Sung and his Manchurian partisans, allocating some of
his time for a tour of Heilongjiang's agroindustrial complex. On his way back
to Pyongyang on August 30, his train made a stop at Tumen, China's small yet
thriving frontier town close to both North Korea and Russia. Several weeks later,
after the election of Kim Jong Il's future successor by the Workers' Party, North
Korea began supplying hundreds of workers to the special China–North Korea
cooperative industrial zones set up in Tumen and elsewhere along the Chinese
side of the border.[3]

The trip was a carefully staged pilgrimage combined with diplomacy. In terms
of pilgrimage, most notable was Kim Jong Il's visit to the old school of North Korea's founding ancestor. The school maintains a bronze statue of Kim Il Sung and
a modest museum for his relics; it also preserves the classroom where Kim studied in the late 1920s as a heritage site. According to a North Korean report, when
Comrade Kim Jong Il entered the classroom, after laying a bouquet of flowers at
the base of the Kim Il Sung statue, he was "immersed in thoughts while looking at
the precious historic objects that contain the bodily odor of our Supreme Leader
from his school years some eighty years back."[4] These relics, kept in Jilin's Yu-

wen school, are important not merely for the national memory of North Korea, China's close ally; they are also meaningful for the political transition that the country is currently undergoing.

In the contemporary North Korean version of Kim Il Sung's biographical history, it was during his brief school years in Jilin that the late North Korean leader first conceived of the military-first, army-as-revolutionary-vanguard political theory. This historical revision depicts the birth of the military-first theory as occurring when the future supreme leader of North Korea revealed to his schoolmates the gift that he had received from his late father back home: a pair of pistols. As discussed earlier, these two pistols together constituted one of the most prominent material symbols in the era of Kim Jong Il's military-first politics. The symbol defines both the content and form of this politics—that is, both the honorable revolutionary heritage that this politics is set to preserve and the principal means of that preservation, which is the revolutionary army and military power. Hence, among the most outstanding images of the North Korean revolution available today is the painting (which is reproduced in a variety of other forms) that depicts the young Kim Il Sung in a school uniform opening an object wrapped in red cloth and showing the meaning-loaded handguns his father handed over to him to his early teenage comrades (also important is the scene of him receiving the guns belonging to his late father from his mother, Kang Ban Sŏk, back home).

The legendary history in Jilin evolves into another pivotal chapter in the genesis of the North Korean revolution and in the descent of Kim Il Sung's revolutionary charisma. We saw earlier another family episode involving the gift of a gun: the single revolver that the ten-year-old Kim Jong Il received from his father and the supreme commander of the North Korean People's Army on a battlefield of the Korean War in 1952. In current North Korean political literacy, the meaning of these gun stories goes beyond the succession of revolutionary authority along Kim's patrilineal line; these stories also embody the moral imperative and collective will to preserve and defend the glorious tradition—the "barrel-of-a-gun spirit" that purports to keep the eminent genealogy of revolution with unwavering political-filial dedication to the exemplary family genealogy and unclenching patriotic-familial loyalty to the leadership of military-first politics. The iconicity of these guns speaks of the supreme principle in the contemporary North Korean revolution, in the words of Kim Jong Il from August 2005: "Our faith in revolution is, in essence, a faith in the leader who guides the revolution." The "leader," in this context, may mean the physically absent founding leader of North Korea or his immortal spirituality. It can also mean the leaders who succeeded the founding hero and follow his legacy faithfully or the line of descent that connects these old and new leaders. Or the term may carry all these variant meanings at once.

Kim Jong Il's pilgrimage to the school was an important gesture to reclaim and renew the semantically multivariate concept of revolutionary leadership. It pointed to a place that keeps the legend of the most important material symbol of his hereditary charisma and the country's contemporary heritage politics. In parallel with this vital historical meaning, the school visit clearly had an equally crucial proactive relevance. The pilgrimage was undertaken during another critical juncture in North Korea's political genealogical history.

A new succession drama has been taking the stage in Pyongyang. Days after Kim Jong Il returned from his pilgrimage to Jilin and Harbin, Pyongyang hosted the third congress of the Workers' Party on September 28, 2010—a rare event in North Korea that has not happened since 1966, despite the fact that the congress represents the crystallization of socialist democracy at the highest institutional level. This historic meeting turned out to be a scrupulously staged political spectacle in which a new order of North Korea's hereditary charismatic politics was to be set in motion publicly.

Hours before the congress opened, Kim Jong Il appointed his youngest son, Kim Jong Un, to the rank of military general, along with the young man's paternal aunt and her husband, as well as three other notables, whom analysts see as together making up a core power circle in charge of a smooth transition of absolute power to the next generation. At the meeting, the delegates elected Kim Jong Un to the powerful position of vice chair of the party's military commission—a key organization within the Workers' Party in charge of overseeing the country's military affairs. Soon afterward, on October 10, the sixty-fifth anniversary of the founding of the North Korean Workers' Party, the sixty-eight-year-old Kim Jong Il and the twenty-eight-year-old Kim Jong Un made their first joint debut to the broad North Korean public.[5] They inspected the military parades together, standing next to each other on the podium. For the large crowd of North Korean citizens assembled for this event, its meaning was crystal clear: a decision had been made concerning the country's future leader. The setting of the podium made it clear who the future exemplary center of the North Korean polity would be, to whom the citizens and the army must continue to dedicate their unity of filial piety and political loyalty. A fairly large number of foreign diplomatic personnel and journalists were also invited to witness the spectacle. For them, the day's military parade sent a lucid message: the North Korean state had decided to replicate the pattern of power transfer put into practice a generation before, and from then on, the outside world would have to relate to North Korea on the basis of recognizing, accepting, and respecting this sovereign decision. The decision for succession was made democratically, in the view of the North Korean state, involving first a gesture of endorsement by the country's singular exemplary authority (the awarding of a high military position to the successor), followed by a unanimous gesture of consent by the party's general assembly and then by a demonstration of allegiance to the decision staged by the People's Army on the day of the Party's anniversary celebration.

The spectacle at the country's capital city was soon followed by a multitude of other local events. Army units across the country began to brief the decision to the rank-and-file soldiers with an emphasis on the army's continuous, vital role in upholding and defending the emerging new leadership just as it had done for the existing center of the North Korean revolution. At the same time, local party organizations held meetings with rank-and-file party members in workplaces, universities, and residential groupings. Their briefings included the news that special gifts to citizens and families were forthcoming from the party hierarchy: small amounts of rice, cooking oil, and alcohol. People were told that the gifts were being given in celebration of the anniversary of the Workers' Party. However, they were under no illusion about what these rare ration items, which they had not seen in recent years even on the birthdays of Kim Il Sung and Kim Jong Il, were actually meant for. In the subsequent weeks, more political-literacy meetings were called by the party and the army. Notable among other important current affairs discussed at these meetings was the news about gifts from China. People were told that the Chinese state leadership had made a tribute to the Dear Leader with the gift of a framed picture of him and Hu Jintao shaking hands after their informal summit meeting in Changchun. Above all, the briefings highlighted China's gift to the Young General, North Korea's designated future successor to the heritage of Kim Il Sung: a picture of the Great Leader seated with Mao taken during their comradely summit meeting in 1953. Moreover, people were told also that China was preparing another significant gift to North Korea: a life-size wax figure of Comrade Kim Jong Suk, paternal grandmother of the Young General and the Mother of Chosun, which, when completed, would be placed next to the existing wax statue of Comrade Kim Il Sung in the sacred inner chamber of the Myohyangsan International Friendship Exhibition Hall.

All these national, local, and international events took place within the short space of two months, between August and October 2010. After Kim Jong Il's sudden death, many more national and local events were hastily organized to accelerate and firm up the succession process left incomplete by the deceased leader. The unfolding of these events drew upon most of the elements of a modern theater state discussed earlier in this book, including mass rallies and spectacles, new mass political-literacy campaigns, and the politics of the gift on both the domestic and international levels. In the ensuing months and possibly years, we will surely see attempts to mobilize music, musicals, art, cinema, and literature to legitimize and secure a real-life political drama of succession. We will probably also witness a new round of on-the-spot-guidance trips by North Korea's nominated new leader. It is reported that the Young General (referred to as "Great Guiding Leader" since his father's death) had already made a number of field visits to unidentified military locations in the company of his father. On New Year's Day in 2012, he went to inspect the famous 105 Armored Division, the unit that is known to have spearheaded the liberation of Seoul during the Korean War, according to North Korea's Central Broadcast, paying close and caring attention to the soldiers' living conditions. The Young General was clearly following in the footsteps of his father, who had made his on-the-spot-guidance visit to the same location in January 2010. The contemporary art of North Korea's theater state now has a tradition to draw upon, whereas in the earlier era, the art of political succession had no exemplars to refer to and thus had to be invented from scratch. It is not certain whether ordinary North Koreans will experience much of the novel and innovative political art in the new drama of hereditary legacy politics; the new succession art may invent some new elements or may primarily follow the old pattern. It remains to be seen whether the future of North Korea's theater state will have much to claim in terms of formal artistic creativity in comparison to its past since the 1970s. In content, however, it is clear that the state's performance confronts great challenges and will require a great deal of creativity and innovative thinking to meet them.

The challenge is both structural and moral. The first part of the present volume focused on the structural aspect. It has been one of our main arguments in this book that North Korea's contemporary statehood is above all a product of the particular mode of succession that the country's leadership happened to choose. Although we spoke about other factors and circumstances, some contingent and others historical, we have proposed that the most preoccupying, determining question in the evolution of the North Korean polity since the 1970s has been the routinization of revolutionary charisma, which in North Korean history turned out to entail hereditary rule. More than anything else, this singularly vital question of preservation concerning the historical life of the polity's founding charismatic, messianic authority shaped the unfolding of North Korea's political and social history. The pursuit of perpetual charisma determined the changing relationship between the party and the army and affected the state's increasing disregard of the economy in proportion to its obsessive concentration on military power and military-led political security. This question of hereditary charisma also played a major role in the evolution of North Korea's foreign policy toward its major allies and enemies and its approaches to South Korea and interaction with the postcolonial world. Above all, this question was the driving force behind North Korea's determined construction of a self-image as a radically self-reliant, self-sufficient, and self-centered political system. At the center of these developments was the singularly focused pursuit of a political mission that all other more powerful revolutionary states were unable to undertake: the realization of a historically transcendent charisma in the form of actualizing a hereditary succession of power.

The North Korean revolution achieved great success in the early state-building era from 1945 to 1950 and again in the postwar national construction drive from 1953 to the 1960s. It created a sturdy and independent state that effectively mobilized the war-torn society, leading it toward rapid and strong industrial economic development. In the subsequent era, the revolution has written another monumental success story, this time in the particular domain of revolutionary politics that concerns mainly the appearances of the state rather than the reality of the economic and political society. During this long era, the pride of revolutionary North Korea has been centered on a revolution in an extremely narrow sense, focusing primarily on questions relating to the formal integrity of the revolutionary state and to the historical durability of the state's exemplary personality. The North Korean state has been spectacularly successful in this constricted domain of political revolution, and it is very proud of its unique, self-made achievement in defending the continuity of the country's revolutionary statehood. This achievement may appear to the outside world, including North Korea's traditional socialist allies, as anachronistic and contrary to modern revolutionary tradition. However, we must acknowledge that the North Korean state's determination to defend its revolutionary heritage, no matter how apparently premodern the outcome may have turned out to be, was, in its inception, nothing short of a political revolution. It was an achievement akin to a political revolution, for no other revolutionary socialist states of the Cold War were able to achieve it. The same is true also in a purely theoretical sense, for this achievement goes against the impermanent nature of charismatic power.

The story of proud success was, however, also a story of tragic failure. While driving itself to turn into a theater state with the determination to battle against the natural mortality of charisma armed with a man-made, magnified, and mass-mobilized politics of art, the state of North Korea became increasingly alienated from the telos of its foundation, which was, like that of other revolutionary postcolonial states, to build a politically independent, yet socially democratic and economically prosperous, community. The sublimation of charismatic authority came with an extreme centralization of political and executive power, which destroyed the democratic principle of socialist revolution. The centralization of power, because of its primary reliance on political cultural means and the mobilization of the population to this activity, came with an increasing negligence and ineptitude on the part of the state in the sphere of economic sustenance and growth. The cumulative effects of this failure in all spheres of state life other than the sphere of cultural production were made brutally clear by the tragic crisis of the mid-1990s, which devastated the single most important foundation of any modern state: the economic and moral integrity of its civil society.

The failure was both moral and structural. To put it in another way, it was a serious structural failure because it was a gross moral failure. In modern times, there is no viable state without a viable society. Clifford Geertz made it crystal clear that a modern state may not be only a theater state. He did so while making a critique of a theory of modern politics that is oblivious to the fact that a state can be made on the basis of an enchanting display, rather than a rational exercise, of power. Although he advanced this historical pluralism of political power, from which insight this book has benefited, he had no illusions about the limits of the theater state in modern times, and on this basis, his pluralistic approach to power closely followed Max Weber's conviction about the limits of charismatic power in modern politics.[6]

It is uncertain whether the third-generation succession, which the current North Korean regime hopes to actualize, will be able to proceed in course. It may well be overtaken by unforeseeable events on the horizon. It is clear, however, that for North Korea to have a future, it must come to terms with the limits of its theater state. It must confront the fact that there is a clear limit in modern history to how far a community can assert radical particularism and radical exceptionalism. It must recover the wisdom that a community's particular authenticity is viable only to the extent that it can be acknowledged and recognized by other communities in the considered, modern spirit of plurality. In order to manage this crucial confrontation with self-identity, it must recover the long-lost, genuinely heroic spirit of its early foundational era. It is necessary for North Korea to return to the historical epoch of the post–Korean War and to extract from it the moral and spiritual strength of a unity of the state and society for the arduous tasks of national rebuilding. The rest of its national history is not a national history but only a history of a state imposed on the society in the guise of national history. North Korea's theater state has to make another political revolution for the future. This time, the revolution will be a struggle to end the life of the theater state, or at least to turn its life from the substance of the state to a mere facade. It is not impossible to undertake this revolution. The evolution of North Korea's theater state has elements that can be positively brought forward. We hope that the future leader of North Korea will make a strong alliance of descent with the founding ancestor of the revolutionary state and only with this ancestor. We hope that he, or they, will cast the age of military-first politics, both its short version from 1994 and its long version from the early 1970s, as a sorry historical episode, or at least an uncharacteristic era of the North Korean revolution. There are several encouraging signs. First among them is the slow recovery of the authority of the Workers' Party as compared to the power of the army. *Rodong Sinmun* asserted on June 30, 2010, that the forthcoming Workers' Party congress, which decided on North Korea's future leader, had "great intentions to increase the people's confidence in our party and in strengthening the might of unity between the party and the people."[7] This move points in the hopeful direction that the relationship between the party and the army will recover its normality in socialist politics by departing from the distorted military-first, party-second form that has prevailed under the rule of Kim Jong Il. In relation to this, it is also encouraging to observe a possible change from a military-focused political economy to an economic policy that returns to an emphasis on socioeconomic integrity. Although this may not indicate that North Korea will embrace market socialism, not to mention an economic liberalization involving the privatization of agriculture, there are signs that the country's leadership, in parallel with the initiative to restore the party's authority, wishes to direct more attention to improving agricultural productivity and the capacity of light industry. The policy directive announced in *Rodong Sinmun* on New Year's Day in 2010 clearly states this change of orientation.[8] The change was also manifested in Kim Jong Il's weeklong visit to China in May 2011. The itinerary of this trip closely resembled, in many ways, Kim Il Sung's important trip to China in October 1991, during which, as mentioned earlier, the late founding leader discussed with his Chinese counterparts the possibility and imperative of North Korea's following in China's footsteps and opening up its economy.[9] From another perspective, this event may be interpreted as an initiative, on the part of North Korean leadership, to show its population and the world that the country is finally ready to return to the last, unachieved wishes of the late great leader after having successfully defended the nation's fragile sovereignty through a policy that privileged its military power over its social economy. This interpretation may bear truth, especially in light of the fact that the hundredth anniversary of Kim Il Sung's birth will take place in 2012, which North Korea has long earmarked as the year in which the country will finally open the door to becoming a "mighty, prosperous, great country."

Notably, North Korea has a strong foreign ally that understands some of this art of political descent. We hope that future leaders will take two gifts from China seriously and only these two: the gift of a portrait of China's and North Korea's founding heroes given to the new leader and the gift of a statue of the Mother of Chosun (not the mother of military-first politics) given to the people of North Korea. The hope is that other future key allies of North Korea, including South Korea, Japan, and the United States, will also understand the meaning of these gifts from North Korea's powerful present ally. We believe that they will, and then, the only remaining thing to do for the upcoming revolution of North Korea will be to break the fantasy of the theater state and to recover from its fragments the single gem that is the real pride of the real North Korean revolution: the achievement of the North Korean miracle in the postwar years made possible by the intimate collaboration between a charismatic leader and the proud people of North Korea, who were willing to endure hardship with a faith and dear hope for a better future. That miracle was achieved not only through the hard work of ordinary North Koreans but also with generous assistance from the international community. True, the shape of the international community has changed dramatically since. Yet, North Korea's immediate international environment in northeastern Asia is growing strong and is capable of giving assistance. North Korea may interpret this international assistance as tribute or a gift from the world acknowledging its stately majesty, if necessary, rather than as aid or investment. Whichever it prefers, however, it must accept this assistance, and it must follow the necessary steps to do so by mending the past mistakes engendered by its military-first politics. The last includes, above all, aborting the army's nuclear-armament program and halting the brutal, immoral economic policy that privileges the power and integrity of the army over the survival and subsistence rights of the people. It must recover the elementary existential and ethical principle of a revolutionary people's army—encapsulated lucidly by the classical saying "Our army is the fish; our people are the water"—that dictates that no people's army survives in history without the support and integrity of the people. For this purpose, it must eventually stop glorifying the history of the Arduous March, both old and new, which is far from a people's history but a history of an army separated and alienated from the people.

Above all, the new North Korean leadership must confront the naked historical lesson and truth that there is indeed a clear limit to the power of the man-made politics of art in resisting the nature of modern political power and authority. It has to recognize the fact that this unwise and arrogant resistance to the natural mortality of charismatic power can have terrible consequences not only for the lives of the people but also for the dignity and heritage of the very authority that the political art seeks to protect from fading into history. It must awaken to the fact that in modern times, it is through following the natural course of events, and only through this humble attitude toward the power of history, that the dignity of the once-charismatic authority may be preserved as a meaningful heritage. Once again, the action that follows this awakening must be to end the political life of the country's theater state. This action requires the courage to initiate a new North Korean revolution that can topple the fantasy of the theater state to restore the order of the state to a rightful shape in modern times as an institution with a tradition, not a choreographer of mystic symbols that are neither grounded in Korea's tradition nor acceptable to the modern world. Now is the time to make another North Korean miracle.

Notes

1. "Segyejajuhwaŭiŏpe ssaŭsin pulmyŏlŭi ŏpjŏpŭn yŏngwŏnhari [His achievements in the honorable effort to bring self-determination to the world will be forever with us]," *Rodong Sinmun*, December 23, 2011. "12wŏlŭi wech'im [Our cries in December]," *Rodong Sinmun*, December 26, 2011.

2. "Chŏngryŏkchŏkin hyŏnjijidokanghanggun [The vigorous on-the-spot guidance]," *Rodong Shinmun,* June 18, 2009.

3. For other details of this trip, see Aidan Foster-Carter, "North Korea: Kim Jong Il Snubs Jimmy Carter in Lead Up to Succession," *East Asia Forum*, September 2, 2010, http://www.eastasiaforum.org/2010/09/02/north-korea-kim-jong -il-snubs-jimmy-carter-in-lead-up-to-succession (accessed October 2010).

4. Chosun jungang t'ongsin [North Korean central broadcast], August 30, 2010.

5. For more about this event, see Ruediger Frank, "Power Restructuring in North Korea: Anointing Kim Jong Il's Successor," *Asia-Pacific Journal*, October 18, 2010, http://www.japanfocus.org/-Ruediger-Frank/3429 (accessed October 2010).

6. Clifford Geertz, *The Interpretation of Cultures* (New York: Basic Books, 1973), 193–233.

7. "Chosŏnrodongdaepyojahoiŭi [Workers' Party congress]," *Rodong Sinmun*, July 30, 2010.

8. "Dasi hanbŏn kyŏngkongŭpkwa nongŏpe pakch'arŭl [Let's bring up agriculture and light industry once more]," *Rodong Sinmun*, January 1, 2010. And the same message was reiterated in the newspaper's New Year editorial in 2011.

9. "Kim Il Sung bangjunghaengjŏk ttara idong [Following the steps of Kim Il Sung's (1991) trip to China],"*Jungang Ilbo*, May 28, 2011.

Bibliography

An, Tai Sung. *North Korea in Transition: From Dictatorship to Dynasty*. Westport, CT: Greenwood Press, 1983.

Anderson, Benedict. *Imagined Communities: Reflections on the Origin and Spread of Nationalism*. New York: Verso, 1991.

Apter, David E. "Yan'an and the Narrative Reconstruction of Reality." In *China in Transformation*, edited by Tu Wei-Ming, 207–32. Cambridge, MA: Harvard University Press, 1994.

Arendt, Hannah. *On Violence*. New York: Harcourt Brace, 1969.

———. *The Human Condition*. Chicago: University of Chicago Press, 1958.

Armstrong, Charles K. "A Socialism of Our Style: North Korean Ideology in a Post-Communist Era." In *North Korean Foreign Relations in the Post–Cold War Era*, edited by Samuel S. Kim, 34–38. New York: Oxford University Press, 1998.

———. "Centering the Periphery: Manchurian Exile(s) and the North Korean State." *Korean Studies* 19 (1995): 1–16.

———. "Juche and North Korea's Global Aspirations." Woodrow Wilson Center North Korea International Documentation Project. Working Paper 1. 2009. http://www.wilsoncenter.org/topics/pubs/NKIDP_WP_1.pdf (accessed April 2009).

———. "Socialism, Sovereignty, and the North Korean Exception." In *North Korea: Toward a Better Understanding*, edited by Sonia Ryang, 41–56. Plymouth, MA: Lexington Books, 2009.

———. *The Koreas*. New York: Routledge, 2007.

———. *The North Korean Revolution, 1945–1950*. Ithaca, NY: Cornell University Press, 2004.

Arrighi, Giovanni. *The Long Twentieth Century: Money, Power, and the Origins of Our Times*. London: Verso, 2010.

Arrighi, Giovanni, Takeshi Hamashita, and Mark Selden, eds. *The Resurgency of East Asia: 500, 150 and 50 Year Perspectives*. London: Routledge, 2003.

Bauman, Zygmunt. "After the Patronage State: A Model in Search of Class Interests." In *The New Great Transformation?: Change and Continuity in East-Central Europe*, edited by Christopher G. A. Bryant and Edmund Mokrzycki, 14–35. New York: Routledge, 1993.

Behrend, Heike. "Power to Heal, Power to Kill." In *Spirit Possession: Modernity and Power in Africa*, edited by Heike Behrend and Ute Luig, 20–33. Oxford: James Currey, 1999.

Binns, Christopher A. P. "The Changing Face of Power: Revolution and Accommodation in the Development of the Soviet Ceremonial System: Part I." *Man* 14 (1979): 585–607.

———. "The Changing Face of Power: Revolution and Accommodation in the Development of the Soviet Ceremonial System: Part II." *Man* 15 (1980): 170–88.

Boddy, Janice. *Wombs and Alien Spirits: Women, Men and the Zār Cult in Northern Sudan*. Madison: University of Wisconsin Press, 1989.

Borneman, John. "Introduction: Theorizing Regime Ends." In *Death of the Father: An Anthropology of the End in Political Authority*, edited by John Borneman, 1–31. Oxford: Berghahn, 2004.

Bradley, Mark P. *Imagining Vietnam and America: The Making of Postcolonial Vietnam, 1919–1950*. Chapel Hill: University of North Carolina Press, 2000.

Brooks, Jeffrey. *Thank You, Comrade Stalin!: Soviet Public Culture from Revolution to Cold War*. Princeton, NJ: Princeton University Press, 2000.

Bryant, Christopher G. A., and Edmund Mokrzycki. "Theorizing the Changes in East-Central Europe." In *The New Great Transformation?: Change and Continuity in East-Central Europe*, edited by Christopher G. A. Bryant and Edmund Mokrzycki, 1–13. New York: Routledge, 1993.

Buck-Morss, Susan. *Dreamworld and Catastrophe: The Passing of Mass Utopian East and West*. Boston: MIT Press, 2002.

Buzo, Adrian. *Guerrilla Dynasty: Politics and Leadership*. London: I. B. Tauris, 1999.

Chakrabarty, Dipesh. *Provincializing Europe: Postcolonial Thought and Historical Difference* Princeton, NJ: Princeton University Press, 2000.

Charny, Joel R. *Acts of Betrayal: The Challenge of Protecting North Koreans in China*. Washington, DC: Refugees International, 2005.

Chatterjee, Partha. *The Nation and Its Fragments: Colonial and Postcolonial Histories*. Princeton, NJ: Princeton University Press, 1993.

Cho, Song-Bak. *Segyerŭl maehoksikinŭn Kim Jong Il ŭi sŏn'gun jŏngch'i* [Kim Jong Il's military-first politics fascinates the world]. Pyongyang: Pyongyang Press, 1999.

Cho, Sung-Ho. *Kim Jong Il changgun ilhwajip* [A collection of anecdotes of General Kim Jong Il]. Pyongyang: Pyongyang Press, 2003.

Choi, Hee-Bok. *Paekdusan nyŏjanggunŭi insaenggwan* [The life philosophy of the woman-general of Paekdu mountains]. Pyongyang: Labor Group Press, 2009.

Choi, Ki-Hwan. *Yŏngwŏnhan t'aeyang Kim Il Sungjusŏk* [Eternal sun, Chairman Kim Il Sung]. Pyongyang: Pyongyang Press, 2002.

Choi, Sun-Ho. *T'albukja gŭdŭlŭi iyagi* [Defectors from North Korea, their stories]. Seoul: Sigongsa, 2008.

Chosŏn daebaekkwa sajŏn [Chosun encyclopedia]. "Chokuk haebang chŏnjaeng [Fatherland Liberation War]." In *Chosŏndaebaekkwasajŏn* [Chosun encyclopedia]. Vol. 17, 501–5. Pyongyang: Baekkwasajŏnch'ulpansa [Encyclopedia press], 2000.

———. "Lee Soo Bok." In *Chosŏndaebaekkwasajŏn* [Chosun encyclopedia]. Vol. 8, 211–12. Pyongyang: Baekkwasajŏnch'ulpansa [Encyclopedia press], 1999.

Chosun misool ch'ulpansa [Pyongyang art press]. *Ŭmakŭi wŏnlo, Kim Jong Il* [The veteran of music, Kim Jong Il]. Pyongyang: Pyongyang Art Press, 1998.

Chosun Pyongyang hwabosa [Chosun Pyongyang art press]. *Sŏn'gun, sŭngliŭi gich'i* [Sŏn'gun, the flag of victory]. Pyongyang: Chosun Pyongyang Art Press, 2003.

Chun, Ha-Chol. *Suryŏngnimŭn yŏngwŏnhi uriwa hamkke kyesinda* [The Supreme Leader is forever with us]. Pyongyang: Workers' Party Press, 1994.

Chun, Je-Hun. *Dongmyongwangrŭn daehan yŏn'gu* [The study on the tomb of King Dongmyung]. Pyongyang: Social Science Press, 1994.

Chun, San-Pil. *Sŏn'gun jŏngchie daehan lihae* [Understanding the *sŏn'gun* politics]. Pyongyang: Pyongyang Press, 2004.

Chun, Young-Sun. "Bukhan 'Arirang' ŭi hyŏndaejŏk pyŏnyonggwa ŭimi [Contemporary transformation and meaning of North Korea's Arirang Festival]." *Hyŏndaebukhanyŏn'gu* [North Korean studies review] 14, no. 1 (2011): 40–75.

———. "Bukhanŭi daejipdanch'ejoyaesulgongyŏn 'Arirang' ŭi jŭngch'ijŏk·munhakyesuljŏk ŭimi [The sociopolitical and literary-artistic meanings of North Korea's Arirang Festival]." *Jungsoyŏn'gu* [Sino-Soviet affairs] 26, no. 2 (August 2002): 131–58.

Chung, Byung-Ho. "Between Defector and Migrant: Identities and Strategies of North Koreans in South Korea." *Korean Studies* 32 (2008): 1–28.

———. "Bukhan kigŭnŭi inryuhakjŏk yŏn'gu [An anthropological study on the North Korean famine]." *T'ongilmunjeyŏn'gu* [Korean journal of unification affairs] 16, no. 1 (2004): 109–40.

———. "Bukhan ŏrini kiawa hankukinryuhakŭi kwaje [North Korean children's famine and the tasks for Korean anthropology]." *Hankukmunhwainryuhak* [Korean cultural anthropology] 32, no. 2 (1999): 155–75.

———. "Kŭkchangkukka bukhanŭi sangjingkwa ŭirye [Symbol and ritual in the theater state of North Korea]." *T'ongilmunjaeyŏn'gu* [Korean journal of unification affairs] 22, no. 2 (2010): 1–42.

———. "Living Dangerously in Two Worlds: The Risks and Tactics of North Korean Refugee Children in China." *Korea Journal* 43, no. 3 (2003): 191–211.

———. "North Korean Famine and Relief Activities of the South Korean NGOs." In *Food Problems in North Korea: Current Situation and Possible Solutions*, edited by Gill-Chin Lim and Namsoo Chang, 239–56. Seoul: Oruem Publishing House, 2003.

Chung, Byung-Ho, Woo-Taek Jun, and Jean-Kyung Chung, eds. *Welkŏm tu koria: Bukjosŏn saramdŭlŭi namhan sali* [Welcome to Korea: North Koreans in South Korea]. Seoul: Hanyang University Press, 2006.

Chung, Chin O. *Pyŏngyang between Peking and Moscow: North Korea's Involvement in the Sino-Soviet Dispute, 1958–1975.* Tuscaloosa, AL: University of Alabama Press, 1978.

Chung, Chin-Hyuk. *Jŏlseŭi wiin'gamum* [The matchless great man's family line]. Pyongyang: Pyongyang Press, 2002.

Chung, Joseph. "North Korea's Economic Development and Capabilities." *Asian Perspective* 11, no. 1 (spring–summer 1987): 45–74.

Cumings, Bruce. *Korea's Place in the Sun: A Modern History.* New York: W. W. Norton, 1997.

———. *North Korea: Another Country.* New York: The New Press, 2004.

———. *The Origins of the Korean War: Liberation and the Emergence of Separate Regimes, 1945–1947.* Princeton, NJ: Princeton University Press, 1981.

Demick, Barbara. *Nothing to Envy: Real Lives in North Korea.* London: Granta, 2010.

Durkheim, Emile. *The Elementary Forms of Religious Life.* Translated by K. E. Fields. New York: The Free Press, 1995.

Dutton, Michael. *Streetlife China.* Cambridge: Cambridge University Press, 1998.

Eberstadt, Nicholas, and Judith Banister. *The Population of North Korea.* Berkeley: Institute of East Asian Studies, University of California, Berkeley, 1992.

Exposición de la amistad internacional, ediciones en lenguas extranjeras. Pyongyang: RPD de Corea, 1982.

Ferguson, Niall. "The Political Economy of the Cold War." Paper presented at the public lecture series by the London School of Economics IDEAS, London, October 18, 2010.

Feuchtwang, Stephan, and Mingming Wang. *Grassroots Charisma: Four Local Leaders in China.* London: Routledge, 2001.

Fitzpatrick, Sheila. *The Cultural Front: Power and Culture in Revolutionary Russia.* Ithaca, NY: Cornell University Press, 1992.

Ford, Glyn, and Soyoung Kim. *North Korea on the Brink: Struggle for Survival.* London: Pluto, 2008.

Foster-Carter, Aidan. "North Korea: Kim Jong-Il Snubs Jimmy Carter in Lead Up to Succession." *East Asia Forum.* September 2, 2010. http://www.eastasia forum.org/2010/09/02/north-korea-kim-jong-il-snubs-jimmy-carter-in-lead-up -to-succession (accessed October 2010).

Fowkes, Reuben. "The Role of Monumental Sculpture in the Construction of Socialist Space in Stalinist Hungary." In *Socialist Spaces: Sites of Everyday Life in the Eastern Bloc*, edited by David Crowley and Susan E. Reid, 65–84. Oxford: Berg, 2002.

Frank, Rudiger. "Power Restructuring in North Korea: Anointing Kim Jong Il's Successor." *Asia-Pacific Journal.* October 18, 2010. http://www.japanfocus .org/-Ruediger-Frank/3429 (accessed October 2010).

———. "The North Korean Economy." In *Handbook on the Northeast and Southeast Asian Economies*, edited by Anis Chowdhury, 298–316. Cheltenham, UK: Edward Elgar, 2007.

Fujitani, Takashi. *Splendid Monarchy: Power and Pageantry in Modern Japan.* Berkeley: University of California Press, 1998.

Fuqua, Jacques L. *Nuclear Endgame: The Need for Engagement with North Korea.* Newport, CT: Praeger, 2007.

Furuta, Hiroshi. "Chūsei to Kōsei: Kitachōsen ideorogi kyōkashijo no nidai kakkiten, 1967, 1987 [Loyalty and filial piety: 1967, 1987 as two major turning points in the history of indoctrination in North Korea]." *Shimonoseki City University Review* 36, nos. 1–2 (1992): 1–94.

———. "Kitachōsenniokeru Jukyō no dentō to shutaishisō no tenkai [Confucian tradition in North Korea and the emergence of *juch'e* ideology]." *Shimonoseki City University Review* 34, no. 3 (1991): 29–71.

———. "Kitachōsenniokeru shūkyōkokka no keisei [The formation of religious state in North Korea]." *Tsukuba Review of Law and Politics* 20 (1996): 51–87.

———. "Pyongyang: Kitachōsenniokeru 'shutai' hōji no ishi to hyōshokūkan [Pyongyang: The will to protect *juch'e* and symbolic space in North Korea]." *Ajiashinseki* [Asian new century], no. 1 (2002): 181–94.

Gabroussenko, Tatiana. *Soldiers on the Cultural Front: Developments in the Early History of North Korean Literature and Literary Policy.* Honolulu: University of Hawaii Press, 2010.

Geertz, Clifford. *Negara: The Theatre State in Nineteenth-Century Bali.* Princeton, NJ: Princeton University Press, 1980.

———. *The Interpretation of Cultures.* New York: Basic Books, 1973.

Gillis, John R., ed. *Commemorations: The Politics of National Identity.* Princeton, NJ: Princeton University Press, 1994.

Goncharov, Sergei, John Lewis, and Litai Xue. *Uncertain Partners: Stalin, Mao, and the Korean War.* Stanford, CA: Stanford University Press, 1993.

Haggard, Stephan, and Marcus Noland. *Famine in North Korea: Markets, Aid, and Reform.* New York: Columbia University Press, 2007.

Halbwachs, Maurice. *On Collective Memory.* Chicago: University of Chicago Press, 1992.

Hann, C. M. "Farewell to the Socialist 'Other.'" In *Postsocialism: Ideals, Ideologies, and Practices in Eurasia*, edited by Chris M. Hann, 1–12. New York: Routledge, 2002.

———. "Socialism and King Stephen's Right Hand." *Religion in Communist Lands* 18, no. 1 (1990): 4–24.

Harrison, Selig S. *Korea Endgame: A Strategy for Reunification and U.S. Disengagement.* Princeton, NJ: Princeton University Press, 2003.

Hassig, Ralph, and Kongdan Oh. *The Hidden People of North Korea: Everyday Life in the Hermit Kingdom.* Lanham, MD: Rowman & Littlefield, 2009.

Hoare, James E., and Susan Pares. *North Korea in the 21st Century: An Interpretative Guide.* Folkestone, UK: Global Oriental, 2005.

Hobsbawm, Eric, and Terence Ranger. Introduction to *The Invention of Tradition*, edited by Eric Hobsbawm and Terence Ranger, 1–14. Cambridge: Cambridge University Press, 1983.

Humphrey, Caroline. *The Unmaking of Soviet Life: Everyday Economies in Russia and Mongolia.* Ithaca, NY: Cornell University Press, 2001.

Hunter, Helen-Louise. *Kim Il-song's North Korea.* Newport, CT: Praeger, 1999.

Isozaki, Atsuhito. "Kimujoniru 'sengunseiji'no honsitsu [The essence of Kim Jong Il's military-first politics]." In *Giki no chosenhanto* [Korean peninsula in crisis], edited by Masao Okonogi, 238–304. Tokyo: Keio University Press, 2006.

Jager, Sheila Miyoshi. *Narratives of Nation Building in Korea: A Genealogy of Patriotism.* Armonk, NY: M. E. Sharpe, 2003.

Jeffries, Ian. *North Korea: A Guide to Economic and Political Developments.* New York: Routledge, 2006.

Jian, Chen. "China's Changing Politics toward the Third World and the End of the Global Cold War." In *The End of the Cold War and the Third World: New Perspectives on Regional Conflict*, edited by Artemy M. Kalinovsky and Sergey Radchenko, 101–21. London: Routledge, 2011.

———. "The Great Transformation: How China Changed in the Long 1970s." Public lecture delivered at the London School of Economics, London, January 22, 2009.

Joo, Hyung-Min. "Visualizing the Invisible Hands: The Shadow Economy in North Korea." *Economy and Society* 39, no. 1 (2010): 110–45.

Joŭnbŏtdŭl [Good friends]. *Bukhansahoi muŏti byŏnhago itnŭnga?* [What changes are taking place in North Korean society?]. Seoul: Jŏngto, 2001.

———. *Bukhansaramdŭli malhanŭn bukhaniyagi* [Tales of North Korea told by North Koreans]. Seoul: Jŏngto, 2000.

Kal, Hong. *Aesthetic Constructions of Korean Nationalism: Spectacle, Politics, and History.* New York: Routledge, 2011.

Kaldor, Mary. *The Imaginary War: Interpretation of East-West Conflict in Europe.* Oxford: Blackwell, 1990.

Kang, Chung-Hi, and Sung-Il Lee. *Yŏngwŏnhi inmingwa hamkke* [Eternally together with the people]. Pyongyang: Pyongyang Press, 2007.

Kang, Jin-Ung. "Bukhanŭi gajokgukgach'ejeŭi hyŏngsŏng [The formation of North Korea's family state system]." *T'ongilmunjeyŏngu* [Unification studies] 13, no. 2 (2001): 323–46.

Kang, Keun-Cho. *Chosŏnkyoyuksa* [History of North Korean education]. Vol. 4. Pyongyang: Social Science Press, 1991.

Kang, Man-Kil. *T'ongilundongsidaeŭi yŏksainsik* [Historical awareness in the era of unification movement]. Seoul: Ch'ŏngsa, 1990.

Kang, Sang-Jung. "Sugisaranai ajia no shinjyochiri o koete: Nihon no chosenkan o chushin ni [Overcoming unchanging mental geography of Asia: Focusing on Japan's view on Korea]." *Ajiashinseki* [Asian new century], no. 1 (2002): 77–107.

Kang, Song-Kil. *Sŏn'gunsidaeŭi jokukŭl gada* [A tour of our fatherland in the military-first era]. Pyongyang: Pyongyang Press, 2002.

Kim, Bong-Ho. *Sŏn'gunŭro uiryŏk ttŏlchinŭn gangkuk* [Our mighty country of military-first politics]. Pyongyang: Pyongyang Press, 2005.

Kim, Byong-Ryong, and Seung-Jung Pak. *Chosŏnminjokŭi wonsijo dan'gun* [The original founding ancestor of the Korean nation, Dangun]. Tokyo: Hakwosubang, 1996.

Kim, Christine. "Politics and Pageantry in Protectorate Korea (1905–10): The Imperial Progresses of Sunjong." *Journal of Asian Studies* 68, no. 3 (2009): 835–59.

Kim, Du-Il. *Sŏn'gunsidae wiinŭi jongch'iwa norae* [The politics and songs of the hero of the military-first era]. Pyongyang: Literature and Arts Press, 2002.

Kim, Eun-Duk. *Koryŏ t'aejo wanggŏn* [The founder king of Koryo, Wanggŏn]. Pyongyang: Science Encyclopedia Press, 1996.

Kim, Gwang-Oon. "The Making of the North Korean State." *Journal of Korean Studies* 12, no. 1 (2007): 15–42.

Kim, Il Sung. *Hyŏkmyŏngjŏk munhakyesulŭl ch'angjakhalde daehayŏ* [On creating revolutionary literature and art]. Pyongyang: Workers' Party Press, 1978.

———. *Segiwa dŏbulŏ* [Together with the century]. Pyongyang: Workers' Party Press, 1992.

Kim, In-Ok. *Kim Jong Il changgun sŏn'gunjŏngch'i liron* [General Kim Jong Il's military-first political theory]. Pyongyang: Pyongyang Press, 2003.

Kim, Ji-Ni. "Bukhansik jonghapgongyŏnyesulŭi jŏngch'akgwa jŏngae [The establishment and development of North Korea's synthetic performance art]." *Hyundaebukhanyŏngu* [North Korean studies review] 11, no. 2 (2008): 137–76.

Kim, Jong Il. "Juch'eŭi dangkŏnsŏlironŭn rodonggyegŭpŭi dangkŏnsŏlesŏ t'ŭlŏjuigonaagaya hal jidojŏk jich'imida [The *juch'e* theory of party construction is the guiding principle for the construction of the party of the working class]." Speech delivered at the Plenum of Central Committee of the Workers' Party, Pyongyang, October 10, 1990.

———. *Kim Jong Il sŏnjip* [Collection of essays by Kim Jong Il]. Vol. 3. Pyongyang: Workers' Party Press, 2010.

———. *Kim Jong Il sŏnjip* [Collection of essays by Kim Jong Il]. Vol. 4. Pyongyang: Workers' Party Press, 2010.

———. *Yŏnghwa yesullon* [Theory of art and cinema]. Pyongyang: Workers' Party Press, 1984.

Kim, Kook-Chin. "An Overview of North Korean–Southeast Asian Relations." In *The Foreign Relations of North Korea*, edited by Jae Kyu Park, Byung Chul Koh, and Tae-Hwan Kwak, 353–78. Boulder, CO: Westview Press, 1987.

Kim, Mike. *Escaping North Korea: Defiance and Hope in the World's Most Repressive Country.* Lanham, MD: Rowman & Littlefield, 2008.

Kim, Seong-Bo. "Bukhanŭi juch'esasang, yuilch'ejewa yugyojŏk jŏnt'ongŭi sanghogwangye [Confucian tradition, *juch'e* ideology, and personality cult in North Korea]." *Sahakyŏngu* [Journal of the historical society of Korea] 61 (2000): 234–52.

Kim, Seong-Bo, Kwang-Su Kim, and Sin-Cheol Lee. *Bukhan hyŏndaesa* [Modern history of North Korea]. Seoul: Ungjin, 2006.

Kim, Suk-Young. "For the Eyes of the Dear Leader: Fashion and Body Politics in North Korean Visual Arts." Lecture given at the US Library of Congress, Washington, DC, March 17, 2009.

———. *Illusive Utopia: Theater, Film, and Everyday Performance in North Korea.* Ann Arbor: University of Michigan Press, 2010.

Kim, Sung-Mo, Sung-Il Tak, and Chul-Man Kim. *Chosŏnŭi jip'danch'ejo* [Mass gymnastics of Chosun] Pyongyang: Foreign Culture Press, 2002.

Kim, U-Kyoung. *Yŏngwŏnhan chuŏk* [Eternal memory]. Pyongyang: Pyongyang Culture and Art Press, 2003.

Kim, Woo-Kyung, Ki-Chun Dong, and Jong-Suk Kim. *Kŭmsusan'ginyŏmgungjŏn chŏnsŏlchip* [Legends of Kŭmsusan memorial palace]. Vols. 1–4. Pyongyang: Literature and Arts Press, 1999.

Kim, Yongho. *North Korean Foreign Policy: Security Dilemma and Succession.* Lanham, MD: Lexington Books, 2011.

Kim, Young C. "North Korea and the Third World." In *North Korea in a Regional and Global Context*, edited by Robert A. Scalapino and Hongkoo Lee, 327–43. Berkeley: Institute of East Asian Studies, University of California, Berkeley, 1986.

Kim Il Sung Jonghap Daehak ch'ulpansa [Kim Il Sung university press]. *Kim Jong Suk dongchi hyŏkmyŏnglyŏksa* [Comrade Kim Jong Suk's revolutionary history]. Pyongyang: Kim Il Sung University Press, 2005.

Kissinger, Henry. *On China.* New York: Allen Lane, 2011.

Kwahak paekkwa sajŏn ch'ulpansa [Science encyclopedia press]. *Jŏngjaronae gwanhan ch'ŏlhakronmunjip* [Philosophical anthology of seed theory]. Pyongyang: Science Encyclopedia Press, 2002.

———. *Munhakyesulsajŏn* [Dictionary of literature and art]. Vol. 1. Pyongyang: Scientific Encyclopedia Press, 1988.

Kwak, Song-Ho. "Bomulgo [The treasure house]." *Chŏngnyŏnmunhak* [Youth literature], no. 7 (2010): 16–17.

Kwon, Heonik. *After the Massacre: Commemoration and Consolation in Ha My and My Lai.* Berkeley: University of California Press, 2006.

———. *Ghosts of War in Vietnam.* Cambridge: Cambridge University Press, 2008.

———. "North Korea's Modern Theatre State." *Korean Studies Forum* 4 (2010): 27–54.

———. "North Korea's Politics of Longing." *Critical Asian Studies* 42 (2010): 3–24.

————. *The Other Cold War.* New York: Columbia University Press, 2010.

Lane, Christel. *Rites of Rulers: Ritual in Industrial Society—the Soviet Case.* Cambridge: Cambridge University Press, 1981.

Lankov, Andrei. *Crisis in North Korea: The Failure of De-Stalinization, 1956.* Honolulu: University of Hawaii Press, 2005.

————. *From Stalin to Kim Il Sung: The Formation of North Korea, 1945–1960.* London: C. Hurst, 2002.

————. "North Korean Refugees in Northeast China." *Asian Survey* 44, no. 6 (2004): 856–73.

————. *North of the DMZ: Essays on Daily Life in North Korea.* Jefferson, NC: McFarland, 2007.

Larkin, John. "North Korea, Mysterious Reform." *Far Eastern Economic Review* 8 (August 2002): 18–19.

Lautze, Sue. *The Famine in North Korea: Humanitarian Responses in Communist Nations.* Cambridge, MA: Feinstein International Famine Center, Tufts University, 1997.

Lee, Byung-Chun, ed. *Kebaldokjewa Pak Chung Hee sidae: Urisidaeŭi jŏngch'ikyŏngjejŏk kiwon* [Developmental dictatorship and Park Chung-Hee era: Political-economic origin of our time]. Seoul: Ch'angbi, 2003.

Lee, Heon-Kyoung. "Kim Il Sung, Kim Jong Il buja usanghwarŭl wihan yugŏjŏk jŏngch'isahoihwa [The personality cults of Kim Il Sung and Kim Jong Il, and the confucianization of politics and society]." *Segyejiyŏkyŏn'gu* [Global area studies] 18 (2002): 89–104.

Lee, Jong-Heun. "Bukhan dodŏkgyŏyukesŏ yugyoyunliŭi bip'angwa suyong [The reception and the criticism of Confucian ethics in the moral education of North Korea]." *T'ongiljŏnlyak* [Unification strategy] 8, no. 1 (2008): 217–49.

Lee, Jong-Ryol. *Jindalae* [The azalea]. Pyongyang: Literature and Art Press, 2007.

Lee, Jong-Suk. *Pundansidaeŭi t'ongilhak* [Unification studies of the division era]. Seoul: Hanul Academy, 1998.

Lee, Moon-Woong. *Bukhan jŏngch'imunhwaŭi hyŏngsŏnggwa gŭ t'ŭkjing* [The formation and characteristics of North Korean political culture]. Seoul: Institute of National Unification, 1976.

Lee, Namhee. *The Making of Minjung: Democracy and the Politics of Representation in South Korea.* Ithaca, NY: Cornell University Press, 2007.

Lee, Woo-Young, ed. *Bukhan dosijuminŭi sajŏkyŏngyŏk yŏn'gu* [Research report on private economy among North Korea's urban residents]. Seoul: Hanul, 2008.

————. *Bukhansahoeŭi sangjingchegye yŏn'gu: Hyŏkmyŏngguhoŭi byŏnhwarŭl jungsimŭro* [A study of symbolic system of North Korean society: Changes in revolutionary slogans]. Seoul: Institute of Unification Studies, 2002.

————. "Munhakyesulŭl tonghaesŏ bon Kim Jol Il sidaeŭi bukhan [North Korea in the era of Kim Jong Il seen through its literature and art]." *Kyŏngjewa sahoi* [Economy and society], no. 49 (2001): 102–23.

Lee, Young-Hee. *Bansegiǔi sinhwa: Hyujŏnsŏn nambukenǔn ch'ǒnsado akmado ǒpta* [A half-century-long myth: No angel or devil across the Armistice line]. Seoul: Samin, 1999.

———. *Saenǔn jwauǔi nalgaero nanda* [Birds need both left and right wings to fly]. Seoul: Dure, 1994.

Leffler, Melvyn P. *For the Soul of Mankind: The United States, the Soviet Union, and the Cold War.* New York: Hill and Wang, 2007.

Lim, Dong-Won. *Pisǔmeikǒ: Nambukgwangyewa bukhaekmunje 20nyǒn* [Peacemaker: Twenty years in inter-Korean relations and in North Korea's nuclear crisis]. Seoul: Jungang, 2008.

Lim, Kun-O. "Baeksŏnghaebang—ŏnlonhaebangi ch'oiusŏnida [Liberation of people: Liberation of press is the first priority]." *Limjingang* [Imjin river], no. 3 (August 2008): 142–43.

———. "Salgi wihan t'albukdo joiinga? [Is it a crime to try to leave North Korea to survive?]." *Limjingang* [Imjin river], no. 4 (March 2009): 27.

MacMillan, Margaret. *Nixon and Mao: The Week That Changed the World.* New York: Random House, 2008.

Malarney, Shaun K. *Culture, Ritual, and Revolution in Vietnam.* New York: RoutledgeCurzon, 2002.

Marr, David G. *Vietnamese Tradition on Trial, 1920–1945.* Berkeley: University of California Press, 1981.

Martin, Bradley K. *Under the Loving Care of the Fatherly Leader: North Korea and the Kim Dynasty.* New York: Thomas Dunne Books, 2004.

Maruyama, Masao. *Thought and Behavior in Modern Japanese Politics.* Edited by Ivan Morris. New York: Oxford University Press, 1969.

Mauss, Marcel. *The Gift.* London: Routledge, 1990 [1922].

McHale, Shawn Frederick. *Print and Power: Confucianism, Communism, and Buddhism in the Making of the Modern Vietnam.* Honolulu: University of Hawaii Press, 2008.

Medlicott, Carol. "Symbol and Sovereignty in North Korea." *SAIS Review* 25, no. 2 (2005): 69–79.

Minjok t'ongil yŏnguwŏn [Research institute for national unification]. *Bukhan jŏngch'isahoiesŏ jŏnt'ongmunhwaǔi yŏkhwal* [The role of traditional culture in the formation of North Korea's political society]. Seoul: Minjokt'ongilyŏnguwon, 1997.

Moon, Katherine. "Beyond Demonization: A Strategy for Human Rights in North Korea." *Current History* (September 2008): 264–66.

Morris-Suzuki, Tessa. "Remembering the Unfinished Conflict: Museums and the Contested Memory of the Korean War." *Asia-Pacific Journal.* July 27, 2009. http://www.japanfocus.org/-Tessa-Morris_Suzuki/3193 (accessed September 13, 2009).

Mosse, George. *Fallen Soldiers: Reshaping the Memory of World Wars.* Oxford: Oxford University Press, 1991.

Munhak yesul jonghap chulpansa [Literature and art press]. *Yŏngsaengŭi mosŭp: Hangilŭi nyŏsŏngyŏngŭng Kim Jong Sukdongch'iŭi t'ansaeng 80 dole jŭŭmhayŏ* [The immortal image: In celebration of the eightieth birth anniversary of the hero of anti-Japan struggle, Kim Jong Suk]. Pyongyang: Literature and Art Press, 1997.

Myers, B. R. *The Cleanest Race: How North Koreans See Themselves and Why It Matters*. Brooklyn, NY: Melville House Publishing, 2010.

Natsios, Andrew S. *The Great North Korean Famine: Famine, Politics, and Foreign Policy*. Washington, DC: US Institute of Peace Press, 2001.

Neocleous, Mark. *Imagining the State*. Maidenhead, UK: Open University Press, 2003.

Oberdorfer, Don. *The Two Koreas: A Contemporary History*. London: Warner Books, 1999.

Ogura, Kizo. *Kankokujin no shikumi* [The composition of Koreans]. Tokyo: Kōdansha, 2001.

Oh, Chang-Un. "Sŏn'gunsidae bukhan nongch'on yŏsŏngŭi hyŏngsanghwa yŏn'gu [Representation of rural women in the military-first era]." *Hyŏndaebukhanyŏn'gu* [North Korean studies review] 13, no. 2 (2010): 84–117.

Oh, Dae-Hyung, and Kyung-Ho Ha. *Dangŭi ryŏngdomit'ae ch'angjakkŏllipdoin daeginyŏmbidŭlŭi sasang yesulsŏng* [The ideological-artistic quality of the commemorative monuments established under the party's leadership]. Pyongyang: Chosun Art Press, 1989.

Oh, Hyun-Chol. *Sŏn'gunryŏngjanggwa sarangŭi segye* [The great general of military-first politics and the world of love]. Pyongyang: Pyongyang Press, 2005.

Ohnuki-Tierney, Emiko. *Kamikaze, Cherry Blossoms, and Nationalisms*. Chicago: University of Chicago Press, 2002.

Okonogi, Masao. "Hajimeni: Rensahōkai no akumu [Introduction: The nightmare of chain collapse]." In *Kitachōsen handobukku* [North Korea handbook], edited by Okonogi Masao, 11–20. Tokyo: Kōdansha, 1997.

Pak, Soon-Sung, and Min Hong, eds. *Bukhanŭi ilsangsegye: Oaech'imgwa soksagim* [Everyday life in North Korea: Cries and whispers]. Seoul: Hanul, 2010.

Palais, James B. *Confucian Statecraft and Korean Institutions*. Seattle: University of Washington Press, 1996.

———. *Politics and Policy in Traditional Korea*. Cambridge, MA: Harvard University Press, 1975.

Park, Han S. *North Korea: The Politics of Unconventional Wisdom*. Boulder, CO: Lynne Rienner Publishers, 2002.

Park, Hyun Ok. *Two Dreams in One Bed: Empire, Social Life, and the Origins of the North Korean Revolution in Manchuria*. Durham, NC: Duke University Press, 2005.

Park, Hyun-Sun. *Hyundae bukhansahoiwa gajok* [Contemporary North Korean society and family]. Seoul: Hanul Academy, 2003.

Park, Jae Kyu. "North Korea's Foreign Policy toward Africa." In *The Foreign Relations of North Korea*, edited by Jae Kyu Park, Byung Chul Koh, and Tae-Hwan Kwak, 436–61. Boulder, CO: Westview Press, 1987.

Park, Su-Won. "She Smiled; She Cried." *Adong munhak* [Children's literature] 4 (2009): 27.

Park, Young-Jung. *Bukhan yŏn'gŭk/ hŭigogŭi bunsŏkkwa chŏnmang* [Analysis and prospect of North Korean theater/play]. Seoul: Yŏn'gŭkkwa in'gan, 2007.

Parry, Jonathan. "The Gift, the Indian Gift and the 'Indian Gift.'" *Man* 21 (1985): 453–73.

Pelley, Patricia M. *Postcolonial Vietnam: New Histories of the National Past.* Durham, NC: Duke University Press, 2002.

Peterson, Glen. *The Power of Words: Literacy and Revolution in South China, 1949–95.* Vancouver: University of British Columbia Press, 1998.

Pine, Frances, and Sue Bridger. "Introduction: Transitions to Post-Socialism and Cultures of Survival." In *Surviving Post-Socialism: Local Strategies and Regional Responses in Eastern Europe and the Former Soviet Union*, edited by Sue Bridger and Frances Pine, 1–15. New York: Routledge, 1997.

Pyongyang ch'ulpansa [Pyongyang press]. *Minjokŭi wŏnsijo dan'gun* [National founding ancestor, Dangun]. Pyongyang: Pyongyang Press, 1994.

———. *Sŏn'gunt'aeyang Kim Jong Il Janggun* [The sun of military-first (politics), General Kim Jong Il]. Vol. 1. Pyongyang: Pyongyang Press, 2006.

———. *Sŏn'gunŭi ŏbŏi Kim Il Sung Janggun* [The father of military-first (politics), General Kim Il Sung]. Vol. 1. Pyongyang: Pyongyang Press, 2007.

———. *Sŏn'gunŭi ŏbŏi Kim Il Sung Janggun* [The father of military-first (politics), General Kim Il Sung]. Vol. 2. Pyongyang: Pyongyang Press, 2007.

———. *Sŏn'gunŭi ŏmŏni Kim Jong Suk nyŏjanggun* [The mother of military-first (politics), Female-General Kim Jong Suk]. Pyongyang: Pyongyang Press, 2007.

Radchenko, Sergey. *Two Suns in the Heavens: The Sino-Soviet Struggle for Supremacy, 1962–1967.* Stanford, CA: Stanford University Press, 2009.

Raheja, Gloria Goodwin. *The Poison in the Gift: Ritual, Presentation, and the Dominant Caste in a North Indian Village.* Chicago: University of Chicago Press, 1988.

Robinson, Joan. "Korean Miracle." *Monthly Review* 16, no. 8 (1965): 541–49.

Robinson, W. Courtland, Myung Ken Lee, Kenneth Hill, and Gilbert Burnham. "Famine, Mortality, and Migration: A Study of North Korean Migrants in China." In *Forced Migration and Mortality*, edited by Holly E. Reed and Charles B. Keely, 69–85. Washington, DC: National Academy Press, 2001.

Ryang, Sonia. "Biopolitics, or the Logic of Sovereign Love: Love's Whereabouts in North Korea." In *North Korea: Toward a Better Understanding*, edited by Sonia Ryang, 57–84. Lanham, MD: Lexington Books, 2009.

Ryu, Kyung-Won. "Tto dasi kinjanggam hŭrŭnŭn sijang [Tensions grow again in the market]." *Limjingang* [Imjin River], no. 4 (March 2009): 122.

Sahoigwahakch'ulp'ansa [Social science press]. *Hangil hyŏkmyŏng munhakye-sul: Kyŏngaehanŭn suryŏng Kim Il Sung dongjiŭi t'ansaeng yesundolkinyŏm* [Anti-Japanese revolutionary literature and art: In celebration of the sixtieth birth anniversary of the esteemed Supreme Leader Kim Il Sung]. Pyongyang: Social Science Press, 1971.

Schmid, Andre. *Korea between Empires*. New York: Columbia University Press, 2002.

Schmitt, Carl. *Theory of the Partisan: Intermediate Commentary on the Concept of the Political*. Translated by G. L. Ulmen. New York: Telos Press, 2007.

Scott, James C. *The Moral Economy of the Peasants*. New Haven, CT: Yale University Press, 1976.

Selden, Mark. "East Asian Regionalism and Its Enemies in Three Epochs: Political Economy and Geopolitics, 16th to 21st Centuries." *Asia-Pacific Journal.* February 25, 2009. http://www.japanfocus.org/-Mark-Selden/3061 (accessed March 8, 2009).

Shu, Kenei (Zhu Jianrong in Chinese). *Motakutō no chōsen sensō* [Mao's Korean war]. Tokyo: Iwanami shoten, 2004.

Smith, Hazel. *Hungry for Peace: International Security, Humanitarian Assistance and Social Change in North Korea*. Washington, DC: US Institute of Peace Press, 2005.

Ssorin-Chaikov, Nikolai, ed. *Dary Vozhdiam/Gifts to Soviet Leaders*. Moscow: Pinakotheke, 2006.

———. "On Heterochrony: Birthday Gifts to Stalin, 1949." *Journal of the Royal Anthropological Institute* 12, no. 2 (2006): 355–75.

Suh, Dae-Sook. *Hyŭndae bukhanŭi jidoja: Kim Il Sunggwa Kim Jong Il* [Leaders of modern North Korea: Kim Il Sung and Kim Jong Il]. Seoul: Ŭlyu, 2000.

———. *Kim Il Sung: The North Korean Leader*. New York: Columbia University Press, 1995.

Suk, Woon-Ki. *Konanŭi haenggun* [Arduous March]. Pyongyang: Literature and Art Press, 1991.

Suzuki, Masayuki. *Kitachōsen: Shakaishugi to dento no kyōmei* [North Korea: The resonance of socialism and tradition]. Tokyo: Tokyo University Press, 1992.

Szalontai, Balázs. *Kim Il Sung in the Khrushchev Era: Soviet-DPRK Relations and the Roots of North Korean Despotism, 1953–1964*. Washington, DC: Woodrow Wilson Center Press, 2005.

Takizawa, Hideki. *Chōsenminzoku no kindaikokka keiseishi jyosetsu* [An introduction to the formation of the modern Korean nation-state]. Tokyo: Ochanomizu shōbo, 2008.

Thompson, E. P. *The Making of the English Working Class*. London: Gollancz, 1963.

T'ongilbu [Ministry of unification]. *Bukhan ihae* [Understanding North Korea]. Seoul: Ministry of Unification 1995.

Turner, Marjorie S. *Joan Robinson and the Americans.* New York: M. E. Sharpe, 1989.

Verdery, Katherine. *What Was Socialism and What Comes Next?* Princeton, NJ: Princeton University Press, 1996.

Vicziany, Marika, David Wright-Neville, and Peter Lentini, eds. *Regional Security in the Asia Pacific: 9/11 and After.* Cheltenham, UK: Edward Elgar, 2004.

Wada, Haruki. *Bukjosŏn: Yugyŏkdaegugkaesŏ jŏnggyukungugkaro* [North Korea: From partisan state to a military state]. Seoul: Dolbegae, 2002.

———. *Kimuiruson to manshu konichisenso* [Kim Il Sung and anti-Japanese war in Manchuria]. Tokyo: Heibonsha, 1992.

———. *Kitachōsen: Yūgekitai kokka no genzai* [North Korea's partisan state today]. Tokyo: Iwanami shoten, 1998.

Wales, Nym, and Kim San. *Song of Arirang: A Korean Communist in the Chinese Revolution.* Rev. ed. San Francisco: Ramparts Press, 1972.

Weber, Max. *The Theory of Social and Economic Organization.* Edited by Talcott Parsons. New York: The Free Press, 1947.

Werbner, Richard. "Smoke from the Barrel of a Gun: Postwars of the Dead, Memory, and Reinscription in Zimbabwe." In *Memory and Postcoloniality*, edited by Richard Werbner, 71–104. London: Zed, 1998.

Westad, Odd Arne. *The Global Cold War.* Cambridge: Cambridge University Press, 2005.

Westad, Odd Arne, and Sophie Quinn-Judge, eds. *The Third Indochina War: Conflict between China, Vietnam and Cambodia, 1972–1979.* London: Routledge, 2006.

Willner, Ann R. *The Spellbinders: Charismatic Political Leadership.* New Haven, CT: Yale University Press, 1984.

Winter, Jay. *Sites of Memory, Sites of Mourning: The Great War in European Cultural History.* Cambridge: Cambridge University Press, 1995.

Woo-Cumings, Meredith. "The Political Ecology of Famine: The North Korean Catastrophe and Its Lessons." Research Paper 31. Asian Development Bank Institute. January 1, 2002. http://www.adbi.org/files/2002.01.rp31.ecology.famine.northkorea.pdf (accessed September 21, 2011).

Woori minjok sŏrodopgi bulkyo undong bonbu [Korean Buddhist sharing movement]. *Bukhansigryangnanŭi silt'ae (Jaryojip)* [Reality of the North Korean food shortage]. Seoul: Joŭnbŏtdŭl, 1998.

Yang, Dali L. *Calamity and Reform in China: State, Rural Society, and Institutional Change since the Great Leap Famine.* Stanford, CA: Stanford University Press, 1996.

Yoshida, Yasuhiko. *Kitachōsen o miru kiku aruku* [Look, hear and walk North Korea]. Tokyo: Heibonsha, 2009.

Yun, U-Chol. *Josŏnrodongdangŭi dodŏk ŭriŭi jŏngch'i* [The moral-loyalty politics of the Workers' Party]. Pyongyang: Social Science Press, 2005.

Zbarsky, Ilya, and Samuel Hutchinson. *Lenin's Embalmers*. London: Harvill Press, 1998.

Zhu, Fang. *Gun Barrel Politics: Party-Army Relations in Mao's China*. Boulder, CO: Westview Press, 1998.

Internet Sources

"Bukhan sigryangnanminŭi saenghwalsang [Life conditions of North Korean food refugees]." CyberHumanRights.com. http://www.cyberhumanrights.com/media/material/5049_1.pdf (accessed March 6, 2010).

Daily NK, May 11, 2009. http://www.dailynk.com/korean/read.php?cataId=nk01300&num=71175 (accessed November 5, 2009).

Memorial speech delivered in the Kim Il Sung University, April 23, 2009. http://www.ournation-school.com/Radio_lecture/w2-72/w2-72.htm (accessed December 19, 2009).

The Character of a Just Man: Who Is General Kim Jong Il? http://www.chongryon.com/k/mc/kim/21-new/2-4.htm (accessed February 17, 2010).

Periodicals

"7.4 Sŏngmyŏngŭn daenamhyŏkmyŏngŭl wihan p'yŏnghwa kongse [July 4th communique is a peace offensive aimed at instigating a revolution in the south]." *Dong-A Ilbo*, September 24, 2009.

"Buk, 'kkŭtkkaji kyŏlp'an bol kŏt' [North, we will settle (the scores) till the end]." *Dong-A Ilbo*, February 23, 2009.

Global People, no. 127, May 16, 2010.

Kang, Tae-Ho. "1991nyŏn, 'Oraedoin mirae' rosŏŭi pukhan [1991, North Korea as an 'ancient future']." *Hangyeore Sinmun*, June 20, 2011.

"Kim Il Sung bangjunghaengjŏk ttara idong [Following the steps of Kim Il Sung's (1991) trip to China]." *Jungang Ilbo*, May 28, 2011.

"North Korea Confirms Kim Jong-Il's Son Will Take Over as Leader." *Guardian*, October 8, 2010.

"North Korean Official Confirms Kim Jong Un as Leader," *Washington Times*, October 8, 2010.

Shin, Sok-Ho. "1970nyŏndaech'o nambukjŏnggwŏn 'jŏkdaejŏk kongsaenggwangye' ipjŭng [The establishment of dictatorship and antagonistic coexistence]." *Dong-A Ilbo*, October 13, 2009.

Uriminjok ggiri [Between us], March 29, 2010.

Womack, Helen, and Tom Harper. "To Russia with Love." *Daily Telegraph*, October 29, 2006.

North Korean Newspaper: *Rodong Sinmun*
[*Rodong Newspaper*]

"A, nae choguk! [Ah, my country!]," *Rodong Sinmun*, September 6, 2009.

"Aegukryŏlsarŭng [The Graves of Patriotic Martyrs]." *Rodong Sinmun*, December 28, 2004.

"Changgunnim saranghasinŭn norae [Song the general cherishes]." *Rodong Sinmun*, July 25, 2000.

"Changgunnimddara sŭngriŭi han'gillo [Following the general toward the road of victory]." *Rodong Sinmun*, July 2, 2004.

Cho, Song-Chol. "Jŏlseŭi uiinŭl gyŏngmohanŭn maninŭi sun'gyŏlhan maŭm [The pure hearts that worship the great human being of all times]." *Rodong Sinmun*, June 1, 2007.

"Chosŏnrodongdaepyojahoeŭi [Workers' Party congress]." *Rodong Sinmun*, June 30, 2010.

"Dasi hanbŏn kyŏngkongŭpkwa nongŏpe pakch'arŭl [Let's bring up agriculture and light industry once more]." *Rodong Sinmun*, January 1, 2010.

"Hyŏkmyŏngga yujanyŏdŭlŭn paekduŭi sŏn'gunjŏnt'ongŭl iŏnagal haeksimgolgandŭlida [The orphans of revolutionary fighters are the spinal core who will lead Paekdu's military-first (politics) tradition]." *Rodong Sinmun*, October 12, 2007.

"Hyŏkmyŏngjŏnt'ongŭl daerŭl iŏ pitnage kyesŭngbalchŏnsikija [Let us be faithful (to the leadership) across generations]." *Rodong Sinmun*, April 25, 1974.

"Inminŭi maŭmsoge yŏngsaenghasinŭn nyŏsa [The woman who leads immortal life in our hearts]." *Rodong Sinmun*, December 22, 2000.

"Jŏngryŏkjŏkin hyŏnjijido kanghaenggun [The passionate on-the-spot-guidance marches]." *Rodong Sinmun*, June 18, 2009.

"Kangkye jŏngsinŭro ŏksege ssawŏnagaja [Let's struggle along forcefully in the spirit of Kangkye]." *Rodong Sinmun*, April 22, 2000.

"Kim Il Sungjusŏknimŭn onŭldo sŏnmulŭl batŭsimnida [Chairman Kim Il Sung continues to receive gifts today]." *Rodong Sinmun*, August 8, 2004.

"Kim Il Sungminjokŭi chonŏmgwa yŏnggwang [Dignity and honor of the people of Kim Il Sung]." *Rodong Sinmun*, July 5, 2009.

"Kim Jong Il changgun—sŏn'gunsŭngriŭi 50nyŏn [General Kim Jong Il—fifty years of sŏn'gun victory]." *Rodong Sinmun*, August 24, 2000.

"Nanŭn Kangyejŏngsinŭl yŏngwŏnhi itjianŭl gŏsipnida [I will never forget the spirit of Kangye]." *Rodong Sinmun*, May 8, 2000.

"Paekdusan nunbora [Snowstorm in Paekdu mountain]." *Rodong Sinmun*, March 21, 2000.

"Pulmyŏlŭi 5nyŏnŭl hoigohamyŏ [Remembering the unforgettable five years]." *Rodong Sinmun*, July 1, 1999.

"Sae segiŭi daegŏljak [The masterpiece of the new century]." *Rodong Sinmun*, July 19, 2002.

"Segyeminjokhaebangt'ujaengsae gili bitnal pulmyŏlŭi ŏbjŏk [Immortal achieve-ment in the world liberation war]." *Rodong Sinmun*, August 17, 2006.

"Sŏn'gunryŏngdonŭn sahoijuŭichosunŭi sŭngriŭi kŭnbonyoin [The military-first political leadership is the foundation for the victory of socialist Korea]." *Rodong Sinmun*, August 24, 2010.

"Sŏngsŭrŏun 3nyŏn [The sacred three years]." *Rodong Sinmun*, July 2, 1997.

"Suryŏngnim purŭsin norae [Song sung by the Supreme Leader]." *Rodong Sinmun*, April 6, 2007.

"T'aeyangŭi noraenŭn yŏngwŏnhamnida [The song of the sun is forever]." *Rodong Sinmun*, April 17, 2008.

"Uri jokukŭi ŏmŏni [Mother of our country]." *Rodong Sinmun*, December 23, 2005.

"Urinŭn hansiksol [We are a single household]." *Rodong Sinmun*, October 3, 2007.

"Urinŭn sŭngrihanda [We shall win]." *Rodong Sinmun*, June 3, 1996.

"Widaehan t'aeyang, jaaeroun ŏbŏi [The great sun, the loving parent]." *Rodong Sinmun*, July 8, 2009.

Media

A State of Mind, directed by Daniel Gordon. Sheffield, UK: VeryMuchSo Produc-tions, 2004.

Chosun jungang t'ongsin [North Korean central broadcast], April 13, 2002.

Chosun jungang t'ongsin [North Korean central broadcast], August 30, 2010.

Index

actors. *See* citizen-actors

Agreement on Reconciliation, Non-Aggression, and Exchanges and Cooperation, 165

Albright, Madeleine, 135

ancestor worship, in Vietnam, 19–20, 61

An Young Ae, 94, 102

Arduous March, 10, 16, 159; ethics of common survival with, 173–78; moral economy and, 162–73; paintings, *175*; poems about, 23, 27, 29; realistic reflections on, 99n51; songs, 173–74. *See also* food crisis

Arendt, Hannah, 61, 92

Arirang Festival, 12, 16, 17, 27, 73; gymnastic fitness displays in, 67n10; with Kim Il Sung and two guns, 96; literary structure of, 56; "Nobody in the world can beat us!," 77; performances, *46*, 129, *130*, 131; power as display in, 46–48; symbolism in, 74

Aristotle, 61

Armstrong, Charles, 4, 16, 81, 111; on collective filial piety, 18; on Third-Worldism, 138–39

army. *See* People's Army

art: background, 17; legacy, 48; mortuary, 73; as political tool, 17; as propaganda and political indoctrination, 4–5; succession, 48. *See also* revolutionary art

authority: leaders with charismatic, 1, 2–3; power converted into legitimate, 43–44, 58; traditional and rational-bureaucratic, 43. *See also* charismatic authority

background art, 17

Bali, 45, 64, 65

the barrel of a gun (*ch'ongdae*), 66; explanation of, 71–75; gift of, 83–87; philosophy, 87–92; political theory of *sŏn'gun* and, 75–83; power of love and power of, 92–96; symbolism in, 74–75, 83, 94

Bauman, Zygmunt, 160

bereavement. *See* Great National Bereavement

Berlin Wall, 49, 135, 162

Borneman, John, 61

Bradley, Mark, 13

Brooks, Jeffrey, 74, 93, 136, 138

Buck-Morss, Susan, 29

Bush, George W., 165

calendars, 71

Cambodia, 134, 153–54

Carter, Jimmy, 135

Castro, Fidel, 134

cemeteries: mass graves and, 110; national, 103–11; in South Korea, 104. *See also specific cemeteries*

Chakrabarty, Dipesh, 14

charismatic authority: completion of, 121–23; impermanence of, 3–4, 44, 48; of leaders, 1, 2–3; social crisis as genesis for, 3; Weber on, 2–3, 43–44, 57, 121–22, 176–77

Chatterjee, Partha, 14–15

Chiang Kai-shek, 137

children: in family state, 155; famine and wandering, *167*; gifts presented to, *157*; with gymnastic fitness displays, 67n10;

About the Authors

Heonik Kwon is professorial senior research fellow at Trinity College, University of Cambridge, and previously taught anthropology at the London School of Economics. He has conducted fieldwork in the former Soviet Union, Vietnam, and, more recently, Korea. Author of several prize-winning books, including *Ghosts of War in Vietnam* and *The Other Cold War*, he is currently directing the international Beyond the Korean War project, which explores the history and memory of the Korean War in local and global contexts.

Byung-Ho Chung is professor of cultural anthropology and director of the Institute of Globalization and Multicultural Studies at Hanyang University, South Korea. He is author of a number of works on North Korean and inter-Korean affairs, including the coedited *Welcome to Korea: North Koreans in South Korea*, and has visited North Korea and China's borders with North Korea on numerous occasions since the mid-1990s. He also has extensive humanitarian and research experience with North Korean youth migrants now settled in China and South Korea.